MznLnx

Missing Links Exam Preps

Exam Prep for

Money and Capital Markets

Rose & Marquis, 10th Edition

The MznLnx Exam Prep is your link from the texbook and lecture to your exams.
The MznLnx Exam Preps are unauthorized and comprehensive reviews of your textbooks.

All material provided by MznLnx and Rico Publications (c) 2010
Textbook publishers and textbook authors do not particpate in or contribute to these reviews.

MznLnx

Rico Publications

Exam Prep for Money and Capital Markets
10th Edition
Rose & Marquis

Publisher: Raymond Houge
Assistant Editor: Michael Rouger
Text and Cover Designer: Lisa Buckner
Marketing Manager: Sara Swagger
Project Manager, Editorial Production: Jerry Emerson
Art Director: Vernon Lowerui

Product Manager: Dave Mason
Editorial Assitant: Rachel Guzmanji
Pedagogy: Debra Long
Cover Image: Jim Reed/Getty Images
Text and Cover Printer: City Printing, Inc.
Compositor: Media Mix, Inc.

(c) 2010 Rico Publications

ALL RIGHTS RESERVED. No part of this work covered by the copyright may be reproduced or used in any form or by an means--graphic, electronic, or mechanical, including photocopying, recording, taping, Web distribution, information storage, and retrieval systems, or in any other manner--without the written permission of the publisher.

Printed in the United States
ISBN:

For more information about our products, contact us at:
Dave.Mason@RicoPublications.com

For permission to use material from this text or product, submit a request online to:
Dave.Mason@RicoPublications.com

Contents

CHAPTER 1
Functions and Roles of the Financial System in the Global Economy   1

CHAPTER 2
Financial Assets, Money, Financial Transactions, and Financial Institutions   10

CHAPTER 3
The Financial Information Marketplace   22

CHAPTER 4
The Future of the Financial System and Trends in the Money and Capital Markets   38

CHAPTER 5
The Determinants of Interest Rates: Competing Ideas   48

CHAPTER 6
Measuring and Calculating Interest Rates and Financial Asset Prices   56

CHAPTER 7
Inflation, Yield Curves, and Duration: Impact on Interest Rates and Asset Prices   64

CHAPTER 8
The Risk Structure of Interest Rates   72

CHAPTER 9
Interest Rate Forecasting and Hedging: Swaps, Financial Futures, and Options   81

CHAPTER 10
Introduction to the Money Market and the Roles Played   92

CHAPTER 11
Commercial Banks, Major Corporations, and Credit Agencies in the Money Market   102

CHAPTER 12
Roles and Services of the Federal Reserve and Other Central Banks   112

CHAPTER 13
The Tools and Goals of Central Bank Monetary Policy   118

CHAPTER 14
The Commercial Banking Industry: Structure, Products, and Management   126

CHAPTER 15
Nonbank Thrift Institutions   137

CHAPTER 16
Mutual Funds, Insurance Companies, Investment Banks, and Other Financial Firms   146

CHAPTER 17
Regulation of the Financial Institutions` Sector   160

CHAPTER 18
Federal, State, and Local Governments Operating in the Financial Markets   172

CHAPTER 19
Business Borrowing: Corporate Bonds, Asset-Backed Securities, Bank Loans   184

CHAPTER 20
The Market for Corporate Stock   195

Contents (Cont.)

CHAPTER 21
  Consumer Lending and Borrowing   209
CHAPTER 22
  The Residential Mortgage Market   219
CHAPTER 23
  International Transactions and Currency Values   227
CHAPTER 24
  International Banking   237
ANSWER KEY   244

TO THE STUDENT

COMPREHENSIVE

The *MznLnx* Exam Prep series is designed to help you pass your exams. Editors at MznLnx review your textbooks and then prepare these practice exams to help you master the textbook material. Unlike study guides, workbooks, and practice tests provided by the texbook publisher and textbook authors, *MznLnx* gives you **all** of the material in each chapter in exam form, not just samples, so you can be sure to nail your exam.

MECHANICAL

The MznLnx Exam Prep series creates exams that will help you learn the subject matter as well as test you on your understanding. Each question is designed to help you master the concept. Just working through the exams, you gain an understanding of the subject--its a simple mechanical process that produces success.

INTEGRATED STUDY GUIDE AND REVIEW

MznLnx is not just a set of exams designed to test you, its also a comprehensive review of the subject content. Each exam question is also a review of the concept, making sure that you will get the answer correct without having to go to other sources of material. You learn as you go! Its the easiest way to pass an exam.

HUMOR

Studying can be tedious and dry. MznLnx's instructional design includes moderate humor within the exam questions on occassion, to break the tedium and revitalize the brain

Chapter 1. Functions and Roles of the Financial System in the Global Economy

1. In finance, the _____ is the system that allows the transfer of money between savers and borrowers.

Put another way: the _____ is a set of complex and closely interconnected financial institutions, markets, instruments, services, practices, and transactions.

   a. 4-4-5 Calendar
   b. Passive income
   c. Financial system
   d. Horizontal merger

2. _____ is the branch of economics that studies the dynamics of exchange rates, foreign investment, and how these affect international trade. It also studies international projects, international investments and capital flows, and trade deficits. It includes the study of futures, options and currency swaps.

   a. A Random Walk Down Wall Street
   b. AAB
   c. ABN Amro
   d. International finance

3. In economics, a _____ is a mechanism that allows people to easily buy and sell (trade) financial securities (such as stocks and bonds), commodities (such as precious metals or agricultural goods), and other fungible items of value at low transaction costs and at prices that reflect the efficient-market hypothesis.

   _____s have evolved significantly over several hundred years and are undergoing constant innovation to improve liquidity.

Both general markets (where many commodities are traded) and specialized markets (where only one commodity is traded) exist.

   a. Secondary market
   b. Cost of carry
   c. Delta hedging
   d. Financial market

4. _____, refers to consumption opportunity gained by an entity within a specified time frame, which is generally expressed in monetary terms. However, for households and individuals, '_____ is the sum of all the wages, salaries, profits, interests payments, rents and other forms of earnings received... in a given period of time.' For firms, _____ generally refers to net-profit: what remains of revenue after expenses have been subtracted.

   a. Accrual
   b. Income
   c. Annual report
   d. OIBDA

5. _____ is a fee paid on borrowed assets. It is the price paid for the use of borrowed money , or, money earned by deposited funds . Assets that are sometimes lent with _____ include money, shares, consumer goods through hire purchase, major assets such as aircraft, and even entire factories in finance lease arrangements.

   a. AAB
   b. Insolvency
   c. A Random Walk Down Wall Street
   d. Interest

6. An _____ is the price a borrower pays for the use of money they do not own, and the return a lender receives for deferring the use of funds, by lending it to the borrower. _____s are normally expressed as a percentage rate over the period of one year.

   _____s targets are also a vital tool of monetary policy and are used to control variables like investment, inflation, and unemployment.

a. AAB
b. ABN Amro
c. A Random Walk Down Wall Street
d. Interest rate

7. A _____ is the price of a single share of a no. of saleable stocks of the company. Once the stock is purchased, the owner becomes a shareholder of the company that issued the share.
a. Whisper numbers
b. Stock split
c. Trading curb
d. Share price

8. _____ refers to making a wide range of secured and unsecured loans to consumers for consumable items such as a car, boat, manufactured home, home equity loan, home equity line of credit, signature loan, signature line of credit, recreational vehicle, or share or certificate of deposit or Stocks and Mutual Funds secured loans.

_____ does not include mortgage loans, typically used for home purchases, which follow some different regulations than consumer loans. Also, consumer loans are different from commercial loans, which can be calculated on a daily basis, rather than 12 monthly payments, and include interest for leap day, such as in Actual/366 loan calculations.

a. Consumer lending
b. Sogflation
c. Primary market
d. Coupon leverage

9. _____ is a legally declared inability or impairment of ability of an individual or organization to pay their creditors. Creditors may file a _____ petition against a debtor ('involuntary _____') in an effort to recoup a portion of what they are owed or initiate a restructuring. In the majority of cases, however, _____ is initiated by the debtor (a 'voluntary _____' that is filed by the bankrupt individual or organization.)
a. Bankruptcy
b. 529 plan
c. Debt settlement
d. 4-4-5 Calendar

10.

A _____ is a type of financial intermediary and a type of bank. Commercial banking is also known as business banking. It is a bank that provides checking accounts, savings accounts, and money market accounts and that accepts time deposits.

a. 7-Eleven
b. 4-4-5 Calendar
c. Commercial bank
d. 529 plan

11. _____ refers to the stock of skills and knowledge embodied in the ability to perform labor so as to produce economic value. Many early economic theories refer to it simply as labor, one of three factors of production, and consider it to be a fungible resource -- homogeneous and easily interchangeable. Other conceptions of labor dispense with these assumptions.
a. Mercantilism
b. Behavioral finance
c. Human capital
d. Market structure

Chapter 1. Functions and Roles of the Financial System in the Global Economy

12. _____ refers to a business or organization attempting to acquire goods or services to accomplish the goals of the enterprise. Though there are several organizations that attempt to set standards in the _____ process, processes can vary greatly between organizations. Typically the word '_____' is not used interchangeably with the word 'procurement', since procurement typically includes Expediting, Supplier Quality, and Traffic and Logistics (T'L) in addition to _____.

   a. 7-Eleven
   b. 529 plan
   c. 4-4-5 Calendar
   d. Purchasing

13. _____ is the value of goods/services compared to the amount paid with a currency. Currency can be either a commodity money, like gold or silver, or fiat currency like US dollars which are the world reserve currency. As Adam Smith noted, having money gives one the ability to 'command' others' labor, so _____ to some extent is power over other people, to the extent that they are willing to trade their labor or goods for money or currency.

   a. Purchasing power
   b. 7-Eleven
   c. 4-4-5 Calendar
   d. 529 plan

14. _____ is the provision of resources (such as granting a loan) by one party to another party where that second party does not reimburse the first party immediately, thereby generating a debt, and instead arranges either to repay or return those resources (or material(s) of equal value) at a later date. The first party is called a creditor, also known as a lender, while the second party is called a debtor, also known as a borrower.

   Movements of financial capital are normally dependent on either _____ or equity transfers.

   a. Warrant
   b. Comparable
   c. Credit
   d. Clearing house

15. _____ is a type of bank account where the money in the account is legally able to be withdrawn immediately upon demand (or 'at call'.) This type of bank account can also be referred to as a 'cheque' or 'checking' or transactional account.

   This type of bank account, allowing immediate conversion of the account balance into cash or withdrawal to another account, can be contrasted with a time deposit (also known as a certificate of deposit or term deposit), where the funds are not legally available for immediate withdrawal by the depositor.

   a. 4-4-5 Calendar
   b. 529 plan
   c. Synthetic lease
   d. Demand deposit

16. _____ is a measure of the ability of a debtor to pay their debts as and when they fall due. It is usually expressed as a ratio or a percentage of current liabilities.

   For a corporation with a published balance sheet there are various ratios used to calculate a measure of liquidity.

   a. Operating profit margin
   b. Operating leverage
   c. Invested capital
   d. Accounting liquidity

17. _____, in bookkeeping, refers to assets, liabilities, income, and expenses recorded on individual pages of the so called book of final entry or ledger. Changes in _____ value are made by chronologically posting debit (DR) and credit (CR) entries to its page. Examples of _____s are cash, _____s receivable, mortgages, loans, land and buildings, common stock, sales, services provided, wages, and payroll overhead.

a. Alpha
b. Option
c. Accretion
d. Account

18. _____ or amalgamation is the act of merging many things into one. In business, it often refers to the mergers or acquisitions of many smaller companies into much larger ones. The financial accounting term of _____ refers to the aggregated financial statements of a group company as consolidated account.
    a. Cost of goods sold
    b. Retained earnings
    c. Consolidation
    d. Write-off

19. _____ is the risk (variability in value) borne by an interest-bearing asset, such as a loan or a bond, due to variability of interest rates. In general, as rates rise, the price of a fixed rate bond will fall, and vice versa. _____ is commonly measured by the bond's duration.
    a. Official bank rate
    b. International Fisher effect
    c. Interest rate risk
    d. A Random Walk Down Wall Street

20. The _____ is a stock exchange based in New York City, New York. It is the largest stock exchange in the world by dollar value of its listed companies securities. As of October 2008, the combined capitalization of all domestic _____ listed companies was $10.1 trillion.
    a. 7-Eleven
    b. 4-4-5 Calendar
    c. New York Stock Exchange
    d. 529 plan

21. _____ is the discipline of identifying, monitoring and limiting risks. In some cases the acceptable risk may be near zero. Risks can come from accidents, natural causes and disasters as well as deliberate attacks from an adversary.
    a. Risk management
    b. FIFO
    c. 4-4-5 Calendar
    d. Penny stock

22. A _____, securities exchange or (in Europe) bourse is a corporation or mutual organization which provides 'trading' facilities for stock brokers and traders, to trade stocks and other securities. _____s also provide facilities for the issue and redemption of securities as well as other financial instruments and capital events including the payment of income and dividends. The securities traded on a _____ include: shares issued by companies, unit trusts and other pooled investment products and bonds.
    a. 529 plan
    b. 4-4-5 Calendar
    c. 7-Eleven
    d. Stock Exchange

23. The _____ is the market for securities, where companies and governments can raise longterm funds. The _____ includes the stock market and the bond market. Financial regulators, such as the U.S. Securities and Exchange Commission, oversee the _____s in their designated countries to ensure that investors are protected against fraud.
    a. Delta neutral
    b. Spot rate
    c. Forward market
    d. Capital market

24. A _____, reserve bank, or monetary authority is the entity responsible for the monetary policy of a country or of a group of member states. It is a bank that can lend money to other banks in times of need. Its primary responsibility is to maintain the stability of the national currency and money supply, but more active duties include controlling subsidized-loan interest rates, and acting as a lender of last resort to the banking sector during times of financial crisis (private banks often being integral to the national financial system.)

Chapter 1. Functions and Roles of the Financial System in the Global Economy

a. 4-4-5 Calendar
c. Central Bank
b. 7-Eleven
d. 529 plan

25. _____ is the process by which the government, or monetary authority of a country controls (i) the supply of money central bank (ii) availability of money, and (iii) cost of money or rate of interest, in order to attain a set of objectives oriented towards the growth and stability of the economy. Monetary theory provides insight into how to craft optimal _____.

_____ is referred to as either being an expansionary policy where an expansionary policy increases the total supply of money in the economy, and a contractionary policy decreases the total money supply.

a. Federal Open Market Committee
c. Tax exemption
b. Natural resources consumption tax
d. Monetary policy

26. In financial accounting, the term _____ is most commonly used to describe any part of shareholders' equity, except for basic share capital. Sometimes, the term is used instead of the term provision; such a use, however, is inconsistent with the terminology suggested by International Accounting Standards Board. For more information about provisions, see provision (accounting.)

a. Treasury stock
c. Closing entries
b. FIFO and LIFO accounting
d. Reserve

27. In the global money market, _____ is an unsecured promissory note with a fixed maturity of one to 270 days.
_____ is a money-market security issued (sold) by large banks and corporations to get money to meet short term debt obligations (for example, payroll), and is only backed by an issuing bank or corporation's promise to pay the face amount on the maturity date specified on the note. Since it is not backed by collateral, only firms with excellent credit ratings from a recognized rating agency will be able to sell their _____ at a reasonable price.

a. Book building
c. Commercial paper
b. Financial distress
d. Trade-off theory

28. _____ is the term used to describe deposits residing in banks that are located outside the borders of the country that issues the currency the deposit is denominated in. For example a deposit denominated in US dollars residing in a Japanese bank is a _____ deposit, or more specifically a Eurodollar deposit.

Key points are the location of the bank and the denomination of the currency, not the nationality of the bank or the owner of the deposit/loan.

a. Eurocurrency
c. A Random Walk Down Wall Street
b. ABN Amro
d. AAB

29. In finance, the _____ is the global financial market for short-term borrowing and lending. It provides short-term liquidity funding for the global financial system. The _____ is where short-term obligations such as Treasury bills, commercial paper and bankers' acceptances are bought and sold.

a. Cramdown
c. Debt-for-equity swap
b. Consumer debt
d. Money market

30. A _____ s a time deposit, a financial product commonly offered to consumers by banks, thrift institutions, and credit unions.

6 *Chapter 1. Functions and Roles of the Financial System in the Global Economy*

They are similar to savings accounts in that they are insured and thus virtually risk-free; they are 'money in the bank'. They are different from savings accounts in that they have a specific, fixed term (often three months, six months, or one to five years), and, usually, a fixed interest rate.

- a. Certificate of deposit
- b. Reserve requirement
- c. Variable rate mortgage
- d. Time deposit

31. A _____ is a bond issued by a corporation. The term is usually applied to longer-term debt instruments, generally with a maturity date falling at least a year after their issue date. (The term 'commercial paper' is sometimes used for instruments with a shorter maturity.)

- a. Government bond
- b. Serial bond
- c. Brady bonds
- d. Corporate bond

32. A _____ is an international bond that is denominated in a currency not native to the country where it is issued. It can be categorised according to the currency in which it is issued. London is one of the centers of the _____ market, but _____s may be traded throughout the world - for example in Singapore or Tokyo.

- a. Education production function
- b. Economic entity
- c. Interest rate option
- d. Eurobond

33. In the United States, _____ are overnight borrowings by banks to maintain their bank reserves at the Federal Reserve. Banks keep reserves at Federal Reserve Banks to meet their reserve requirements and to clear financial transactions. Transactions in the _____ market enable depository institutions with reserve balances in excess of reserve requirements to lend reserves to institutions with reserve deficiencies.

- a. Federal funds rate
- b. Federal funds
- c. 4-4-5 Calendar
- d. Regulation T

34. In business and finance, a _____ (also referred to as equity _____) of stock means a _____ of ownership in a corporation (company.) In the plural, stocks is often used as a synonym for _____s especially in the United States, but it is less commonly used that way outside of North America.

In the United Kingdom, South Africa, and Australia, stock can also refer to completely different financial instruments such as government bonds or, less commonly, to all kinds of marketable securities.

- a. Bucket shop
- b. Share
- c. Procter ' Gamble
- d. Margin

35. In finance, a _____ is a debt security, in which the authorized issuer owes the holders a debt and, depending on the terms of the _____, is obliged to pay interest (the coupon) and/or to repay the principal at a later date, termed maturity.

Thus a _____ is a loan: the issuer is the borrower, the _____ holder is the lender, and the coupon is the interest. _____s provide the borrower with external funds to finance long-term investments, or, in the case of government _____s, to finance current expenditure.

Chapter 1. Functions and Roles of the Financial System in the Global Economy

a. Puttable bond
b. Bond
c. Catastrophe bonds
d. Convertible bond

36. A _____ is a fungible, negotiable instrument representing financial value. They are broadly categorized into debt securities (such as banknotes, bonds and debentures), and equity securities; e.g., common stocks. The company or other entity issuing the _____ is called the issuer.
   a. Securities lending
   b. Book entry
   c. Security
   d. Tracking stock

37. The _____ is the over-the-counter financial market in contracts for future delivery, so called forward contracts. Forward contracts are personalized between parties. The _____ is a general term used to describe the informal market by which these contracts are entered into.
   a. Limits to arbitrage
   b. Delta hedging
   c. Spot rate
   d. Forward market

38. In finance, a _____ is a standardized contract, to buy or sell a specified commodity of standardized quality at a certain date in the future, at a market determined price (the futures price.)

The price is determined by the instantaneous equilibrium between the forces of supply and demand among competing buy and sell orders on the exchange at the time of the purchase or sale of the contract.

In many cases, the items may be such non-traditional 'commodities' as foreign currencies, commercial or government paper [e.g., bonds], or 'baskets' of corporate equity ['stock indices'] or other financial instruments.

   a. Repurchase agreement
   b. Financial future
   c. Heston model
   d. Futures contract

39. The _____ is that part of the capital markets that deals with the issuance of new securities. Companies, governments or public sector institutions can obtain funding through the sale of a new stock or bond issue. This is typically done through a syndicate of securities dealers.
   a. Primary market
   b. Peer group analysis
   c. Sector rotation
   d. Volatility clustering

40. The _____ is the financial market where previously issued securities and financial instruments such as stock, bonds, options, and futures are bought and sold. The term '_____' is also used refer to the market for any used goods or assets, or an alternative use for an existing product or asset where the customer base is the second market

With primary issuances of securities or financial instruments, or the primary market, investors purchase these securities directly from issuers such as corporations issuing shares in an IPO or private placement, or directly from the federal government in the case of treasuries.

   a. Financial market
   b. Performance attribution
   c. Secondary market
   d. Delta neutral

Chapter 1. Functions and Roles of the Financial System in the Global Economy

41. The _____ or cash market is a commodities or securities market in which goods are sold for cash and delivered immediately. Contracts bought and sold on these markets are immediately effective. _____s can operate wherever the infrastructure exists to conduct the transaction.
   a. Non-deliverable forward
   b. Currency swap
   c. Foreign exchange controls
   d. Spot market

42. In business and accounting, _____s are everything of value that is owned by a person or company. The balance sheet of a firm records the monetary value of the _____s owned by the firm. The two major _____ classes are tangible _____s and intangible _____s.
   a. EBITDA
   b. Accounts payable
   c. Income
   d. Asset

43. An _____ is a contract written by a seller that conveys to the buyer the right -- but not the obligation -- to buy (in the case of a call _____) or to sell (in the case of a put _____) a particular asset, such as a piece of property such as, among others, a futures contract. In return for granting the _____, the seller collects a payment (the premium) from the buyer.

   For example, buying a call _____ provides the right to buy a specified quantity of a security at a set strike price at some time on or before expiration, while buying a put _____ provides the right to sell.

   a. Option
   b. AT'T Mobility LLC
   c. Amortization
   d. Annuity

44. In economics and finance, _____ is the practice of taking advantage of a price differential between two or more markets: striking a combination of matching deals that capitalize upon the imbalance, the profit being the difference between the market prices. When used by academics, an _____ is a transaction that involves no negative cash flow at any probabilistic or temporal state and a positive cash flow in at least one state; in simple terms, a risk-free profit.
   a. Issuer
   b. Efficient-market hypothesis
   c. Initial margin
   d. Arbitrage

45. _____ (in a financial context) is the assumption of the risk of loss, in return for the uncertain possibility of a reward. Only if one may safely say that a particular position involves no risk may one say, strictly speaking, that such a position represents an 'investment.' Financial _____ involves the buying, holding, selling, and short-selling of stocks, bonds, commodities, currencies, collectibles, real estate, derivatives, or any valuable financial instrument to profit from fluctuations in its price as opposed to buying it for use or for income via methods such as dividends or interest. _____ represents one of four market roles in Western financial markets, distinct from hedging, long- or short-term investing, and arbitrage.
   a. Market anomaly
   b. Forward market
   c. Speculation
   d. Central Securities Depository

46. A _____ is a professionally managed type of collective investment scheme that pools money from many investors and invests it in stocks, bonds, short-term money market instruments, and/or other securities. The _____ will have a fund manager that trades the pooled money on a regular basis. Currently, the worldwide value of all _____s totals more than $26 trillion.

Since 1940, there have been three basic types of investment companies in the United States: open-end funds, also known in the US as _____s; unit investment trusts (UITs); and closed-end funds.

a. Trust company
b. Net asset value
c. Financial intermediary
d. Mutual fund

47. The U.S. _____ is an independent agency of the United States government which holds primary responsibility for enforcing the federal securities laws and regulating the securities industry, the nation's stock and options exchanges, and other electronic securities markets. The SEC was created by section 4 of the SEC of 1934 (now codified as 15 U.S.C. §78d and commonly referred to as the 1934 Act.)
a. 529 plan
b. 4-4-5 Calendar
c. Securities and Exchange Commission
d. 7-Eleven

48. A _____ assesses the credit worthiness of an individual, corporation, or even a country. _____s are calculated from financial history and current assets and liabilities. Typically, a _____ tells a lender or investor the probability of the subject being able to pay back a loan.
a. Credit cycle
b. Debenture
c. Credit report monitoring
d. Credit rating

Chapter 2. Financial Assets, Money, Financial Transactions, and Financial Institutions

1. In business and accounting, _____s are everything of value that is owned by a person or company. The balance sheet of a firm records the monetary value of the _____s owned by the firm. The two major _____ classes are tangible _____s and intangible _____s.
   a. Income
   b. Asset
   c. Accounts payable
   d. EBITDA

2. _____ refers to a business or organization attempting to acquire goods or services to accomplish the goals of the enterprise. Though there are several organizations that attempt to set standards in the _____ process, processes can vary greatly between organizations. Typically the word '_____' is not used interchangeably with the word 'procurement', since procurement typically includes Expediting, Supplier Quality, and Traffic and Logistics (T'L) in addition to _____.
   a. 529 plan
   b. 4-4-5 Calendar
   c. 7-Eleven
   d. Purchasing

3. _____, in bookkeeping, refers to assets, liabilities, income, and expenses recorded on individual pages of the so called book of final entry or ledger. Changes in _____ value are made by chronologically posting debit (DR) and credit (CR) entries to its page. Examples of _____s are cash, _____s receivable, mortgages, loans, land and buildings, common stock, sales, services provided, wages, and payroll overhead.
   a. Accretion
   b. Option
   c. Alpha
   d. Account

4. _____ is a file or account that contains money that a person or company owes to suppliers, but hasn't paid yet (a form of debt.) When you receive an invoice you add it to the file, and then you remove it when you pay. Thus, the A/P is a form of credit that suppliers offer to their purchasers by allowing them to pay for a product or service after it has already been received.
   a. Outstanding balance
   b. Earnings before interest, taxes, depreciation and amortization
   c. Accounts payable
   d. Accrual

5. In the global money market, _____ is an unsecured promissory note with a fixed maturity of one to 270 days. _____ is a money-market security issued (sold) by large banks and corporations to get money to meet short term debt obligations (for example, payroll), and is only backed by an issuing bank or corporation's promise to pay the face amount on the maturity date specified on the note. Since it is not backed by collateral, only firms with excellent credit ratings from a recognized rating agency will be able to sell their _____ at a reasonable price.
   a. Book building
   b. Financial distress
   c. Trade-off theory
   d. Commercial paper

6. _____ is a form of corporation equity ownership represented in the securities. It is dangerous in comparison to preferred shares and some other investment options, in that in the event of bankruptcy, _____ investors receive their funds after preferred stockholders, bondholders, creditors, etc. On the other hand, common shares on average perform better than preferred shares or bonds over time.
   a. Stock market bubble
   b. Stock split
   c. Stop-limit order
   d. Common stock

7. A _____ is a bond issued by a corporation. The term is usually applied to longer-term debt instruments, generally with a maturity date falling at least a year after their issue date. (The term 'commercial paper' is sometimes used for instruments with a shorter maturity.)

a. Serial bond	b. Government bond
c. Brady bonds	d. Corporate bond

8. _____ is that which is owed; usually referencing assets owed, but the term can cover other obligations. In the case of assets, _____ is a means of using future purchasing power in the present before a summation has been earned. Some companies and corporations use _____ as a part of their overall corporate finance strategy.

a. Debt	b. Credit cycle
c. Partial Payment	d. Cross-collateralization

9. A _____ is a financial contract whose value is derived from the value of something else (known as the underlying.) The underlying on which a _____ is based can be an asset, weather conditions bonds or other forms of credit.

a. 529 plan	b. 7-Eleven
c. 4-4-5 Calendar	d. Derivative

10. A _____ is a futures contract on a short term interest rate (STIR.) Contracts vary, but are often defined on an interest rate index such as 3-month sterling or US dollar LIBOR.

They are traded across a wide range of currencies, including the G12 country currencies and many others.

a. Real estate derivatives	b. Notional amount
c. Dual currency deposit	d. Financial future

11. In finance, the _____ is the global financial market for short-term borrowing and lending. It provides short-term liquidity funding for the global financial system. The _____ is where short-term obligations such as Treasury bills, commercial paper and bankers' acceptances are bought and sold.

a. Consumer debt	b. Cramdown
c. Money market	d. Debt-for-equity swap

12. An _____ is a contract written by a seller that conveys to the buyer the right -- but not the obligation -- to buy (in the case of a call _____) or to sell (in the case of a put _____) a particular asset, such as a piece of property such as, among others, a futures contract. In return for granting the _____, the seller collects a payment (the premium) from the buyer.

For example, buying a call _____ provides the right to buy a specified quantity of a security at a set strike price at some time on or before expiration, while buying a put _____ provides the right to sell.

a. AT'T Mobility LLC	b. Option
c. Amortization	d. Annuity

13. An _____ is defined as 'a promise which meets the requirements for the formation of a contract and limits the promisor's power to revoke an offer.' Restatement (Second) of Contracts § 25 (1981.)

Quite simply, an _____ is a type of contract that protects an offeree from an offeror's ability to revoke the contract.

Consideration for the _____ is still required as it is still a form of contract.

Chapter 2. Financial Assets, Money, Financial Transactions, and Financial Institutions

a. A Random Walk Down Wall Street
b. AAB
c. ABN Amro
d. Option contract

14. _____ is typically a higher ranking stock than voting shares, and its terms are negotiated between the corporation and the investor.

_____ usually carry no voting rights, but may carry superior priority over common stock in the payment of dividends and upon liquidation. _____ may carry a dividend that is paid out prior to any dividends to common stock holders.

a. Second lien loan
b. Follow-on offering
c. Trade-off theory
d. Preferred stock

15. A _____ is the price of a single share of a no. of saleable stocks of the company. Once the stock is purchased, the owner becomes a shareholder of the company that issued the share.
a. Whisper numbers
b. Trading curb
c. Stock split
d. Share price

16. In business and finance, a _____ (also referred to as equity _____) of stock means a _____ of ownership in a corporation (company.) In the plural, stocks is often used as a synonym for _____s especially in the United States, but it is less commonly used that way outside of North America.

In the United Kingdom, South Africa, and Australia, stock can also refer to completely different financial instruments such as government bonds or, less commonly, to all kinds of marketable securities.

a. Margin
b. Share
c. Procter ' Gamble
d. Bucket shop

17. In finance, a _____ is a debt security, in which the authorized issuer owes the holders a debt and, depending on the terms of the _____, is obliged to pay interest (the coupon) and/or to repay the principal at a later date, termed maturity.

Thus a _____ is a loan: the issuer is the borrower, the _____ holder is the lender, and the coupon is the interest. _____s provide the borrower with external funds to finance long-term investments, or, in the case of government _____s, to finance current expenditure.

a. Catastrophe bonds
b. Bond
c. Puttable bond
d. Convertible bond

18. A _____ is an exchange of promises between two or more parties to do an act which is enforceable in a court of law. It is where an unqualified offer meets a qualified acceptance and the parties reach Consensus ad Idem. The parties must have the necessary capacity to _____ and the _____ must not be either trifling, indeterminate, impossible or illegal.
a. 529 plan
b. 7-Eleven
c. 4-4-5 Calendar
d. Contract

Chapter 2. Financial Assets, Money, Financial Transactions, and Financial Institutions

19. In finance, the _____ is the system that allows the transfer of money between savers and borrowers.

Put another way: the _____ is a set of complex and closely interconnected financial institutions, markets, instruments, services, practices, and transactions.

- a. Passive income
- b. Horizontal merger
- c. 4-4-5 Calendar
- d. Financial system

20. In finance, a _____ is a standardized contract, to buy or sell a specified commodity of standardized quality at a certain date in the future, at a market determined price (the futures price.)

The price is determined by the instantaneous equilibrium between the forces of supply and demand among competing buy and sell orders on the exchange at the time of the purchase or sale of the contract.

In many cases, the items may be such non-traditional 'commodities' as foreign currencies, commercial or government paper [e.g., bonds], or 'baskets' of corporate equity ['stock indices'] or other financial instruments.

- a. Futures contract
- b. Repurchase agreement
- c. Heston model
- d. Financial future

21. A _____ is a fungible, negotiable instrument representing financial value. They are broadly categorized into debt securities (such as banknotes, bonds and debentures), and equity securities; e.g., common stocks. The company or other entity issuing the _____ is called the issuer.
- a. Book entry
- b. Security
- c. Securities lending
- d. Tracking stock

22. In financial accounting, a _____ or statement of financial position is a summary of a person's or organization's balances. Assets, liabilities and ownership equity are listed as of a specific date, such as the end of its financial year. A _____ is often described as a snapshot of a company's financial condition.
- a. Statement on Auditing Standards No. 70: Service Organizations
- b. Statement of retained earnings
- c. Financial statements
- d. Balance sheet

23. The _____ is a private, not-for-profit organization whose primary purpose is to develop generally accepted accounting principles (GAAP) within the United States in the public's interest. The Securities and Exchange Commission (SEC) designated the _____ as the organization responsible for setting accounting standards for public companies in the U.S. It was created in 1973, replacing the Accounting Principles Board and the Committee on Accounting Procedure of the American Institute of Certified Public Accountants. The _____'s mission is 'to establish and improve standards of financial accounting and reporting for the guidance and education of the public, including issuers, auditors, and users of financial information.'

The _____ is not a governmental body.

- a. PlaNet Finance
- b. MRU Holdings
- c. Credit karma
- d. FASB

Chapter 2. Financial Assets, Money, Financial Transactions, and Financial Institutions

24. _____ are formal records of a business' financial activities.

_____ provide an overview of a business' financial condition in both short and long term. There are four basic _____:

1. **Balance sheet**: also referred to as statement of financial position or condition, reports on a company's assets, liabilities, and net equity as of a given point in time.
2. **Income statement**: also referred to as Profit and Loss statement (or a 'P'L'), reports on a company's income, expenses, and profits over a period of time.
3. **Statement of retained earnings**: explains the changes in a company's retained earnings over the reporting period.
4. **Statement of cash flows**: reports on a company's cash flow activities, particularly its operating, investing and financing activities.

a. Notes to the Financial Statements
b. Statement on Auditing Standards No. 70: Service Organizations
c. Financial statements
d. Statement of retained earnings

25. In the theory of capital structure _____ is the name for a firm using its profits as a source of capital for new investment, rather than a) distributing them to firm's owners or other investors and b) obtaining capital elsewhere. It is to be contrasted with external financing which consists of new money from outside of the firm brought in for investment. _____ is generally thought to be less expensive for the firm than external financing because the firm does not have to incur transaction costs to obtain it, nor does it have to pay the taxes associated with paying dividends.
    a. Operating ratio
    b. Employee stock option
    c. Underwriting contract
    d. Internal financing

26. In business, _____ is the total assets minus total outside liabilities of an individual or a company. For a company, this is called shareholders' equity and may be referred to as book value. _____ is stated as at a particular point in time.
    a. Certified International Investment Analyst
    b. Moneylender
    c. Restructuring
    d. Net worth

27. _____ or financing is to provide capital (funds), which means money for a project, a person, a business or any other private or public institutions.

Those funds can be allocated for either short term or long term purposes. The health fund is a new way of _____ private healthcare centers.

a. Proxy fight
b. Product life cycle
c. Synthetic CDO
d. Funding

28. In the theory of capital structure, _____ is the phrase used to describe funds that firms obtain from outside of the firm. It is contrasted to internal financing which consists mainly of profits retained by the firm for investment. There are many kinds of _____.
    a. Ownership equity
    b. External financing
    c. Adjustment
    d. Asset-backed commercial paper

Chapter 2. Financial Assets, Money, Financial Transactions, and Financial Institutions

29. _____ are defined as identifiable non-monetary assets that cannot be seen, touched or physically measured, which are created through time and/or effort and that are identifiable as a separate asset. There are two primary forms of intangibles - legal intangibles (such as trade secrets (e.g., customer lists), copyrights, patents, trademarks, and goodwill) and competitive intangibles (such as knowledge activities (know-how, knowledge), collaboration activities, leverage activities, and structural activities.) Legal intangibles generate legal property rights defensible in a court of law.
   a. ABN Amro
   b. AAB
   c. A Random Walk Down Wall Street
   d. Intangible assets

30. _____ is the amount by which a government, private company, or individual's spending exceeds income over a particular period of time, the opposite of budget surplus.

When the expenditures of a government to individuals and corporations) are greater than its tax revenues, it creates a deficit in the government budget; such a deficit is known as _____. This causes the government to borrow capital from the 'world market', increasing further debt, debt service and interest rates

   a. Deficit spending
   b. 4-4-5 Calendar
   c. 529 plan
   d. 7-Eleven

31. In finance, a _____ is the party in a loan agreement which receives money or other instrument from a lender and promises to repay the lender in a specified time.
   a. Debt management plan
   b. Borrower
   c. Line of credit
   d. Cash credit

32. _____ is a fee paid on borrowed assets. It is the price paid for the use of borrowed money , or, money earned by deposited funds . Assets that are sometimes lent with _____ include money, shares, consumer goods through hire purchase, major assets such as aircraft, and even entire factories in finance lease arrangements.
   a. AAB
   b. A Random Walk Down Wall Street
   c. Insolvency
   d. Interest

33. In the United States, _____ are overnight borrowings by banks to maintain their bank reserves at the Federal Reserve. Banks keep reserves at Federal Reserve Banks to meet their reserve requirements and to clear financial transactions. Transactions in the _____ market enable depository institutions with reserve balances in excess of reserve requirements to lend reserves to institutions with reserve deficiencies.
   a. Federal funds
   b. 4-4-5 Calendar
   c. Federal funds rate
   d. Regulation T

34. In financial accounting, the term _____ is most commonly used to describe any part of shareholders' equity, except for basic share capital. Sometimes, the term is used instead of the term provision; such a use, however, is inconsistent with the terminology suggested by International Accounting Standards Board. For more information about provisions, see provision (accounting.)
   a. FIFO and LIFO accounting
   b. Closing entries
   c. Treasury stock
   d. Reserve

35. In economics, _____ is the total amount of money available in an economy at a particular point in time. There are several ways to define 'money', but each includes currency in circulation and demand deposits.

Chapter 2. Financial Assets, Money, Financial Transactions, and Financial Institutions

_____ data are recorded and published.

a. 7-Eleven
b. 4-4-5 Calendar
c. 529 plan
d. Money supply

36. A _____ is a measure of the average price of consumer goods and services purchased by households. The _____ can be used to index (i.e., adjust for the effects of inflation) wages, salaries, pensions, or regulated or contracted prices. The _____ is, along with the population census and the National Income and Product Accounts, one of the most closely watched national economic statistics.

a. Divisia index
b. 4-4-5 Calendar
c. 529 plan
d. Consumer price index

37. _____ in economics is a persistent decrease in the general price level of goods and services - a negative inflation rate. When the inflation rate slows down (decreases, but remains positive), this is known as disinflation.

Inflation destroys real value in money.

a. Deflation
b. Fixed exchange rate
c. Recession
d. Mercantilism

38. The _____ is one of the measures of national income and input for a given country's economy. _____ is defined as the total cost of all finished goods and services produced within the country in a stipulated period of time (usually a 365-day year.) It is sometimes regarded as the sum of profits added at every level of production (the intermediate stages) of all final goods and services produced within a country in a stipulated timeframe, and it is rarely given a monetary value.

a. Recession
b. Macroeconomics
c. Behavioral finance
d. Gross domestic product

39. In economics, _____ is a rise in the general level of prices of goods and services in an economy over a period of time. The term '_____' once referred to increases in the money supply (monetary _____); however, economic debates about the relationship between money supply and price levels have led to its primary use today in describing price _____. _____ can also be described as a decline in the real value of money--a loss of purchasing power in the medium of exchange which is also the monetary unit of account.

a. A Random Walk Down Wall Street
b. AAB
c. ABN Amro
d. Inflation

40. A _____ is a normalized average (typically a weighted average) of prices for a given class of goods or services in a given region, during a given interval of time. It is a statistic designed to help to compare how these prices, taken as a whole, differ between time periods or geographical locations.

a. Transfer pricing
b. Discounts and allowances
c. Price discrimination
d. Price Index

41. _____ is the value of goods/services compared to the amount paid with a currency. Currency can be either a commodity money, like gold or silver, or fiat currency like US dollars which are the world reserve currency. As Adam Smith noted, having money gives one the ability to 'command' others' labor, so _____ to some extent is power over other people, to the extent that they are willing to trade their labor or goods for money or currency.

Chapter 2. Financial Assets, Money, Financial Transactions, and Financial Institutions 17

    a. 7-Eleven
    c. 4-4-5 Calendar
    b. 529 plan
    d. Purchasing power

42. In economics, _____ refers to any price or value expressed in money of the day, as opposed to real value, which adjusts for the effect of inflation. Examples include a bundle of commodities, such as gross domestic product, and income. For a series of _____s in successive years, different values could be because of differences in the price level, an index of prices.
    a. Future value
    c. Biflation
    b. Financial transaction
    d. Nominal value

43. In economics, business, and accounting, a _____ is the value of money that has been used up to produce something, and hence is not available for use anymore. In business, the _____ may be one of acquisition, in which case the amount of money expended to acquire it is counted as _____. In this case, money is the input that is gone in order to acquire the thing.
    a. Sliding scale fees
    c. Marginal cost
    b. Cost
    d. Fixed costs

44. _____ are government bonds issued by the United States Department of the Treasury through the Bureau of the Public Debt. They are the debt financing instruments of the U.S. Federal government, and they are often referred to simply as Treasuries or Treasurys. There are four types of marketable _____: Treasury bills, Treasury notes, Treasury bonds, and Treasury Inflation Protected Securities (TIPS.)
    a. Treasury securities
    c. 4-4-5 Calendar
    b. Treasury Inflation Protected Securities
    d. Treasury Inflation-Protected Securities

45. An _____ is the price a borrower pays for the use of money they do not own, and the return a lender receives for deferring the use of funds, by lending it to the borrower. _____s are normally expressed as a percentage rate over the period of one year.

_____s targets are also a vital tool of monetary policy and are used to control variables like investment, inflation, and unemployment.

    a. A Random Walk Down Wall Street
    c. ABN Amro
    b. AAB
    d. Interest rate

46. _____ is the risk (variability in value) borne by an interest-bearing asset, such as a loan or a bond, due to variability of interest rates. In general, as rates rise, the price of a fixed rate bond will fall, and vice versa. _____ is commonly measured by the bond's duration.
    a. Interest rate risk
    c. Official bank rate
    b. A Random Walk Down Wall Street
    d. International Fisher effect

47. _____ is a legally declared inability or impairment of ability of an individual or organization to pay their creditors. Creditors may file a _____ petition against a debtor ('involuntary _____') in an effort to recoup a portion of what they are owed or initiate a restructuring. In the majority of cases, however, _____ is initiated by the debtor (a 'voluntary _____' that is filed by the bankrupt individual or organization.)

a. 4-4-5 Calendar
b. Debt settlement
c. 529 plan
d. Bankruptcy

48. _____ is the provision of resources (such as granting a loan) by one party to another party where that second party does not reimburse the first party immediately, thereby generating a debt, and instead arranges either to repay or return those resources (or material(s) of equal value) at a later date. The first party is called a creditor, also known as a lender, while the second party is called a debtor, also known as a borrower.

Movements of financial capital are normally dependent on either _____ or equity transfers.

a. Warrant
b. Comparable
c. Clearing house
d. Credit

49. A _____ is a cooperative financial institution that is owned and controlled by its members, and operated for the purpose of promoting thrift, providing credit at reasonable rates, and providing other financial services to its members. Many _____s exist to further community development or sustainable international development on a local level. Worldwide, _____ systems vary significantly in terms of total system assets and average institution asset size since _____s exist in a wide range of sizes, ranging from volunteer operations with a handful of members to institutions with several billion dollars in assets and hundreds of thousands of members.

a. Credit Union Service Organization
b. Credit union
c. Corporate credit union
d. Fi-linx

50. A _____ is a pool of assets forming an independent legal entity that are bought with the contributions to a pension plan for the exclusive purpose of financing pension plan benefits.

_____s are important shareholders of listed and private companies. They are especially important to the stock market where large institutional investors like the Ontario Teachers' Pension Plan dominate.

a. Leveraged buyout
b. Limited liability company
c. Leverage
d. Pension fund

51. A _____ is a financial institution that specializes in accepting savings deposits and making mortgage and other loans. The S'L or thrift term is mainly used in the United States; similar institutions in the United Kingdom, Ireland and some Commonwealth countries include building societies and trustee savings banks.

They are often mutually held, meaning that the depositors and borrowers are members with voting rights, and have the ability to direct the financial and managerial goals of the organization, not unlike the poliyholders of a mutual insurance company.

a. Person-to-person lending
b. Savings and loan association
c. Mutual fund
d. Net asset value

52. _____ or amalgamation is the act of merging many things into one. In business, it often refers to the mergers or acquisitions of many smaller companies into much larger ones. The financial accounting term of _____ refers to the aggregated financial statements of a group company as consolidated account.

Chapter 2. Financial Assets, Money, Financial Transactions, and Financial Institutions

a. Cost of goods sold
b. Retained earnings
c. Write-off
d. Consolidation

53. An _____ is a company whose main business is holding securities of other companies purely for investment purposes. The _____ invests money on behalf of its shareholders who in turn share in the profits and losses.
   a. Unit investment trust
   b. Investment company
   c. AAB
   d. A Random Walk Down Wall Street

54. Money funds (or _____, money market mutual funds) are mutual funds that invest in short-term debt instruments.

_____, also known as principal stability funds, seek to limit exposure to losses due to credit, market and liquidity risks.
_____, in the United States, are regulated by the Securities and Exchange Commission's (SEC) Investment Company Act of 1940.

   a. Stock fund
   b. Money market funds
   c. Closed-end fund
   d. Mutual fund fees and expenses

55. A _____ is a professionally managed type of collective investment scheme that pools money from many investors and invests it in stocks, bonds, short-term money market instruments, and/or other securities. The _____ will have a fund manager that trades the pooled money on a regular basis. Currently, the worldwide value of all _____s totals more than $26 trillion.

Since 1940, there have been three basic types of investment companies in the United States: open-end funds, also known in the US as _____s; unit investment trusts (UITs); and closed-end funds.

   a. Trust company
   b. Financial intermediary
   c. Mutual fund
   d. Net asset value

56. A _____ is a tax designation for a corporation investing in real estate that reduces or eliminates corporate income taxes. In return, _____s are required to distribute 95% of their income, which may be taxable in the hands of the investors. The _____ structure was designed to provide a similar structure for investment in real estate as mutual funds provide for investment in stocks.
   a. Real Estate Investment Trust
   b. REIT
   c. Liquidation value
   d. Real estate investing

57. A _____ or _____ is a tax designation for a corporation investing in real estate that reduces or eliminates corporate income taxes. In return, _____s are required to distribute 95% of their income, which may be taxable in the hands of the investors. The _____ structure was designed to provide a similar structure for investment in real estate as mutual funds provide for investment in stocks.
   a. Liquidation value
   b. Tenancy
   c. Real estate investment trust
   d. Real estate investing

58. A _____ or bank is a financial institution whose primary activity is to act as a payment agent for customers and to borrow and lend money.

Chapter 2. Financial Assets, Money, Financial Transactions, and Financial Institutions

The first modern bank was founded in Italy in Genoa in 1406, its name was Banco di San Giorgio (Bank of St. George.) Many other financial activities were added over time.

- a. Black Sea Trade and Development Bank
- b. Bought deal
- c. 4-4-5 Calendar
- d. Banker

59. The institution most often referenced by the word '_____' is a public or publicly traded _____, the shares of which are traded on a public stock exchange (e.g., the New York Stock Exchange or Nasdaq in the United States) where shares of stock of _____s are bought and sold by and to the general public. Most of the largest businesses in the world are publicly traded _____s. However, the majority of _____s are said to be closely held, privately held or close _____s, meaning that no ready market exists for the trading of shares.
- a. Depository Trust Company
- b. Federal Home Loan Mortgage Corporation
- c. Corporation
- d. Protect

60. Explicit _____ is a measure implemented in many countries to protect bank depositors, in full or in part, from losses caused by a bank's inability to pay its debts when due. _____ systems are one component of a financial system safety net that promotes financial stability.
- a. Reserve requirement
- b. Banking panic
- c. Time deposit
- d. Deposit Insurance

61. _____ in finance is a risk management technique, related to hedging, that mixes a wide variety of investments within a portfolio. Because the fluctuations of a single security have less impact on a diverse portfolio, _____ minimizes the risk from any one investment.

A simple example of _____ is the following: On a particular island the entire economy consists of two companies: one that sells umbrellas and another that sells sunscreen.

- a. 529 plan
- b. 4-4-5 Calendar
- c. Diversification
- d. 7-Eleven

62. _____, in microeconomics, are the cost advantages that a business obtains due to expansion. _____ may be utilized by any size firm expanding its scale of operation.
- a. Uniform Commercial Code
- b. Employee Retirement Income Security Act
- c. Articles of incorporation
- d. Economies of scale

63. The _____ is a United States government corporation created by the Glass-Steagall Act of 1933. It provides deposit insurance, which guarantees the safety of checking and savings deposits in member banks, currently up to $250,000 per depositor per bank. Insured deposits are backed by the full faith and credit of the United States.
- a. Federal Deposit Insurance Corporation
- b. Ford Foundation
- c. FASB
- d. NYSE Group

64. _____ refer to services provided by the finance industry.

Chapter 2. Financial Assets, Money, Financial Transactions, and Financial Institutions   21

The finance industry encompasses a broad range of organizations that deal with the management of money. Among these organizations are banks, credit card companies, insurance companies, consumer finance companies, stock brokerages, investment funds and some government sponsored enterprises.

a. Financial services
b. Cost of carry
c. Delta hedging
d. Financial instruments

65. _____ is a life of security. It may also refer to the final payment date of a loan or other financial instrument, at which point all remaining interest and principal is due to be paid.

1, 3, 6 months _____ band can be calculated by using 30-day per month periods.

a. Primary market
b. Replacement cost
c. False billing
d. Maturity

66. In finance, _____, also known as return on investment is the ratio of money gained or lost on an investment relative to the amount of money invested. The amount of money gained or lost may be referred to as interest, profit/loss, gain/loss, or net income/loss. The money invested may be referred to as the asset, capital, principal, or the cost basis of the investment.

a. Composiition of Creditors
b. Doctrine of the Proper Law
c. Stock or scrip dividends
d. Rate of return

67. _____ most frequently refers to the standard deviation of the continuously compounded returns of a financial instrument with a specific time horizon. It is often used to quantify the risk of the instrument over that time period. _____ is typically expressed in annualized terms, and it may either be an absolute number ($5) or a fraction of the mean (5%).

a. Portfolio insurance
b. Volatility
c. Currency swap
d. Seasoned equity offering

68. In economics, _____ is the removal of intermediaries in a supply chain: 'cutting out the middleman'. Instead of going through traditional distribution channels, which had some type of intermediate (such as a distributor, wholesaler, broker, or agent), companies may now deal with every customer directly, for example via the Internet. One important factor is a drop in the cost of servicing customers directly.

a. Disintermediation
b. 7-Eleven
c. 4-4-5 Calendar
d. 529 plan

69. In finance, _____ (or gearing) is borrowing money to supplement existing funds for investment in such a way that the potential positive or negative outcome is magnified and/or enhanced. It generally refers to using borrowed funds, or debt, so as to attempt to increase the returns to equity. Deleveraging is the action of reducing borrowings.

a. Pension fund
b. Leverage
c. Financial endowment
d. Limited partnership

Chapter 3. The Financial Information Marketplace

1. In economics and contract theory, _____ deals with the study of decisions in transactions where one party has more or better information than the other. This creates an imbalance of power in transactions which can sometimes cause the transactions to go awry. Examples of this problem are adverse selection and moral hazard.
   - a. A Random Walk Down Wall Street
   - b. ABN Amro
   - c. AAB
   - d. Information asymmetry

2. In economics, business, and accounting, a _____ is the value of money that has been used up to produce something, and hence is not available for use anymore. In business, the _____ may be one of acquisition, in which case the amount of money expended to acquire it is counted as _____. In this case, money is the input that is gone in order to acquire the thing.
   - a. Sliding scale fees
   - b. Marginal cost
   - c. Fixed costs
   - d. Cost

3. A _____, is a mathematical formalization of a trajectory that consists of taking successive random steps. The results of _____ analysis have been applied to computer science, physics, ecology, economics and a number of other fields as a fundamental model for random processes in time. For example, the path traced by a molecule as it travels in a liquid or a gas, the search path of a foraging animal, the price of a fluctuating stock and the financial status of a gambler can all be modeled as _____s.
   - a. 4-4-5 Calendar
   - b. 529 plan
   - c. 7-Eleven
   - d. Random walk

4. A _____ is a fungible, negotiable instrument representing financial value. They are broadly categorized into debt securities (such as banknotes, bonds and debentures), and equity securities; e.g., common stocks. The company or other entity issuing the _____ is called the issuer.
   - a. Securities lending
   - b. Tracking stock
   - c. Book entry
   - d. Security

5. The U.S. _____ is an independent agency of the United States government which holds primary responsibility for enforcing the federal securities laws and regulating the securities industry, the nation's stock and options exchanges, and other electronic securities markets. The SEC was created by section 4 of the SEC of 1934 (now codified as 15 U.S.C. § 78d and commonly referred to as the 1934 Act.)
   - a. 7-Eleven
   - b. 4-4-5 Calendar
   - c. 529 plan
   - d. Securities and Exchange Commission

6. _____ is the provision of resources (such as granting a loan) by one party to another party where that second party does not reimburse the first party immediately, thereby generating a debt, and instead arranges either to repay or return those resources (or material(s) of equal value) at a later date. The first party is called a creditor, also known as a lender, while the second party is called a debtor, also known as a borrower.

   Movements of financial capital are normally dependent on either _____ or equity transfers.

   - a. Comparable
   - b. Clearing house
   - c. Warrant
   - d. Credit

7. A _____ assesses the credit worthiness of an individual, corporation, or even a country. _____s are calculated from financial history and current assets and liabilities. Typically, a _____ tells a lender or investor the probability of the subject being able to pay back a loan.

a. Credit cycle
b. Credit report monitoring
c. Debenture
d. Credit rating

8. _____ is the trading of a corporation's stock or other securities (e.g. bonds or stock options) by individuals with potential access to non-public information about the company. In most countries, trading by corporate insiders such as officers, key employees, directors, and large shareholders may be legal, if this trading is done in a way that does not take advantage of non-public information. However, the term is frequently used to refer to a practice in which an insider or a related party trades based on material non-public information obtained during the performance of the insider's duties at the corporation, or otherwise in breach of a fiduciary duty or other relationship of trust and confidence or where the non-public information was misappropriated from the company.
   a. Open outcry
   b. Intellidex
   c. Equity investment
   d. Insider trading

9. The institution most often referenced by the word '_____' is a public or publicly traded _____, the shares of which are traded on a public stock exchange (e.g., the New York Stock Exchange or Nasdaq in the United States) where shares of stock of _____s are bought and sold by and to the general public. Most of the largest businesses in the world are publicly traded _____s. However, the majority of _____s are said to be closely held, privately held or close _____s, meaning that no ready market exists for the trading of shares.
   a. Federal Home Loan Mortgage Corporation
   b. Protect
   c. Depository Trust Company
   d. Corporation

10. '_____' is a 1970 paper by the economist George Akerlof. It discusses information asymmetry, which occurs when the seller knows more about a product than the buyer. Akerlof, Michael Spence, and Joseph Stiglitz jointly received the Nobel Memorial Prize in Economic Sciences in 2001 for their research related to asymmetric information.
    a. 7-Eleven
    b. 4-4-5 Calendar
    c. The Market for Lemons: Quality Uncertainty and the Market Mechanism
    d. 529 plan

11. In economics, _____ is the removal of intermediaries in a supply chain: 'cutting out the middleman'. Instead of going through traditional distribution channels, which had some type of intermediate (such as a distributor, wholesaler, broker, or agent), companies may now deal with every customer directly, for example via the Internet. One important factor is a drop in the cost of servicing customers directly.
    a. 7-Eleven
    b. 4-4-5 Calendar
    c. Disintermediation
    d. 529 plan

12. Behavioral economics and _____ are closely related fields that have evolved to be a separate branch of economic and financial analysis which applies scientific research on human and social, cognitive and emotional factors to better understand economic decisions by, say, consumers, borrowers, investors, and how they affect market prices, returns and the allocation of resources.

The field is primarily concerned with the bounds of rationality (selfishness, self-control) of economic agents. Behavioral models typically integrate insights from psychology with neo-classical economic theory.

   a. Recession
   b. Medium of exchange
   c. Market structure
   d. Behavioral finance

24 *Chapter 3. The Financial Information Marketplace*

13. Explicit _____ is a measure implemented in many countries to protect bank depositors, in full or in part, from losses caused by a bank's inability to pay its debts when due. _____ systems are one component of a financial system safety net that promotes financial stability.
   a. Deposit Insurance
   b. Reserve requirement
   c. Banking panic
   d. Time deposit

14. The _____ is a United States government corporation created by the Glass-Steagall Act of 1933. It provides deposit insurance, which guarantees the safety of checking and savings deposits in member banks, currently up to $250,000 per depositor per bank. Insured deposits are backed by the full faith and credit of the United States.
   a. FASB
   b. Ford Foundation
   c. Federal Deposit Insurance Corporation
   d. NYSE Group

15. In statistics, _____ has two related meanings:

   - the arithmetic _____
   - the expected value of a random variable, which is also called the population _____.

   It is sometimes stated that the '_____' is average. This is incorrect if '_____' is taken in the specific sense of 'arithmetic _____' as there are different types of averages: the _____, median, and mode. Other simple statistical analyses use measures of spread, such as range, interquartile range, or standard deviation. For a real-valued random variable X, the _____ is the expectation of X. Note that not every probability distribution has a defined _____; see the Cauchy distribution for an example.

   a. Harmonic mean
   b. Sample size
   c. Probability distribution
   d. Mean

16. In financial accounting, the term _____ is most commonly used to describe any part of shareholders' equity, except for basic share capital. Sometimes, the term is used instead of the term provision; such a use, however, is inconsistent with the terminology suggested by International Accounting Standards Board. For more information about provisions, see provision (accounting.)
   a. FIFO and LIFO accounting
   b. Treasury stock
   c. Reserve
   d. Closing entries

17. A _____ is any actual or hypothesized stock market trend based on the calendar, such as rises and falls associated with particular days of the week or months of the year.

Examples include:

- Halloween indicator (or the 'Sell in May' principle)
- January effect
- Mark Twain effect
- Monday effect
- Weekend effect
- Turn-of-the-Month effect
- Holiday effect

a. 4-4-5 Calendar
c. 7-Eleven

b. 529 plan
d. Calendar effect

18. _____, consists of the buying and selling of products or services over electronic systems such as the Internet and other computer networks. The amount of trade conducted electronically has grown extraordinarily with widespread Internet usage. The use of commerce is conducted in this way, spurring and drawing on innovations in electronic funds transfer, supply chain management, Internet marketing, online transaction processing, electronic data interchange (EDI), inventory management systems, and automated data collection systems.

a. ABN Amro
c. AAB

b. A Random Walk Down Wall Street
d. Electronic commerce

19. An _____ is a company whose main business is holding securities of other companies purely for investment purposes. The _____ invests money on behalf of its shareholders who in turn share in the profits and losses.

a. AAB
c. A Random Walk Down Wall Street

b. Unit investment trust
d. Investment Company

20. In the United States, the Financial Industry Regulatory Authority (FINRA) is a self-regulatory organization (SRO) under the Securities Exchange Act of 1934, successor to the _____.

FINRA is responsible for regulatory oversight of all securities firms that do business with the public; professional training, testing and licensing of registered persons; arbitration and mediation; market regulation by contract for The NASDAQ Stock Market, Inc., the American Stock Exchange LLC, and the International Securities Exchange, LLC; and industry utilities, such as Trade Reporting Facilities and other over-the-counter operations.

a. 7-Eleven
c. 529 plan

b. 4-4-5 Calendar
d. NASD

21. In the United States, the Financial Industry Regulatory Authority (FINRA) is a self-regulatory organization (SRO) under the Securities Exchange Act of 1934, successor to the _____, Inc.

FINRA is responsible for regulatory oversight of all securities firms that do business with the public; professional training, testing and licensing of registered persons; arbitration and mediation; market regulation by contract for The NASDAQ Stock Market, Inc., the American Stock Exchange LLC, and the International Securities Exchange, LLC; and industry utilities, such as Trade Reporting Facilities and other over-the-counter operations.

a. National Association of Securities Dealers
c. 7-Eleven

b. 529 plan
d. 4-4-5 Calendar

22. The term _____ usually refers to a company that is permitted to offer its registered securities for sale to the general public, typically through a stock exchange, or occasionally a company whose stock is traded over the counter via market makers who use non-exchange quotation services.

The term '_____' may also refer to a company owned by the government.

a. General partnership	b. Corporation
c. First Prudential Markets	d. Public Company

23. The _____ (sometimes called 'Peekaboo') is a private-sector, non-profit corporation created by the Sarbanes-Oxley Act, a 2002 United States federal law, to oversee the auditors of public companies. Its stated purpose is to 'protect the interests of investors and further the public interest in the preparation of informative, fair, and independent audit reports'. Although a private entity, the _____ has many government-like regulatory functions, making it in some ways similar to the private Self Regulatory Organizations (SROs) that regulate stock markets and other aspects of the financial markets in the United States.

a. Financial Crimes Enforcement Network	b. Gamelan Council
c. World Trade Organization	d. Public Company Accounting Oversight Board

24. The U.S. Securities and Exchange Commission's (SEC's) Regulation Fair Disclosure, also commonly referred to as _____ was an SEC ruling implemented in October 2000 (.) It mandated that all publicly traded companies must disclose material information to all investors at the same time.

The regulation sought to stamp out selective disclosure, in which some investors (often large institutional investors) received market moving information before others (often smaller, individual investors.)

a. Commodity Pool Operator	b. Regulation Fair Disclosure
c. Revenue recognition	d. Regulation FD

25. The _____ is a federally mandated non-profit corporation in the United States that protects securities investors from harm if a broker-dealer company fails. Investors are not insured for any potential loss while invested in the market.

Congress created _____ in 1970 through the _____ (15 U.S.C.

a. Williams Act	b. Rule 144A
c. Prudent man rule	d. SIPC

26. The _____ of 2002 (Pub.L. 107-204, 116 Stat. 745, enacted July 30, 2002), also known as the Public Company Accounting Reform and Investor Protection Act of 2002 and commonly called Sarbanes-Oxley, Sarbox or SOX, is a United States federal law enacted on July 30, 2002 in response to a number of major corporate and accounting scandals including those affecting Enron, Tyco International, Adelphia, Peregrine Systems and WorldCom.

a. Foreign Corrupt Practices Act	b. Blue sky law
c. Duty of loyalty	d. Sarbanes-Oxley Act

27. Congress enacted the _____, in the aftermath of the stock market crash of 1929 and during the ensuing Great Depression. It requires that any offer or sale of securities using the means and instrumentalities of interstate commerce be registered pursuant to the 1933 Act, unless an exemption from registration exists under the law.

a. Securities Act of 1933	b. 529 plan
c. 7-Eleven	d. 4-4-5 Calendar

Chapter 3. The Financial Information Marketplace

28. The _____ of 1934 is a law governing the secondary trading of securities (stocks, bonds, and debentures) in the United States of America. The Act, 48 Stat. 881 (enacted June 6, 1934), codified at 15 U.S.C. § 78a et seq., was a sweeping piece of legislation. The Act and related statutes form the basis of regulation of the financial markets and their participants in the United States.

   a. 4-4-5 Calendar
   b. 7-Eleven
   c. 529 plan
   d. Securities Exchange Act

29. The _____ of 1970 codified at 15 U.S.C. § 78aaa through 15 U.S.C. § 78lll, established the Securities Investor Protection Corporation (SIPC). Most brokers and dealers registered under the Securities Exchange Act of 1934 are required to be members of the SIPC.

   The SIPC maintains a fund that is intended to protect investors against the misappropriation of their funds and of most types of securities in the event of the failure of their broker.

   a. Quiet period
   b. McFadden Act
   c. Fiduciary
   d. Securities Investor Protection Act

30. The _____ is a federally mandated non-profit corporation in the United States that protects securities investors from harm if a broker-dealer company fails. Investors are not insured for any potential loss while invested in the market.

   Congress created _____ in 1970 through the Securities Investor Protection Act (15 U.S.C.

   a. SIPC
   b. Prudent man rule
   c. Securities Investor Protection Corporation
   d. Rule 144A

31. In banking and finance, _____ denotes all activities from the time a commitment is made for a transaction until it is settled. _____ is necessary because the speed of trades is much faster than the cycle time for completing the underlying transaction.

   In its widest sense _____ involves the management of post-trading, pre-settlement credit exposures, to ensure that trades are settled in accordance with market rules, even if a buyer or seller should become insolvent prior to settlement.

   a. Clearing house
   b. Share
   c. Procter ' Gamble
   d. Clearing

32. The goals of _____ are to establish different market settings and environments to observe experimentally and analyze agents' behavior and the resulting characteristics of trading flows, information diffusion and aggregation, price setting mechanism and returns processes. This can happen for instance by conducting trading simulations or establishing and studying the behaviour of people in artificial competitive market-like settings.

   Researchers in _____ can study to what extent existing financial economics theory makes valid predictions and attempt to discover new principles on which theory can be extended.

a. Experimental Finance
b. Alternative display facility
c. Intelligent investor
d. Earnings growth

33. A _____ is a bond issued by a corporation. The term is usually applied to longer-term debt instruments, generally with a maturity date falling at least a year after their issue date. (The term 'commercial paper' is sometimes used for instruments with a shorter maturity.)
a. Brady bonds
b. Serial bond
c. Government bond
d. Corporate bond

34. _____ is that which is owed; usually referencing assets owed, but the term can cover other obligations. In the case of assets, _____ is a means of using future purchasing power in the present before a summation has been earned. Some companies and corporations use _____ as a part of their overall corporate finance strategy.
a. Partial Payment
b. Cross-collateralization
c. Debt
d. Credit cycle

35. _____ refers to any type of investment that yields a regular (or fixed) return.

For example, if you lend money to a borrower and the borrower has to pay interest once a month, you have been issued a fixed-income security. When a company does this, it is often called a bond or corporate bank debt (although preferred stock is also sometimes considered to be _____).

a. 4-4-5 Calendar
b. Bond market
c. 529 plan
d. Fixed income

36. _____ is a fee paid on borrowed assets. It is the price paid for the use of borrowed money, or, money earned by deposited funds. Assets that are sometimes lent with _____ include money, shares, consumer goods through hire purchase, major assets such as aircraft, and even entire factories in finance lease arrangements.
a. Insolvency
b. A Random Walk Down Wall Street
c. AAB
d. Interest

37. An _____ is the price a borrower pays for the use of money they do not own, and the return a lender receives for deferring the use of funds, by lending it to the borrower. _____s are normally expressed as a percentage rate over the period of one year.

_____s targets are also a vital tool of monetary policy and are used to control variables like investment, inflation, and unemployment.

a. ABN Amro
b. Interest rate
c. AAB
d. A Random Walk Down Wall Street

38. A _____ is the price of a single share of a no. of saleable stocks of the company. Once the stock is purchased, the owner becomes a shareholder of the company that issued the share.
a. Trading curb
b. Stock split
c. Whisper numbers
d. Share price

Chapter 3. The Financial Information Marketplace

39. _____ are government bonds issued by the United States Department of the Treasury through the Bureau of the Public Debt. They are the debt financing instruments of the U.S. Federal government, and they are often referred to simply as Treasuries or Treasurys. There are four types of marketable _____: Treasury bills, Treasury notes, Treasury bonds, and Treasury Inflation Protected Securities (TIPS.)
   a. Treasury Inflation Protected Securities
   b. Treasury securities
   c. Treasury Inflation-Protected Securities
   d. 4-4-5 Calendar

40. In finance, the term _____ describes the amount in cash that returns to the owners of a security. Normally it does not include the price variations, at the difference of the total return. _____ applies to various stated rates of return on stocks (common and preferred, and convertible), fixed income instruments (bonds, notes, bills, strips, zero coupon), and some other investment type insurance products (e.g. annuities.)
   a. Yield to maturity
   b. Macaulay duration
   c. 4-4-5 Calendar
   d. Yield

41. In finance, a _____ is a debt security, in which the authorized issuer owes the holders a debt and, depending on the terms of the _____, is obliged to pay interest (the coupon) and/or to repay the principal at a later date, termed maturity.

Thus a _____ is a loan: the issuer is the borrower, the _____ holder is the lender, and the coupon is the interest. _____s provide the borrower with external funds to finance long-term investments, or, in the case of government _____s, to finance current expenditure.

   a. Puttable bond
   b. Catastrophe bonds
   c. Convertible bond
   d. Bond

42. A _____ is the highest price that a buyer (i.e., bidder) is willing to pay for a good. It is usually referred to simply as the 'bid.'

In bid and ask, the _____ stands in contrast to the ask price or 'offer', and the difference between the two is called the bid/ask spread.

An unsolicited bid or offer is when a person or company receives a bid even though they are not looking to sell.

   a. Settlement date
   b. Mid price
   c. Political risk
   d. Bid price

43. A _____ is a payment made by a corporation to its shareholder members. When a corporation earns a profit or surplus, that money can be put to two uses: it can either be re-invested in the business (called retained earnings), or it can be paid to the shareholders as a _____. Many corporations retain a portion of their earnings and pay the remainder as a _____.

   a. Dividend yield
   b. Dividend
   c. Dividend puzzle
   d. Special dividend

44. The _____ on a company stock is the company's annual dividend payments divided by its market cap, or the dividend per share divided by the price per share. It is often expressed as a percentage.

Dividend payments on preferred shares are stipulated by the prospectus.

a. Dividend imputation
b. Special dividend
c. Dividend yield
d. Dividend reinvestment plan

45. The _____ is one of several stock market indices, created by nineteenth-century Wall Street Journal editor and Dow Jones ' Company co-founder Charles Dow. Dow compiled the index to gauge the performance of the industrial sector of the American stock market. It is the second-oldest U.S. market index, after the Dow Jones Transportation Average, which Dow also created.

a. 7-Eleven
b. 529 plan
c. 4-4-5 Calendar
d. Dow Jones Industrial Average

46. _____ is an American publishing and financial information firm.

The company was founded in 1882 by three reporters: Charles Dow, Edward Jones, and Charles Bergstresser. Like The New York Times and the Washington Post, the company was in recent years publicly traded but privately controlled.

a. Federal National Mortgage Association
b. Holding company
c. Dow Jones ' Company
d. The Dun ' Bradstreet Corporation

47. In business and finance, a _____ (also referred to as equity _____) of stock means a _____ of ownership in a corporation (company.) In the plural, stocks is often used as a synonym for _____s especially in the United States, but it is less commonly used that way outside of North America.

In the United Kingdom, South Africa, and Australia, stock can also refer to completely different financial instruments such as government bonds or, less commonly, to all kinds of marketable securities.

a. Share
b. Margin
c. Procter ' Gamble
d. Bucket shop

48. An _____ is a contract written by a seller that conveys to the buyer the right -- but not the obligation -- to buy (in the case of a call _____) or to sell (in the case of a put _____) a particular asset, such as a piece of property such as, among others, a futures contract. In return for granting the _____, the seller collects a payment (the premium) from the buyer.

For example, buying a call _____ provides the right to buy a specified quantity of a security at a set strike price at some time on or before expiration, while buying a put _____ provides the right to sell.

a. Annuity
b. AT'T Mobility LLC
c. Amortization
d. Option

49. _____ are those dividends paid out in form of additional stock shares of the issuing corporation or other corporation They are usually issued in proportion to shares owned (for example for every 100 shares of stock owned, 5% stock dividend will yield 5 extra shares). If this payment involves the issue of new shares, this is very similar to a stock split in that it increases the total number of shares while lowering the price of each share and does not change the market capitalization or the total value of the shares held
- a. Database auditing
- b. The Hong Kong Securities Institute
- c. Time-based currency
- d. Stock or scrip dividends

50. A _____ is a method of measuring a section of the stock market. Many indices are cited by news or financial services firms and are used to benchmark the performance of portfolios such as mutual funds.
- a. Stop order
- b. Program trading
- c. Trading curb
- d. Stock market index

51. The _____ of a stock is a measure of the price paid for a share relative to the annual income or profit earned by the firm per share. It is a financial ratio used for valuation: a higher _____ means that investors are paying more for each unit of income, so the stock is more expensive compared to one with lower _____.

The _____ has units of years, which can be interpreted as 'number of years of earnings to pay back purchase price'.

- a. Return of capital
- b. Quick ratio
- c. Sustainable growth rate
- d. P/E ratio

52. In the global money market, _____ is an unsecured promissory note with a fixed maturity of one to 270 days. _____ is a money-market security issued (sold) by large banks and corporations to get money to meet short term debt obligations (for example, payroll), and is only backed by an issuing bank or corporation's promise to pay the face amount on the maturity date specified on the note. Since it is not backed by collateral, only firms with excellent credit ratings from a recognized rating agency will be able to sell their _____ at a reasonable price.
- a. Commercial paper
- b. Financial distress
- c. Book building
- d. Trade-off theory

53. In finance, the _____ of a financial asset measures the sensitivity of the asset's price to interest rate movements, expressed as a number of years. The reason for expressing this sensitivity in years is that the time that will elapse until a cash flow is received allows more interest to accumulate. Therefore the price of an asset with long term cashflows has more interest rate sensitivity than an asset with cashflows in the near future.
- a. 4-4-5 Calendar
- b. Yield to maturity
- c. Macaulay duration
- d. Duration

54. In economics, _____ is a rise in the general level of prices of goods and services in an economy over a period of time. The term '_____' once referred to increases in the money supply (monetary _____); however, economic debates about the relationship between money supply and price levels have led to its primary use today in describing price _____. _____ can also be described as a decline in the real value of money--a loss of purchasing power in the medium of exchange which is also the monetary unit of account.
- a. A Random Walk Down Wall Street
- b. AAB
- c. ABN Amro
- d. Inflation

Chapter 3. The Financial Information Marketplace

55. _____ is the risk (variability in value) borne by an interest-bearing asset, such as a loan or a bond, due to variability of interest rates. In general, as rates rise, the price of a fixed rate bond will fall, and vice versa. _____ is commonly measured by the bond's duration.
- a. International Fisher effect
- b. A Random Walk Down Wall Street
- c. Official bank rate
- d. Interest rate risk

56. The _____ is an American stock exchange. It is the largest electronic screen-based equity securities trading market in the United States. With approximately 3,200 companies, it has more trading volume per day than any other stock exchange in the world.
- a. 529 plan
- b. 7-Eleven
- c. 4-4-5 Calendar
- d. NASDAQ

57. The _____ is a stock exchange based in New York City, New York. It is the largest stock exchange in the world by dollar value of its listed companies securities. As of October 2008, the combined capitalization of all domestic _____ listed companies was $10.1 trillion.
- a. New York Stock Exchange
- b. 7-Eleven
- c. 529 plan
- d. 4-4-5 Calendar

58. A _____, securities exchange or (in Europe) bourse is a corporation or mutual organization which provides 'trading' facilities for stock brokers and traders, to trade stocks and other securities. _____s also provide facilities for the issue and redemption of securities as well as other financial instruments and capital events including the payment of income and dividends. The securities traded on a _____ include: shares issued by companies, unit trusts and other pooled investment products and bonds.
- a. 529 plan
- b. 4-4-5 Calendar
- c. 7-Eleven
- d. Stock Exchange

59. In economics, _____ is a measure of the relative satisfaction from or desirability of consumption of various goods and services. Given this measure, one may speak meaningfully of increasing or decreasing _____, and thereby explain economic behavior in terms of attempts to increase one's _____. For illustrative purposes, changes in _____ are sometimes expressed in units called utils.
- a. Utility function
- b. AAB
- c. Utility
- d. A Random Walk Down Wall Street

60. In finance, the _____ is the relation between the interest rate (or cost of borrowing) and the time to maturity of the debt for a given borrower in a given currency. For example, the current U.S. dollar interest rates paid on U.S. Treasury securities for various maturities are closely watched by many traders, and are commonly plotted on a graph such as the one on the right which is informally called 'the _____.' More formal mathematical descriptions of this relation are often called the term structure of interest rates.

The yield of a debt instrument is the annualized percentage increase in the value of the investment.

- a. 529 plan
- b. Yield curve
- c. 7-Eleven
- d. 4-4-5 Calendar

61. A _____ is a unit that is equal to 1/100th of a percentage point. It is frequently used to express percentage point changes of less than 1%. It avoids the ambiguity between relative and absolute discussions about rates.

a. 4-4-5 Calendar
b. Bond market
c. 529 plan
d. Basis point

62. _____ is a legal entity that develops, registers and sells securities for the purpose of financing its operations. _____s may be domestic or foreign governments, corporations or investment trusts. _____s are legally responsible for the obligations of the issue and for reporting financial conditions, material developments and any other operational activities as required by the regulations of their jurisdictions.
   a. Arbitrage
   b. Initial margin
   c. Efficient-market hypothesis
   d. Issuer

63. _____ is the discipline of identifying, monitoring and limiting risks. In some cases the acceptable risk may be near zero. Risks can come from accidents, natural causes and disasters as well as deliberate attacks from an adversary.
   a. FIFO
   b. 4-4-5 Calendar
   c. Penny stock
   d. Risk Management

64. The _____ is a free-trade and professional association that promotes and advocates issues important to the banking industry in the United States. The _____'s national headquarters are in Washington, D.C. In addition to its trade association mission, the _____ also performs educational components for consumers through its Educational Foundation affiliate.

While the _____ works on a national level, it also is supported by state operated offices (sometimes referred to as 'Leagues') which focus attention on state level support.

   a. ABN Amro
   b. A Random Walk Down Wall Street
   c. American Bankers Association
   d. AAB

65. A _____ or bank is a financial institution whose primary activity is to act as a payment agent for customers and to borrow and lend money.

The first modern bank was founded in Italy in Genoa in 1406, its name was Banco di San Giorgio (Bank of St. George.)

Many other financial activities were added over time.

   a. 4-4-5 Calendar
   b. Black Sea Trade and Development Bank
   c. Bought deal
   d. Banker

66. A _____ is a cooperative financial institution that is owned and controlled by its members, and operated for the purpose of promoting thrift, providing credit at reasonable rates, and providing other financial services to its members. Many _____s exist to further community development or sustainable international development on a local level. Worldwide, _____ systems vary significantly in terms of total system assets and average institution asset size since _____s exist in a wide range of sizes, ranging from volunteer operations with a handful of members to institutions with several billion dollars in assets and hundreds of thousands of members.
   a. Fi-linx
   b. Credit Union Service Organization
   c. Corporate credit union
   d. Credit Union

Chapter 3. The Financial Information Marketplace

67. A _____ (U.S.), or credit reference agency (UK) is a company that collects information from various sources and provides consumer credit information on individual consumers for a variety of uses. This helps lenders assess credit worthiness, the ability to pay back a loan, and can affect the interest rate and other terms of a loan. Interest rates are not the same for everyone, but instead can be based on risk-based pricing, a form of price discrimination based on the different expected risks of different borrowers, as set out in their credit rating.

a. Probability of default
b. Reserve requirement
c. Credit bureau
d. Wall Street Journal prime rate

68. The _____ provide stable, on-demand, low-cost funding to American financial institutions for home mortgage loans, small business, rural, agricultural, and economic development lending. With their members, the _____ank System represents the largest collective source of home mortgage and community credit in the United States. The banks do not provide loans directly to individuals, only to other banks.

a. 529 plan
b. 4-4-5 Calendar
c. Federal Home Loan Banks
d. 7-Eleven

69. In the United States, _____ are overnight borrowings by banks to maintain their bank reserves at the Federal Reserve. Banks keep reserves at Federal Reserve Banks to meet their reserve requirements and to clear financial transactions. Transactions in the _____ market enable depository institutions with reserve balances in excess of reserve requirements to lend reserves to institutions with reserve deficiencies.

a. Federal funds rate
b. 4-4-5 Calendar
c. Regulation T
d. Federal funds

70. A _____, securities analyst, research analyst, equity analyst, or investment analyst is a person who performs financial analysis for external or internal clients as a core part of the job.

An analyst studies companies and other entities to arrive at the estimate of their financial value. It is normally done by analyzing financial reports, aided by follow-up interviews with company representatives and industry experts.

a. Financial Analyst
b. Stockbroker
c. Purchasing manager
d. Portfolio manager

71. The _____ is the national association of U.S. investment companies. _____ encourages adherence to high ethical standards, promotes public understanding of funds and investing, and advances the interests of investment funds and their shareholders, directors, and advisers.

As of July 1, 2008, _____ membership included 9,067 mutual funds, 675 closed-end funds, 625 exchange-traded funds (ETFs), and three sponsors of unit investment trust (UITs.)

a. A Random Walk Down Wall Street
b. AAB
c. ABN Amro
d. Investment Company Institute

72. A _____, reserve bank, or monetary authority is the entity responsible for the monetary policy of a country or of a group of member states. It is a bank that can lend money to other banks in times of need. Its primary responsibility is to maintain the stability of the national currency and money supply, but more active duties include controlling subsidized-loan interest rates, and acting as a lender of last resort to the banking sector during times of financial crisis (private banks often being integral to the national financial system.)

Chapter 3. The Financial Information Marketplace 35

a. 7-Eleven
c. 529 plan

b. 4-4-5 Calendar
d. Central bank

73. _____ is the removal or simplification of government rules and regulations that constrain the operation of market forces. _____ does not mean elimination of laws against fraud, but eliminating or reducing government control of how business is done, thereby moving toward a more free market.

The stated rationale for '_____' is often that fewer and simpler regulations will lead to a raised level of competitiveness, therefore higher productivity, more efficiency and lower prices overall.

a. Value added
c. Demand shock

b. Deregulation
d. Supply shock

74. The _____ (NYSE: FNM), commonly known as Fannie Mae, is a stockholder-owned corporation chartered by Congress in 1968 as a government sponsored enterprise (GSE), but founded in 1938 during the Great Depression. The corporation's purpose is to purchase and securitize mortgages in order to ensure that funds are consistently available to the institutions that lend money to home buyers.

On September 7, 2008, James Lockhart, director of the Federal Housing Finance Agency (FHFA), announced that Fannie Mae and Freddie Mac were being placed into conservatorship of the FHFA.

a. General partnership
c. The Depository Trust ' Clearing Corporation

b. SPDR
d. Federal National Mortgage Association

75. _____, in bookkeeping, refers to assets, liabilities, income, and expenses recorded on individual pages of the so called book of final entry or ledger. Changes in _____ value are made by chronologically posting debit (DR) and credit (CR) entries to its page. Examples of _____s are cash, _____s receivable, mortgages, loans, land and buildings, common stock, sales, services provided, wages, and payroll overhead.
a. Alpha
c. Accretion

b. Option
d. Account

76. The _____ is one of the measures of national income and input for a given country's economy. _____ is defined as the total cost of all finished goods and services produced within the country in a stipulated period of time (usually a 365-day year.) It is sometimes regarded as the sum of profits added at every level of production (the intermediate stages) of all final goods and services produced within a country in a stipulated timeframe, and it is rarely given a monetary value.
a. Macroeconomics
c. Recession

b. Behavioral finance
d. Gross domestic product

77. _____, refers to consumption opportunity gained by an entity within a specified time frame, which is generally expressed in monetary terms. However, for households and individuals, '_____ is the sum of all the wages, salaries, profits, interests payments, rents and other forms of earnings received... in a given period of time.' For firms, _____ generally refers to net-profit: what remains of revenue after expenses have been subtracted.
a. OIBDA
c. Annual report

b. Income
d. Accrual

78. In financial accounting, a _____ or statement of financial position is a summary of a person's or organization's balances. Assets, liabilities and ownership equity are listed as of a specific date, such as the end of its financial year. A _____ is often described as a snapshot of a company's financial condition.
   a. Financial statements
   b. Statement of retained earnings
   c. Statement on Auditing Standards No. 70: Service Organizations
   d. Balance sheet

79. The _____ is a private, not-for-profit organization whose primary purpose is to develop generally accepted accounting principles (GAAP) within the United States in the public's interest. The Securities and Exchange Commission (SEC) designated the _____ as the organization responsible for setting accounting standards for public companies in the U.S. It was created in 1973, replacing the Accounting Principles Board and the Committee on Accounting Procedure of the American Institute of Certified Public Accountants. The _____'s mission is 'to establish and improve standards of financial accounting and reporting for the guidance and education of the public, including issuers, auditors, and users of financial information.'

The _____ is not a governmental body.

   a. PlaNet Finance
   b. FASB
   c. Credit karma
   d. MRU Holdings

80. _____ are formal records of a business' financial activities.

   _____ provide an overview of a business' financial condition in both short and long term. There are four basic _____:

   1. **Balance sheet**: also referred to as statement of financial position or condition, reports on a company's assets, liabilities, and net equity as of a given point in time.
   2. **Income statement**: also referred to as Profit and Loss statement (or a 'P'L'), reports on a company's income, expenses, and profits over a period of time.
   3. **Statement of retained earnings**: explains the changes in a company's retained earnings over the reporting period.
   4. **Statement of cash flows**: reports on a company's cash flow activities, particularly its operating, investing and financing activities.

   a. Statement on Auditing Standards No. 70: Service Organizations
   b. Notes to the Financial Statements
   c. Statement of retained earnings
   d. Financial statements

81. _____ is the price at which an asset would trade in a competitive Walrasian auction setting. _____ is often used interchangeably with open _____, fair value or fair _____, although these terms have distinct definitions in different standards, and may differ in some circumstances.

International Valuation Standards defines _____ as 'the estimated amount for which a property should exchange on the date of valuation between a willing buyer and a willing seller in an arm'e;s-length transaction after proper marketing wherein the parties had each acted knowledgeably, prudently, and without compulsion.'

_____ is a concept distinct from market price, which is 'e;the price at which one can transact'e;, while _____ is 'e;the true underlying value'e; according to theoretical standards.

a. Wrap account
c. Debt restructuring
b. T-Model
d. Market value

38 Chapter 4. The Future of the Financial System and Trends in the Money and Capital Markets

1. The _____ is the market for securities, where companies and governments can raise longterm funds. The _____ includes the stock market and the bond market. Financial regulators, such as the U.S. Securities and Exchange Commission, oversee the _____s in their designated countries to ensure that investors are protected against fraud.
   a. Capital market
   b. Spot rate
   c. Delta neutral
   d. Forward market

2. _____ or amalgamation is the act of merging many things into one. In business, it often refers to the mergers or acquisitions of many smaller companies into much larger ones. The financial accounting term of _____ refers to the aggregated financial statements of a group company as consolidated account.
   a. Consolidation
   b. Write-off
   c. Cost of goods sold
   d. Retained earnings

3. _____ is the removal or simplification of government rules and regulations that constrain the operation of market forces. _____ does not mean elimination of laws against fraud, but eliminating or reducing government control of how business is done, thereby moving toward a more free market.

   The stated rationale for '_____' is often that fewer and simpler regulations will lead to a raised level of competitiveness, therefore higher productivity, more efficiency and lower prices overall.

   a. Deregulation
   b. Value added
   c. Demand shock
   d. Supply shock

4. _____ is the term used to describe deposits residing in banks that are located outside the borders of the country that issues the currency the deposit is denominated in. For example a deposit denominated in US dollars residing in a Japanese bank is a _____ deposit, or more specifically a Eurodollar deposit.

   Key points are the location of the bank and the denomination of the currency, not the nationality of the bank or the owner of the deposit/loan.

   a. Eurocurrency
   b. ABN Amro
   c. A Random Walk Down Wall Street
   d. AAB

5. In economics, a _____ is a mechanism that allows people to easily buy and sell (trade) financial securities (such as stocks and bonds), commodities (such as precious metals or agricultural goods), and other fungible items of value at low transaction costs and at prices that reflect the efficient-market hypothesis.

   _____s have evolved significantly over several hundred years and are undergoing constant innovation to improve liquidity.

   Both general markets (where many commodities are traded) and specialized markets (where only one commodity is traded) exist.

   a. Secondary market
   b. Delta hedging
   c. Cost of carry
   d. Financial market

6. _____ refer to services provided by the finance industry.

Chapter 4. The Future of the Financial System and Trends in the Money and Capital Markets

The finance industry encompasses a broad range of organizations that deal with the management of money. Among these organizations are banks, credit card companies, insurance companies, consumer finance companies, stock brokerages, investment funds and some government sponsored enterprises.

a. Financial instruments
b. Delta hedging
c. Cost of carry
d. Financial services

7. In finance, the _____ is the system that allows the transfer of money between savers and borrowers.

Put another way: the _____ is a set of complex and closely interconnected financial institutions, markets, instruments, services, practices, and transactions.

a. 4-4-5 Calendar
b. Horizontal merger
c. Passive income
d. Financial system

8. The phrase _____ refers to the aspect of corporate strategy, corporate finance and management dealing with the buying, selling and combining of different companies that can aid, finance, or help a growing company in a given industry grow rapidly without having to create another business entity.

An acquisition, also known as a takeover, is the buying of one company (the 'target') by another. An acquisition may be friendly or hostile.

a. 529 plan
b. 7-Eleven
c. Mergers and acquisitions
d. 4-4-5 Calendar

9. In finance, the _____ is the global financial market for short-term borrowing and lending. It provides short-term liquidity funding for the global financial system. The _____ is where short-term obligations such as Treasury bills, commercial paper and bankers' acceptances are bought and sold.

a. Debt-for-equity swap
b. Cramdown
c. Money market
d. Consumer debt

10. _____ is the incidence or process of transferring ownership of a business, enterprise, agency or public service from the public sector (government) to the private sector (business.) In a broader sense, _____ refers to transfer of any government function to the private sector including governmental functions like revenue collection and law enforcement.

The term '_____' also has been used to describe two unrelated transactions. The first is a buyout, by the majority owner, of all shares of a public corporation or holding company's stock, privatizing a publicly traded stock. The second is a demutualization of a mutual organization or cooperative to form a joint stock company.

a. 7-Eleven
b. Privatization
c. 529 plan
d. 4-4-5 Calendar

11.

Chapter 4. The Future of the Financial System and Trends in the Money and Capital Markets

A _____ is a type of financial intermediary and a type of bank. Commercial banking is also known as business banking. It is a bank that provides checking accounts, savings accounts, and money market accounts and that accepts time deposits.

a. Commercial bank
b. 7-Eleven
c. 529 plan
d. 4-4-5 Calendar

12. _____ in finance is a risk management technique, related to hedging, that mixes a wide variety of investments within a portfolio. Because the fluctuations of a single security have less impact on a diverse portfolio, _____ minimizes the risk from any one investment.

A simple example of _____ is the following: On a particular island the entire economy consists of two companies: one that sells umbrellas and another that sells sunscreen.

a. Diversification
b. 529 plan
c. 7-Eleven
d. 4-4-5 Calendar

13. The institution most often referenced by the word '_____' is a public or publicly traded _____, the shares of which are traded on a public stock exchange (e.g., the New York Stock Exchange or Nasdaq in the United States) where shares of stock of _____s are bought and sold by and to the general public. Most of the largest businesses in the world are publicly traded _____s. However, the majority of _____s are said to be closely held, privately held or close _____s, meaning that no ready market exists for the trading of shares.

a. Federal Home Loan Mortgage Corporation
b. Depository Trust Company
c. Protect
d. Corporation

14. Explicit _____ is a measure implemented in many countries to protect bank depositors, in full or in part, from losses caused by a bank's inability to pay its debts when due. _____ systems are one component of a financial system safety net that promotes financial stability.

a. Banking panic
b. Time deposit
c. Reserve requirement
d. Deposit Insurance

15. The _____ is a United States government corporation created by the Glass-Steagall Act of 1933. It provides deposit insurance, which guarantees the safety of checking and savings deposits in member banks, currently up to $250,000 per depositor per bank. Insured deposits are backed by the full faith and credit of the United States.

a. Federal Deposit Insurance Corporation
b. Ford Foundation
c. NYSE Group
d. FASB

16. In financial accounting, the term _____ is most commonly used to describe any part of shareholders' equity, except for basic share capital. Sometimes, the term is used instead of the term provision; such a use, however, is inconsistent with the terminology suggested by International Accounting Standards Board. For more information about provisions, see provision (accounting.)

a. FIFO and LIFO accounting
b. Reserve
c. Treasury stock
d. Closing entries

Chapter 4. The Future of the Financial System and Trends in the Money and Capital Markets   41

17. _____ has been viewed as a process of increasing involvement of enterprises in international markets, although there is no agreed definition of _____ or international entrepreneurship. There are several _____ theories which try to explain why there are international activities.

Adam Smith claimed that a country should specialise in, and export, commodities in which it had an absolute advantage.

a. Internationalization
c. A Random Walk Down Wall Street
b. AAB
d. ABN Amro

18. _____ is a fee paid on borrowed assets. It is the price paid for the use of borrowed money , or, money earned by deposited funds . Assets that are sometimes lent with _____ include money, shares, consumer goods through hire purchase, major assets such as aircraft, and even entire factories in finance lease arrangements.
a. Interest
c. Insolvency
b. AAB
d. A Random Walk Down Wall Street

19. An _____ is the price a borrower pays for the use of money they do not own, and the return a lender receives for deferring the use of funds, by lending it to the borrower. _____s are normally expressed as a percentage rate over the period of one year.

_____s targets are also a vital tool of monetary policy and are used to control variables like investment, inflation, and unemployment.

a. ABN Amro
c. Interest rate
b. A Random Walk Down Wall Street
d. AAB

20. _____ is the risk (variability in value) borne by an interest-bearing asset, such as a loan or a bond, due to variability of interest rates. In general, as rates rise, the price of a fixed rate bond will fall, and vice versa. _____ is commonly measured by the bond's duration.
a. A Random Walk Down Wall Street
c. Interest rate risk
b. Official bank rate
d. International Fisher effect

21. _____ is the discipline of identifying, monitoring and limiting risks. In some cases the acceptable risk may be near zero. Risks can come from accidents, natural causes and disasters as well as deliberate attacks from an adversary.
a. FIFO
c. 4-4-5 Calendar
b. Penny stock
d. Risk management

22. A mutual shareholder or _____ is an individual or company (including a corporation) that legally owns one or more shares of stock in a joint stock company. A company's shareholders collectively own that company. Thus, the typical goal of such companies is to enhance shareholder value.
a. Trading curb
c. Stockholder
b. Stock market bubble
d. Limit order

23. A _____ is a foreign exchange agreement between two parties to exchange principal and fixed rate interest payments on a loan in one currency for principal and fixed rate interest payments on an equal (regarding net present value) loan in another currency. They are motivated by comparative advantage.

Chapter 4. The Future of the Financial System and Trends in the Money and Capital Markets

a. Foreign exchange market
b. Currency pair
c. Currency swap
d. Forex swap

24. A _____ is a futures contract on a short term interest rate (STIR.) Contracts vary, but are often defined on an interest rate index such as 3-month sterling or US dollar LIBOR.

They are traded across a wide range of currencies, including the G12 country currencies and many others.

a. Real estate derivatives
b. Financial future
c. Notional amount
d. Dual currency deposit

25. An _____ is a contract written by a seller that conveys to the buyer the right -- but not the obligation -- to buy (in the case of a call _____) or to sell (in the case of a put _____) a particular asset, such as a piece of property such as, among others, a futures contract. In return for granting the _____, the seller collects a payment (the premium) from the buyer.

For example, buying a call _____ provides the right to buy a specified quantity of a security at a set strike price at some time on or before expiration, while buying a put _____ provides the right to sell.

a. Annuity
b. Amortization
c. AT'T Mobility LLC
d. Option

26. An _____ is defined as 'a promise which meets the requirements for the formation of a contract and limits the promisor's power to revoke an offer.' Restatement (Second) of Contracts § 25 (1981.)

Quite simply, an _____ is a type of contract that protects an offeree from an offeror's ability to revoke the contract.

Consideration for the _____ is still required as it is still a form of contract.

a. ABN Amro
b. A Random Walk Down Wall Street
c. AAB
d. Option contract

27. In finance, a _____ is a derivative in which two counterparties agree to exchange one stream of cash flows against another stream. These streams are called the legs of the _____.

The cash flows are calculated over a notional principal amount, which is usually not exchanged between counterparties.

a. Swap
b. Volatility arbitrage
c. Local volatility
d. Volatility swap

28. In economics and finance, _____ is the practice of taking advantage of a price differential between two or more markets: striking a combination of matching deals that capitalize upon the imbalance, the profit being the difference between the market prices. When used by academics, an _____ is a transaction that involves no negative cash flow at any probabilistic or temporal state and a positive cash flow in at least one state; in simple terms, a risk-free profit.

Chapter 4. The Future of the Financial System and Trends in the Money and Capital Markets

a. Issuer
b. Initial margin
c. Efficient-market hypothesis
d. Arbitrage

29. A _____ is an exchange of promises between two or more parties to do an act which is enforceable in a court of law. It is where an unqualified offer meets a qualified acceptance and the parties reach Consensus ad Idem. The parties must have the necessary capacity to _____ and the _____ must not be either trifling, indeterminate, impossible or illegal.
    a. 4-4-5 Calendar
    b. 7-Eleven
    c. Contract
    d. 529 plan

30. _____ is the provision of resources (such as granting a loan) by one party to another party where that second party does not reimburse the first party immediately, thereby generating a debt, and instead arranges either to repay or return those resources (or material(s) of equal value) at a later date. The first party is called a creditor, also known as a lender, while the second party is called a debtor, also known as a borrower.

    Movements of financial capital are normally dependent on either _____ or equity transfers.

    a. Clearing house
    b. Comparable
    c. Warrant
    d. Credit

31. In finance, a _____ is a standardized contract, to buy or sell a specified commodity of standardized quality at a certain date in the future, at a market determined price (the futures price.)

    The price is determined by the instantaneous equilibrium between the forces of supply and demand among competing buy and sell orders on the exchange at the time of the purchase or sale of the contract.

    In many cases, the items may be such non-traditional 'commodities' as foreign currencies, commercial or government paper [e.g., bonds], or 'baskets' of corporate equity ['stock indices'] or other financial instruments.

    a. Heston model
    b. Repurchase agreement
    c. Financial future
    d. Futures contract

32. An _____ is a derivative in which one party exchanges a stream of interest payments for another party's stream of cash flows. _____s can be used by hedgers to manage their fixed or floating assets and liabilities. They can also be used by speculators to replicate unfunded bond exposures to profit from changes in interest rates.
    a. Interest rate Swap
    b. Implied volatility
    c. International Swaps and Derivatives Association
    d. Equity swap

33. In finance, a _____ is collateral that the holder of a position in securities, options, or futures contracts has to deposit to cover the credit risk of his counterparty (most often his broker.) This risk can arise if the holder has done any of the following:

    - borrowed cash from the counterparty to buy securities or options,
    - sold securities or options short, or
    - entered into a futures contract.

Chapter 4. The Future of the Financial System and Trends in the Money and Capital Markets

The collateral can be in the form of cash or securities, and it is deposited in a _____ account. On U.S. futures exchanges, '_____' was formally called performance bond.

_____ buying is buying securities with cash borrowed from a broker, using other securities as collateral.

a. Share
c. Margin
b. Procter ' Gamble
d. Credit

34. In economics and contract theory, _____ deals with the study of decisions in transactions where one party has more or better information than the other. This creates an imbalance of power in transactions which can sometimes cause the transactions to go awry. Examples of this problem are adverse selection and moral hazard.
    a. AAB
    b. A Random Walk Down Wall Street
    c. ABN Amro
    d. Information asymmetry

35. In financial accounting, a _____ or statement of financial position is a summary of a person's or organization's balances. Assets, liabilities and ownership equity are listed as of a specific date, such as the end of its financial year. A _____ is often described as a snapshot of a company's financial condition.
    a. Financial statements
    b. Statement of retained earnings
    c. Statement on Auditing Standards No. 70: Service Organizations
    d. Balance sheet

36. The _____ is a private, not-for-profit organization whose primary purpose is to develop generally accepted accounting principles (GAAP) within the United States in the public's interest. The Securities and Exchange Commission (SEC) designated the _____ as the organization responsible for setting accounting standards for public companies in the U.S. It was created in 1973, replacing the Accounting Principles Board and the Committee on Accounting Procedure of the American Institute of Certified Public Accountants. The _____'s mission is 'to establish and improve standards of financial accounting and reporting for the guidance and education of the public, including issuers, auditors, and users of financial information.'

The _____ is not a governmental body.

a. PlaNet Finance
c. Credit karma
b. MRU Holdings
d. FASB

37. _____ are formal records of a business' financial activities.

Chapter 4. The Future of the Financial System and Trends in the Money and Capital Markets

_____ provide an overview of a business' financial condition in both short and long term. There are four basic _____:

1. **Balance sheet**: also referred to as statement of financial position or condition, reports on a company's assets, liabilities, and net equity as of a given point in time.
2. **Income statement**: also referred to as Profit and Loss statement (or a 'P'L'), reports on a company's income, expenses, and profits over a period of time.
3. **Statement of retained earnings**: explains the changes in a company's retained earnings over the reporting period.
4. **Statement of cash flows**: reports on a company's cash flow activities, particularly its operating, investing and financing activities.

a. Statement of retained earnings
b. Financial statements
c. Notes to the Financial Statements
d. Statement on Auditing Standards No. 70: Service Organizations

38. In economics, business, and accounting, a _____ is the value of money that has been used up to produce something, and hence is not available for use anymore. In business, the _____ may be one of acquisition, in which case the amount of money expended to acquire it is counted as _____. In this case, money is the input that is gone in order to acquire the thing.
a. Fixed costs
b. Cost
c. Marginal cost
d. Sliding scale fees

39. _____ is a structured finance process that involves pooling and repackaging of cash-flow-producing financial assets into securities, which are then sold to investors. The term '_____' is derived from the fact that the form of financial instruments used to obtain funds from the investors are securities. As a portfolio risk backed by amortizing cash flows - and unlike general corporate debt - the credit quality of securitized debt is non-stationary due to changes in volatility that are time- and structure-dependent.
a. Special journals
b. The Glass-Steagall Act of 1933
c. Reputational risk
d. Securitization

40. _____ is subcontracting a process, such as product design or manufacturing, to a third-party company. The decision to outsource is often made in the interest of lowering cost or making better use of time and energy costs, redirecting or conserving energy directed at the competencies of a particular business, or to make more efficient use of land, labor, capital, (information) technology and resources. _____ became part of the business lexicon during the 1980s.
a. Exchange Rate Mechanism
b. AT'T Inc.
c. OTC Bulletin Board
d. Outsourcing

41. The _____ Act is an Act of the 106th United States Congress which repealed part of the Glass-Steagall Act of 1933, opening up competition among banks, securities companies and insurance companies. The Glass-Steagall Act prohibited any one institution from acting as both an investment bank and a commercial bank, or as both a bank and an insurer.

The _____ Act (GLBA) allowed commercial and investment banks to consolidate.

46 Chapter 4. The Future of the Financial System and Trends in the Money and Capital Markets

    a. 7-Eleven
    c. 4-4-5 Calendar
    b. Gramm-Leach-Bliley
    d. 529 plan

42. A _____ is a company that owns other companies' outstanding stock. It usually refers to a company which does not produce goods or services itself, rather its only purpose is owning shares of other companies. They allow the reduction of risk for the owners and can allow the ownership and control of a number of different companies.
    a. Privately held company
    b. MRU Holdings
    c. Federal National Mortgage Association
    d. Holding company

43. A _____, in business matters, is an entity that is controlled by a bigger and more powerful entity. The controlled entity is called a company, corporation, or limited liability company, and the controlling entity is called its parent (or the parent company.) The reason for this distinction is that a lone company cannot be a _____ of any organization; only an entity representing a legal fiction as a separate entity can be a _____.
    a. Subsidiary
    b. 529 plan
    c. Joint stock company
    d. 4-4-5 Calendar

44. A _____ is a fungible, negotiable instrument representing financial value. They are broadly categorized into debt securities (such as banknotes, bonds and debentures), and equity securities; e.g., common stocks. The company or other entity issuing the _____ is called the issuer.
    a. Securities lending
    b. Book entry
    c. Security
    d. Tracking stock

45. The U.S. _____ is an independent agency of the United States government which holds primary responsibility for enforcing the federal securities laws and regulating the securities industry, the nation's stock and options exchanges, and other electronic securities markets. The SEC was created by section 4 of the SEC of 1934 (now codified as 15 U.S.C. Â§ 78d and commonly referred to as the 1934 Act.)
    a. 7-Eleven
    b. 529 plan
    c. 4-4-5 Calendar
    d. Securities and Exchange Commission

46. A _____ assesses the credit worthiness of an individual, corporation, or even a country. _____s are calculated from financial history and current assets and liabilities. Typically, a _____ tells a lender or investor the probability of the subject being able to pay back a loan.
    a. Debenture
    b. Credit report monitoring
    c. Credit cycle
    d. Credit rating

47. _____ consists of the sale of goods or merchandise from a fixed location, such as a department store, boutique or kiosk in small or individual lots for direct consumption by the purchaser. _____ may include subordinated services, such as delivery. Purchasers may be individuals or businesses.
    a. 4-4-5 Calendar
    b. 7-Eleven
    c. 529 plan
    d. Retailing

48. A _____ is a system (including physical or electronic infrastructure and associated procedures and protocols) used to settle financial transactions in bond markets, currency markets, and futures, derivatives or options markets, or to transfer funds between financial institutions. Due to the backing of modern fiat currencies with government bonds, _____s are a core part of modern monetary systems.

a. Payment system
c. 7-Eleven
b. 4-4-5 Calendar
d. 529 plan

49. _____ is a type of trade policy that allows traders to act and transact without interference from government. Thus, the policy permits trading partners mutual gains from trade, with goods and services produced according to the theory of comparative advantage.

Under a _____ policy, prices are a reflection of true supply and demand, and are the sole determinant of resource allocation.

a. Free Trade
c. Seasoned equity offering
b. Yield spread
d. Monte Carlo methods

50. The _____ was the outcome of the failure of negotiating governments to create the International Trade Organization (ITO). _____ was formed in 1947 and lasted until 1994, when it was replaced by the World Trade Organization. The Bretton Woods Conference had introduced the idea for an organization to regulate trade as part of a larger plan for economic recovery after World War II.

a. 529 plan
c. 4-4-5 Calendar
b. General Agreement on Tariffs and Trade
d. 7-Eleven

51. The _____ is a trilateral trade bloc in North America created by the governments of the United States, Canada, and Mexico. The agreement creating the trade bloc came into force on January 1, 1994. It superseded the Canada-United States Free Trade Agreement between the U.S. and Canada.

a. 4-4-5 Calendar
c. 529 plan
b. 7-Eleven
d. North American Free Trade Agreement

1. The terms _____, nominal _____, and effective _____ describe the interest rate for a whole year (annualized), rather than just a monthly fee/rate, as applied on a loan, mortgage, credit card, etc. Those terms have formal, legal definitions in some countries or legal jurisdictions, but in general:

- The nominal _____ is the simple-interest rate (for a year.)
- The effective _____ is the fee+compound interest rate (calculated across a year.)

The nominal _____ is calculated as: the rate, for a payment period, multiplied by the number of payment periods in a year. However, the exact legal definition of 'effective _____' can vary greatly in each jurisdiction, depending on the type of fees included, such as participation fees, loan origination fees, monthly service charges, or late fees. The effective _____ has been called the 'mathematically-true' interest rate for each year. The computation for the effective _____, as the fee+compound interest rate, can also vary depending on whether the up-front fees, such as origination or participation fees, are added to the entire amount, or treated as a short-term loan due in the first payment.

a. A Random Walk Down Wall Street
b. Annual percentage rate
c. AAB
d. ABN Amro

2. In finance, the _____ of a financial asset measures the sensitivity of the asset's price to interest rate movements, expressed as a number of years. The reason for expressing this sensitivity in years is that the time that will elapse until a cash flow is received allows more interest to accumulate. Therefore the price of an asset with long term cashflows has more interest rate sensitivity than an asset with cashflows in the near future.

a. Duration
b. 4-4-5 Calendar
c. Macaulay duration
d. Yield to maturity

3. In economics, _____ is a rise in the general level of prices of goods and services in an economy over a period of time. The term '_____' once referred to increases in the money supply (monetary _____); however, economic debates about the relationship between money supply and price levels have led to its primary use today in describing price _____.
_____ can also be described as a decline in the real value of money--a loss of purchasing power in the medium of exchange which is also the monetary unit of account.

a. AAB
b. ABN Amro
c. Inflation
d. A Random Walk Down Wall Street

4. _____ is a fee paid on borrowed assets. It is the price paid for the use of borrowed money, or, money earned by deposited funds. Assets that are sometimes lent with _____ include money, shares, consumer goods through hire purchase, major assets such as aircraft, and even entire factories in finance lease arrangements.

a. Insolvency
b. AAB
c. Interest
d. A Random Walk Down Wall Street

5. An _____ is the price a borrower pays for the use of money they do not own, and the return a lender receives for deferring the use of funds, by lending it to the borrower. _____s are normally expressed as a percentage rate over the period of one year.

_____s targets are also a vital tool of monetary policy and are used to control variables like investment, inflation, and unemployment.

Chapter 5. The Determinants of Interest Rates: Competing Ideas   49

a. AAB
b. ABN Amro
c. A Random Walk Down Wall Street
d. Interest rate

6. _____ is the risk (variability in value) borne by an interest-bearing asset, such as a loan or a bond, due to variability of interest rates. In general, as rates rise, the price of a fixed rate bond will fall, and vice versa. _____ is commonly measured by the bond's duration.
   a. Official bank rate
   b. International Fisher effect
   c. Interest rate risk
   d. A Random Walk Down Wall Street

7. In finance, the term _____ describes the amount in cash that returns to the owners of a security. Normally it does not include the price variations, at the difference of the total return. _____ applies to various stated rates of return on stocks (common and preferred, and convertible), fixed income instruments (bonds, notes, bills, strips, zero coupon), and some other investment type insurance products (e.g. annuities.)
   a. 4-4-5 Calendar
   b. Macaulay duration
   c. Yield to maturity
   d. Yield

8. In finance, the _____ is the relation between the interest rate (or cost of borrowing) and the time to maturity of the debt for a given borrower in a given currency. For example, the current U.S. dollar interest rates paid on U.S. Treasury securities for various maturities are closely watched by many traders, and are commonly plotted on a graph such as the one on the right which is informally called 'the _____.' More formal mathematical descriptions of this relation are often called the term structure of interest rates.

The yield of a debt instrument is the annualized percentage increase in the value of the investment.

   a. 529 plan
   b. 7-Eleven
   c. 4-4-5 Calendar
   d. Yield curve

9. A _____ is a unit that is equal to 1/100th of a percentage point. It is frequently used to express percentage point changes of less than 1%. It avoids the ambiguity between relative and absolute discussions about rates.
   a. Bond market
   b. 4-4-5 Calendar
   c. 529 plan
   d. Basis point

10. _____ is the provision of resources (such as granting a loan) by one party to another party where that second party does not reimburse the first party immediately, thereby generating a debt, and instead arranges either to repay or return those resources (or material(s) of equal value) at a later date. The first party is called a creditor, also known as a lender, while the second party is called a debtor, also known as a borrower.

Movements of financial capital are normally dependent on either _____ or equity transfers.

   a. Clearing house
   b. Comparable
   c. Warrant
   d. Credit

11. _____ refers to making a wide range of secured and unsecured loans to consumers for consumable items such as a car, boat, manufactured home, home equity loan, home equity line of credit, signature loan, signature line of credit, recreational vehicle, or share or certificate of deposit or Stocks and Mutual Funds secured loans.

_____ does not include mortgage loans, typically used for home purchases, which follow some different regulations than consumer loans. Also, consumer loans are different from commercial loans, which can be calculated on a daily basis, rather than 12 monthly payments, and include interest for leap day, such as in Actual/366 loan calculations.

 a. Sogflation
 b. Coupon leverage
 c. Primary market
 d. Consumer lending

12. _____ is a legally declared inability or impairment of ability of an individual or organization to pay their creditors. Creditors may file a _____ petition against a debtor ('involuntary _____') in an effort to recoup a portion of what they are owed or initiate a restructuring. In the majority of cases, however, _____ is initiated by the debtor (a 'voluntary _____' that is filed by the bankrupt individual or organization.)

 a. Debt settlement
 b. 529 plan
 c. 4-4-5 Calendar
 d. Bankruptcy

13. The _____ is the interest rate that it is assumed can be obtained by investing in financial instruments with no default risk. However, the financial instrument can carry other types of risk, e.g. market risk (the risk of changes in market interest rates), liquidity risk (the risk of being unable to sell the instrument for cash at short notice without significant costs) etc.

Though a truly risk-free asset exists only in theory, in practice most professionals and academics use short-dated government bonds of the currency in question.

 a. London Interbank Bid Rate
 b. London Interbank Offered Rate
 c. Cash accumulation equation
 d. Risk-free Interest rate

14. _____ is the difference between price and the costs of bringing to market whatever it is that is accounted as an enterprise (whether by harvest, extraction, manufacture, or purchase) in terms of the component costs of delivered goods and/or services and any operating or other expenses.

A key difficulty in measuring profit is in defining costs. Pure economic monetary profits can be zero or negative even in competitive equilibrium when accounted monetized costs exceed monetized price.

 a. AAB
 b. Accounting profit
 c. Economic profit
 d. A Random Walk Down Wall Street

15. In economics, _____ (or 'discounting') pertains to how large a premium a consumer will place on enjoyment nearer in time over more remote enjoyment.

There is no absolute distinction that separates 'high' and 'low' _____, only comparisons with others either individually or in aggregate. Someone with a high _____ is focused substantially on their well-being in the present and the immediate future compared to the average, while someone with low _____ places more emphasis than average on their well-being in the further future.

a. 4-4-5 Calendar
b. 529 plan
c. 7-Eleven
d. Time preference

16.

A _____ is a type of financial intermediary and a type of bank. Commercial banking is also known as business banking. It is a bank that provides checking accounts, savings accounts, and money market accounts and that accepts time deposits.

a. Commercial bank
b. 4-4-5 Calendar
c. 7-Eleven
d. 529 plan

17. The _____ is a capital budgeting metric used by firms to decide whether they should make investments. It is an indicator of the efficiency or quality of an investment, as opposed to net present value (NPV), which indicates value or magnitude.

The IRR is the annualized effective compounded return rate which can be earned on the invested capital, i.e., the yield on the investment.

a. ABN Amro
b. A Random Walk Down Wall Street
c. AAB
d. Internal rate of return

18. In finance, _____, also known as return on investment is the ratio of money gained or lost on an investment relative to the amount of money invested. The amount of money gained or lost may be referred to as interest, profit/loss, gain/loss, or net income/loss. The money invested may be referred to as the asset, capital, principal, or the cost basis of the investment.

a. Doctrine of the Proper Law
b. Composiition of Creditors
c. Stock or scrip dividends
d. Rate of return

19. In economics, business, and accounting, a _____ is the value of money that has been used up to produce something, and hence is not available for use anymore. In business, the _____ may be one of acquisition, in which case the amount of money expended to acquire it is counted as _____. In this case, money is the input that is gone in order to acquire the thing.

a. Sliding scale fees
b. Cost
c. Marginal cost
d. Fixed costs

20. The _____ is an expected return that the provider of capital plans to earn on their investment.

Capital (money) used for funding a business should earn returns for the capital providers who risk their capital. For an investment to be worthwhile, the expected return on capital must be greater than the _____.

a. Weighted average cost of capital
b. 4-4-5 Calendar
c. Cost of capital
d. Capital intensity

Chapter 5. The Determinants of Interest Rates: Competing Ideas

21. A _____ is a fungible, negotiable instrument representing financial value. They are broadly categorized into debt securities (such as banknotes, bonds and debentures), and equity securities; e.g., common stocks. The company or other entity issuing the _____ is called the issuer.
   a. Tracking stock
   b. Book entry
   c. Securities lending
   d. Security

22. A _____ is a bond issued by a corporation. The term is usually applied to longer-term debt instruments, generally with a maturity date falling at least a year after their issue date. (The term 'commercial paper' is sometimes used for instruments with a shorter maturity.)
   a. Brady bonds
   b. Serial bond
   c. Government bond
   d. Corporate bond

23. _____ is a measure of the ability of a debtor to pay their debts as and when they fall due. It is usually expressed as a ratio or a percentage of current liabilities.

For a corporation with a published balance sheet there are various ratios used to calculate a measure of liquidity.

   a. Operating profit margin
   b. Operating leverage
   c. Invested capital
   d. Accounting liquidity

24. John Maynard Keynes developed the _____ of Interest in the General Theory of Employment Interest and Money. The primary consideration of the _____ is the demand for money as an asset, as a means for holding wealth. Interest rates, he argues, cannot be a reward for savings as such because, if a person hoards his savings in cash, keeping it under his mattress say, he will receive no interest, although he has nevertheless, refrained from consuming all his current income.
   a. 7-Eleven
   b. 529 plan
   c. Liquidity preference
   d. 4-4-5 Calendar

25. In business and accounting, _____s are everything of value that is owned by a person or company. The balance sheet of a firm records the monetary value of the _____s owned by the firm. The two major _____ classes are tangible _____s and intangible _____s.
   a. EBITDA
   b. Asset
   c. Income
   d. Accounts payable

26. In finance, a _____ is a debt security, in which the authorized issuer owes the holders a debt and, depending on the terms of the _____, is obliged to pay interest (the coupon) and/or to repay the principal at a later date, termed maturity.

Thus a _____ is a loan: the issuer is the borrower, the _____ holder is the lender, and the coupon is the interest. _____s provide the borrower with external funds to finance long-term investments, or, in the case of government _____s, to finance current expenditure.

   a. Puttable bond
   b. Catastrophe bonds
   c. Bond
   d. Convertible bond

Chapter 5. The Determinants of Interest Rates: Competing Ideas

27. _____ or net present worth (NPW) is defined as the total present value (PV) of a time series of cash flows. It is a standard method for using the time value of money to appraise long-term projects. Used for capital budgeting, and widely throughout economics, it measures the excess or shortfall of cash flows, in present value terms, once financing charges are met.

   a. Negative gearing
   b. Present value of costs
   c. Tax shield
   d. Net present value

28. _____ is the value on a given date of a future payment or series of future payments, discounted to reflect the time value of money and other factors such as investment risk. _____ calculations are widely used in business and economics to provide a means to compare cash flows at different times on a meaningful 'like to like' basis.

The most commonly applied model of the time value of money is compound interest.

   a. Present value
   b. Net present value
   c. Present value of benefits
   d. Negative gearing

29. _____ are cash, evidence of an ownership interest in an entity or deliver, cash or another financial instrument.

   _____ can be categorized by form depending on whether they are cash instruments or derivative instruments:

   - Cash instruments are _____ whose value is determined directly by markets. They can be divided into securities, which are readily transferable, and other cash instruments such as loans and deposits, where both borrower and lender have to agree on a transfer.
   - Derivative instruments are _____ which derive their value from the value and characteristics of one or more underlying assets. They can be divided into exchange-traded derivatives and over-the-counter (OTC) derivatives.

Alternatively, _____ can be categorized by 'asset class' depending on whether they are equity based (reflecting ownership of the issuing entity) or debt based (reflecting a loan the investor has made to the issuing entity.) If it is debt, it can be further categorised into short term (less than one year) or long term.

Foreign Exchange instruments and transactions are neither debt nor equity based and belong in their own category.

   a. Financial services
   b. Secondary market
   c. Cost of carry
   d. Financial instruments

30. In economics, _____ is the total amount of money available in an economy at a particular point in time. There are several ways to define 'money', but each includes currency in circulation and demand deposits.

   _____ data are recorded and published.

a. Money supply
b. 7-Eleven
c. 529 plan
d. 4-4-5 Calendar

31. _____, in bookkeeping, refers to assets, liabilities, income, and expenses recorded on individual pages of the so called book of final entry or ledger. Changes in _____ value are made by chronologically posting debit (DR) and credit (CR) entries to its page. Examples of _____s are cash, _____s receivable, mortgages, loans, land and buildings, common stock, sales, services provided, wages, and payroll overhead.
  a. Option
  b. Account
  c. Alpha
  d. Accretion

32. _____ in economics is a persistent decrease in the general price level of goods and services - a negative inflation rate. When the inflation rate slows down (decreases, but remains positive), this is known as disinflation.

Inflation destroys real value in money.

  a. Deflation
  b. Mercantilism
  c. Recession
  d. Fixed exchange rate

33. In financial accounting, the term _____ is most commonly used to describe any part of shareholders' equity, except for basic share capital. Sometimes, the term is used instead of the term provision; such a use, however, is inconsistent with the terminology suggested by International Accounting Standards Board. For more information about provisions, see provision (accounting.)
  a. FIFO and LIFO accounting
  b. Reserve
  c. Closing entries
  d. Treasury stock

34. _____ is the process by which the government, or monetary authority of a country controls (i) the supply of money central bank (ii) availability of money, and (iii) cost of money or rate of interest, in order to attain a set of objectives oriented towards the growth and stability of the economy. Monetary theory provides insight into how to craft optimal _____.

_____ is referred to as either being an expansionary policy where an expansionary policy increases the total supply of money in the economy, and a contractionary policy decreases the total money supply.

  a. Federal Open Market Committee
  b. Natural resources consumption tax
  c. Tax exemption
  d. Monetary policy

35. A _____, reserve bank, or monetary authority is the entity responsible for the monetary policy of a country or of a group of member states. It is a bank that can lend money to other banks in times of need. Its primary responsibility is to maintain the stability of the national currency and money supply, but more active duties include controlling subsidized-loan interest rates, and acting as a lender of last resort to the banking sector during times of financial crisis (private banks often being integral to the national financial system.)
  a. 4-4-5 Calendar
  b. 7-Eleven
  c. 529 plan
  d. Central Bank

Chapter 5. The Determinants of Interest Rates: Competing Ideas

36. _____ is an economic model based on price, utility and quantity in a market. It predicts that in a competitive market, price will function to equalize the quantity demanded by consumers, and the quantity supplied by producers, resulting in an economic equilibrium of price and quantity. Similarly, an increase in the number of workers tends to result in lower wages and vice-versa.
   a. Loan participation
   b. Price channel
   c. Rural credit cooperatives
   d. Supply and demand

37. An _____ is a security whose value and income payments are derived from and collateralized (or 'backed') by a specified pool of underlying assets. The pool of assets is typically a group of small and illiquid assets that are unable to be sold individually. Pooling the assets allows them to be sold to general investors, a process called securitization, and allows the risk of investing in the underlying assets to be diversified because each security will represent a fraction of the total value of the diverse pool of underlying assets.
   a. Asset-backed security
   b. A Random Walk Down Wall Street
   c. ABN Amro
   d. AAB

38. _____, refers to consumption opportunity gained by an entity within a specified time frame, which is generally expressed in monetary terms. However, for households and individuals, '_____ is the sum of all the wages, salaries, profits, interests payments, rents and other forms of earnings received... in a given period of time.' For firms, _____ generally refers to net-profit: what remains of revenue after expenses have been subtracted.
   a. OIBDA
   b. Accrual
   c. Income
   d. Annual report

39. The institution most often referenced by the word '_____' is a public or publicly traded _____, the shares of which are traded on a public stock exchange (e.g., the New York Stock Exchange or Nasdaq in the United States) where shares of stock of _____s are bought and sold by and to the general public. Most of the largest businesses in the world are publicly traded _____s. However, the majority of _____s are said to be closely held, privately held or close _____s, meaning that no ready market exists for the trading of shares.
   a. Federal Home Loan Mortgage Corporation
   b. Corporation
   c. Depository Trust Company
   d. Protect

Chapter 6. Measuring and Calculating Interest Rates and Financial Asset Prices

1. The terms _____ , nominal _____ , and effective _____ describe the interest rate for a whole year (annualized), rather than just a monthly fee/rate, as applied on a loan, mortgage, credit card, etc. Those terms have formal, legal definitions in some countries or legal jurisdictions, but in general:

    - The nominal _____ is the simple-interest rate (for a year.)
    - The effective _____ is the fee+compound interest rate (calculated across a year.)

    The nominal _____ is calculated as: the rate, for a payment period, multiplied by the number of payment periods in a year. However, the exact legal definition of 'effective _____' can vary greatly in each jurisdiction, depending on the type of fees included, such as participation fees, loan origination fees, monthly service charges, or late fees. The effective _____ has been called the 'mathematically-true' interest rate for each year. The computation for the effective _____, as the fee+compound interest rate, can also vary depending on whether the up-front fees, such as origination or participation fees, are added to the entire amount, or treated as a short-term loan due in the first payment.

    a. AAB
    b. ABN Amro
    c. A Random Walk Down Wall Street
    d. Annual percentage rate

2. A _____ is a unit that is equal to 1/100th of a percentage point. It is frequently used to express percentage point changes of less than 1%. It avoids the ambiguity between relative and absolute discussions about rates.

    a. Basis point
    b. 4-4-5 Calendar
    c. 529 plan
    d. Bond market

3. In finance, the _____ of a financial asset measures the sensitivity of the asset's price to interest rate movements, expressed as a number of years. The reason for expressing this sensitivity in years is that the time that will elapse until a cash flow is received allows more interest to accumulate. Therefore the price of an asset with long term cashflows has more interest rate sensitivity than an asset with cashflows in the near future.

    a. Duration
    b. 4-4-5 Calendar
    c. Macaulay duration
    d. Yield to maturity

4. In economics, _____ is a rise in the general level of prices of goods and services in an economy over a period of time. The term '_____' once referred to increases in the money supply (monetary _____); however, economic debates about the relationship between money supply and price levels have led to its primary use today in describing price _____. _____ can also be described as a decline in the real value of money--a loss of purchasing power in the medium of exchange which is also the monetary unit of account.

    a. A Random Walk Down Wall Street
    b. Inflation
    c. ABN Amro
    d. AAB

5. _____ is a fee paid on borrowed assets. It is the price paid for the use of borrowed money , or, money earned by deposited funds . Assets that are sometimes lent with _____ include money, shares, consumer goods through hire purchase, major assets such as aircraft, and even entire factories in finance lease arrangements.

    a. Interest
    b. AAB
    c. Insolvency
    d. A Random Walk Down Wall Street

6. An _____ is the price a borrower pays for the use of money they do not own, and the return a lender receives for deferring the use of funds, by lending it to the borrower. _____s are normally expressed as a percentage rate over the period of one year.

Chapter 6. Measuring and Calculating Interest Rates and Financial Asset Prices 57

_____s targets are also a vital tool of monetary policy and are used to control variables like investment, inflation, and unemployment.

a. ABN Amro
c. A Random Walk Down Wall Street
b. Interest rate
d. AAB

7. _____ is the risk (variability in value) borne by an interest-bearing asset, such as a loan or a bond, due to variability of interest rates. In general, as rates rise, the price of a fixed rate bond will fall, and vice versa. _____ is commonly measured by the bond's duration.

a. Official bank rate
c. Interest rate risk
b. A Random Walk Down Wall Street
d. International Fisher effect

8. In finance, the term _____ describes the amount in cash that returns to the owners of a security. Normally it does not include the price variations, at the difference of the total return. _____ applies to various stated rates of return on stocks (common and preferred, and convertible), fixed income instruments (bonds, notes, bills, strips, zero coupon), and some other investment type insurance products (e.g. annuities.)

a. 4-4-5 Calendar
c. Yield
b. Macaulay duration
d. Yield to maturity

9. In finance, the _____ is the relation between the interest rate (or cost of borrowing) and the time to maturity of the debt for a given borrower in a given currency. For example, the current U.S. dollar interest rates paid on U.S. Treasury securities for various maturities are closely watched by many traders, and are commonly plotted on a graph such as the one on the right which is informally called 'the _____.' More formal mathematical descriptions of this relation are often called the term structure of interest rates.

The yield of a debt instrument is the annualized percentage increase in the value of the investment.

a. 529 plan
c. 7-Eleven
b. 4-4-5 Calendar
d. Yield curve

10. In finance, a _____ is a debt security, in which the authorized issuer owes the holders a debt and, depending on the terms of the _____, is obliged to pay interest (the coupon) and/or to repay the principal at a later date, termed maturity.

Thus a _____ is a loan: the issuer is the borrower, the _____ holder is the lender, and the coupon is the interest. _____s provide the borrower with external funds to finance long-term investments, or, in the case of government _____s, to finance current expenditure.

a. Puttable bond
c. Catastrophe bonds
b. Convertible bond
d. Bond

11. _____ is that which is owed; usually referencing assets owed, but the term can cover other obligations. In the case of assets, _____ is a means of using future purchasing power in the present before a summation has been earned. Some companies and corporations use _____ as a part of their overall corporate finance strategy.

58 Chapter 6. Measuring and Calculating Interest Rates and Financial Asset Prices

a. Cross-collateralization
c. Credit cycle
b. Partial Payment
d. Debt

12. A _____ is a fungible, negotiable instrument representing financial value. They are broadly categorized into debt securities (such as banknotes, bonds and debentures), and equity securities; e.g., common stocks. The company or other entity issuing the _____ is called the issuer.

a. Security
c. Securities lending
b. Book entry
d. Tracking stock

13. A '_____' is a 'Charge' that is paid to obtain the right to delay a payment. Essentially, the payer purchases the right to make a given payment in the future instead of in the Present. The '_____', or 'Charge' that must be paid to delay the payment, is simply the difference between what the payment amount would be if it were paid in the present and what the payment amount would be paid if it were paid in the future.

a. Risk modeling
c. Discount
b. Risk aversion
d. Value at risk

14. The _____ is an interest rate a central bank charges depository institutions that borrow reserves from it.

The term _____ has two meanings:

- the same as interest rate; the term 'discount' does not refer to the meaning of the word, but to the purpose of using the quantity, such as computations of present value, e.g. net present value / discounted cash flow

- the annual effective _____, which is the annual interest divided by the capital including that interest; this rate is lower than the interest rate; it corresponds to using the value after a year as the nominal value, and seeing the initial value as the nominal value minus a discount; it is used for Treasury Bills and similar financial instruments

The annual effective _____ is the annual interest divided by the capital including that interest, which is the interest rate divided by 100% plus the interest rate. It is the annual discount factor to be applied to the future cash flow, to find the discount, subtracted from a future value to find the value one year earlier.

For example, suppose there is a government bond that sells for $95 and pays $100 in a year's time.

a. Stochastic volatility
c. Black-Scholes
b. Discount rate
d. Fisher equation

15. _____ is the term used to describe deposits residing in banks that are located outside the borders of the country that issues the currency the deposit is denominated in. For example a deposit denominated in US dollars residing in a Japanese bank is a _____ deposit, or more specifically a Eurodollar deposit.

Key points are the location of the bank and the denomination of the currency, not the nationality of the bank or the owner of the deposit/loan.

Chapter 6. Measuring and Calculating Interest Rates and Financial Asset Prices

a. A Random Walk Down Wall Street
b. AAB
c. Eurocurrency
d. ABN Amro

16. _____, in finance and accounting, means stated value or face value. From this comes the expressions at par (at the _____), over par (over _____) and under par (under _____.)

The term '_____' has several meanings depending on context and geography.

a. Global Squeeze
b. Par value
c. Sinking fund
d. FIDC

17. _____ mature in one year or less. Like zero-coupon bonds, they do not pay interest prior to maturity; instead they are sold at a discount of the par value to create a positive yield to maturity. Many regard _____ as the least risky investment available to U.S. investors.

a. 4-4-5 Calendar
b. Treasury securities
c. Treasury Inflation Protected Securities
d. Treasury bills

18. In finance, the _____ is the global financial market for short-term borrowing and lending. It provides short-term liquidity funding for the global financial system. The _____ is where short-term obligations such as Treasury bills, commercial paper and bankers' acceptances are bought and sold.

a. Consumer debt
b. Cramdown
c. Debt-for-equity swap
d. Money market

19. In finance, _____, also known as return on investment is the ratio of money gained or lost on an investment relative to the amount of money invested. The amount of money gained or lost may be referred to as interest, profit/loss, gain/loss, or net income/loss. The money invested may be referred to as the asset, capital, principal, or the cost basis of the investment.

a. Composiition of Creditors
b. Doctrine of the Proper Law
c. Stock or scrip dividends
d. Rate of return

20. A _____ or market-based mechanism is any of a wide variety of ways to match up buyers and sellers.

An example of a _____ uses announced bid and ask prices. Generally speaking, when two parties wish to engage in a trade, the purchaser will announce a price he is willing to pay (the bid price) and seller will announce a price he is willing to accept (the ask price).

a. 529 plan
b. Price mechanism
c. 4-4-5 Calendar
d. 7-Eleven

21. The _____ for securities is the difference between the price quoted by a market maker for an immediate sale and an immediate purchase The size of the bid-offer spread in a given commodity is a measure of the liquidity of the market.

The trader initiating the transaction is said to demand liquidity, and the other party to the transaction supplies liquidity.

Chapter 6. Measuring and Calculating Interest Rates and Financial Asset Prices

a. Trade-off
b. Capital outflow
c. Defined contribution plan
d. Bid/offer spread

22. A _____ is a bond issued by a corporation. The term is usually applied to longer-term debt instruments, generally with a maturity date falling at least a year after their issue date. (The term 'commercial paper' is sometimes used for instruments with a shorter maturity.)
    a. Brady bonds
    b. Serial bond
    c. Corporate bond
    d. Government bond

23. The coupon or _____ of a bond is the amount of interest paid per year expressed as a percentage of the face value of the bond.

For example if you hold $10,000 nominal of a bond described as a 4.5% loan stock, you will receive $450 in interest each year (probably in two installments of $225 each.)

Not all bonds have coupons.

   a. Puttable bond
   b. Zero-coupon bond
   c. Revenue bonds
   d. Coupon rate

24. The _____ or redemption yield is the yield promised to the bondholder on the assumption that the bond or other fixed-interest security such as gilts will be held to maturity, that all coupon and principal payments will be made and coupon payments are reinvested at the bond's promised yield at the same rate as invested. It is a measure of the return of the bond. This technique in theory allows investors to calculate the fair value of different financial instruments.
    a. 4-4-5 Calendar
    b. Yield to maturity
    c. Yield
    d. Macaulay duration

25. _____ is a life of security. It may also refer to the final payment date of a loan or other financial instrument, at which point all remaining interest and principal is due to be paid.

1, 3, 6 months _____ band can be calculated by using 30-day per month periods.

   a. Primary market
   b. Replacement cost
   c. False billing
   d. Maturity

26. _____ is the value on a given date of a future payment or series of future payments, discounted to reflect the time value of money and other factors such as investment risk. _____ calculations are widely used in business and economics to provide a means to compare cash flows at different times on a meaningful 'like to like' basis.

The most commonly applied model of the time value of money is compound interest.

   a. Present value of benefits
   b. Negative gearing
   c. Net present value
   d. Present value

Chapter 6. Measuring and Calculating Interest Rates and Financial Asset Prices 61

27. _____ is the concept of adding accumulated interest back to the principal, so that interest is earned on interest from that moment on. The act of declaring interest to be principal is called compounding (i.e., interest is compounded.) A loan, for example, may have its interest compounded every month: in this case, a loan with $100 principal and 1% interest per month would have a balance of $101 at the end of the first month.
   a. Risk management
   b. Penny stock
   c. 4-4-5 Calendar
   d. Compound interest

28. _____ are government bonds issued by the United States Department of the Treasury through the Bureau of the Public Debt. They are the debt financing instruments of the U.S. Federal government, and they are often referred to simply as Treasuries or Treasurys. There are four types of marketable _____: Treasury bills, Treasury notes, Treasury bonds, and Treasury Inflation Protected Securities (TIPS.)
   a. Treasury Inflation Protected Securities
   b. Treasury securities
   c. Treasury Inflation-Protected Securities
   d. 4-4-5 Calendar

29. A _____ is the price of a single share of a no. of saleable stocks of the company. Once the stock is purchased, the owner becomes a shareholder of the company that issued the share.
   a. Whisper numbers
   b. Stock split
   c. Trading curb
   d. Share price

30. A _____ is a property interest created by agreement or by operation of law over assets to secure the performance of an obligation, usually the payment of a debt. It gives the beneficiary of the _____ certain preferential rights in the disposition of secured assets. Such rights vary according to the type of _____, but in most cases, a holder of the _____ is entitled to seize, and usually sell, the property to discharge the debt that the _____ secures.
   a. FIDC
   b. Netting
   c. Retention ratio
   d. Security interest

31. _____ are a form of British government bond (gilt), dating originally from the 18th century. _____ are one of the rare examples of an actual perpetuity: although they may be redeemed by the British government, they are unlikely to do so in the foreseeable future.

In 1752, the Chancellor of the Exchequer and Prime Minister Sir Henry Pelham converted all outstanding issues of redeemable government stock into one bond, Consolidated 3.5% Annuities, in order to reduce the coupon rate paid on the government debt.

   a. Brady bonds
   b. Consols
   c. Serial bond
   d. Revenue bonds

32. A _____ is a payment made by a corporation to its shareholder members. When a corporation earns a profit or surplus, that money can be put to two uses: it can either be re-invested in the business (called retained earnings), or it can be paid to the shareholders as a _____. Many corporations retain a portion of their earnings and pay the remainder as a _____.
   a. Special dividend
   b. Dividend
   c. Dividend puzzle
   d. Dividend yield

33. _____ refers to any type of investment that yields a regular (or fixed) return.

For example, if you lend money to a borrower and the borrower has to pay interest once a month, you have been issued a fixed-income security. When a company does this, it is often called a bond or corporate bank debt (although preferred stock is also sometimes considered to be _____).

a. 529 plan
c. Fixed income
b. Bond market
d. 4-4-5 Calendar

34. A _____ is an annuity in which the periodic payments begin on a fixed date and continue indefinitely. It is sometimes referred to as a perpetual annuity. Fixed coupon payments on permanently invested (irredeemable) sums of money are prime examples of these. Scholarships paid perpetually from an endowment fit the definition of _____.

a. Perpetuity
c. Stochastic volatility
b. Current yield
d. LIBOR market model

35. _____ are cash, evidence of an ownership interest in an entity or deliver, cash or another financial instrument.

_____ can be categorized by form depending on whether they are cash instruments or derivative instruments:

- Cash instruments are _____ whose value is determined directly by markets. They can be divided into securities, which are readily transferable, and other cash instruments such as loans and deposits, where both borrower and lender have to agree on a transfer.
- Derivative instruments are _____ which derive their value from the value and characteristics of one or more underlying assets. They can be divided into exchange-traded derivatives and over-the-counter (OTC) derivatives.

Alternatively, _____ can be categorized by 'asset class' depending on whether they are equity based (reflecting ownership of the issuing entity) or debt based (reflecting a loan the investor has made to the issuing entity.) If it is debt, it can be further categorised into short term (less than one year) or long term.

Foreign Exchange instruments and transactions are neither debt nor equity based and belong in their own category.

a. Financial services
c. Secondary market
b. Cost of carry
d. Financial instruments

36. In business and finance, a _____ (also referred to as equity _____) of stock means a _____ of ownership in a corporation (company.) In the plural, stocks is often used as a synonym for _____s especially in the United States, but it is less commonly used that way outside of North America.

In the United Kingdom, South Africa, and Australia, stock can also refer to completely different financial instruments such as government bonds or, less commonly, to all kinds of marketable securities.

Chapter 6. Measuring and Calculating Interest Rates and Financial Asset Prices 63

a. Bucket shop
b. Margin
c. Share
d. Procter ' Gamble

37. An _____ is a contract written by a seller that conveys to the buyer the right -- but not the obligation -- to buy (in the case of a call _____) or to sell (in the case of a put _____) a particular asset, such as a piece of property such as, among others, a futures contract. In return for granting the _____, the seller collects a payment (the premium) from the buyer.

For example, buying a call _____ provides the right to buy a specified quantity of a security at a set strike price at some time on or before expiration, while buying a put _____ provides the right to sell.

a. AT'T Mobility LLC
b. Annuity
c. Option
d. Amortization

38. The _____ is the market for securities, where companies and governments can raise longterm funds. The _____ includes the stock market and the bond market. Financial regulators, such as the U.S. Securities and Exchange Commission, oversee the _____s in their designated countries to ensure that investors are protected against fraud.

a. Forward market
b. Spot rate
c. Delta neutral
d. Capital market

39. _____ is the provision of resources (such as granting a loan) by one party to another party where that second party does not reimburse the first party immediately, thereby generating a debt, and instead arranges either to repay or return those resources (or material(s) of equal value) at a later date. The first party is called a creditor, also known as a lender, while the second party is called a debtor, also known as a borrower.

Movements of financial capital are normally dependent on either _____ or equity transfers.

a. Comparable
b. Clearing house
c. Warrant
d. Credit

40. The _____ of 1968 is a United States federal law designed to protect consumers in credit transactions, by requiring clear disclosure of key terms of the lending arrangement and all costs. The statute is contained in Title I of the Consumer Credit Protection Act, as amended (15 U.S.C. § 1601 et seq.).

a. Fair Credit Reporting Act
b. Fair Credit Billing Act
c. Regulation Q
d. Truth in Lending Act

41. _____ expresses an annual rate of interest taking into account the effect of compounding, usually for deposit or investment products (such as a certificate of deposit.) It is analogous to the Annual percentage rate (APR), which is used for loans. In some jurisdictions, the use and definition of _____ may be regulated by a government agency, in which case it would generally be capitalized.

a. Annual percentage yield
b. A Random Walk Down Wall Street
c. ABN Amro
d. AAB

Chapter 7. Inflation, Yield Curves, and Duration: Impact on Interest Rates and Asset Prices

1. A _____ is a measure of the average price of consumer goods and services purchased by households. The _____ can be used to index (i.e., adjust for the effects of inflation) wages, salaries, pensions, or regulated or contracted prices. The _____ is, along with the population census and the National Income and Product Accounts, one of the most closely watched national economic statistics.
   - a. 4-4-5 Calendar
   - b. 529 plan
   - c. Divisia index
   - d. Consumer price index

2. In finance, the _____ of a financial asset measures the sensitivity of the asset's price to interest rate movements, expressed as a number of years. The reason for expressing this sensitivity in years is that the time that will elapse until a cash flow is received allows more interest to accumulate. Therefore the price of an asset with long term cashflows has more interest rate sensitivity than an asset with cashflows in the near future.
   - a. 4-4-5 Calendar
   - b. Macaulay duration
   - c. Duration
   - d. Yield to maturity

3. The _____ is one of the measures of national income and input for a given country's economy. _____ is defined as the total cost of all finished goods and services produced within the country in a stipulated period of time (usually a 365-day year.) It is sometimes regarded as the sum of profits added at every level of production (the intermediate stages) of all final goods and services produced within a country in a stipulated timeframe, and it is rarely given a monetary value.
   - a. Behavioral finance
   - b. Recession
   - c. Gross domestic product
   - d. Macroeconomics

4. In economics, _____ is a rise in the general level of prices of goods and services in an economy over a period of time. The term '_____' once referred to increases in the money supply (monetary _____); however, economic debates about the relationship between money supply and price levels have led to its primary use today in describing price _____. _____ can also be described as a decline in the real value of money--a loss of purchasing power in the medium of exchange which is also the monetary unit of account.
   - a. Inflation
   - b. ABN Amro
   - c. A Random Walk Down Wall Street
   - d. AAB

5. _____ is a fee paid on borrowed assets. It is the price paid for the use of borrowed money, or, money earned by deposited funds. Assets that are sometimes lent with _____ include money, shares, consumer goods through hire purchase, major assets such as aircraft, and even entire factories in finance lease arrangements.
   - a. AAB
   - b. A Random Walk Down Wall Street
   - c. Insolvency
   - d. Interest

6. An _____ is the price a borrower pays for the use of money they do not own, and the return a lender receives for deferring the use of funds, by lending it to the borrower. _____s are normally expressed as a percentage rate over the period of one year.

   _____s targets are also a vital tool of monetary policy and are used to control variables like investment, inflation, and unemployment.

   - a. Interest rate
   - b. A Random Walk Down Wall Street
   - c. ABN Amro
   - d. AAB

Chapter 7. Inflation, Yield Curves, and Duration: Impact on Interest Rates and Asset Prices

7. _____ is the risk (variability in value) borne by an interest-bearing asset, such as a loan or a bond, due to variability of interest rates. In general, as rates rise, the price of a fixed rate bond will fall, and vice versa. _____ is commonly measured by the bond's duration.
   a. Official bank rate
   b. A Random Walk Down Wall Street
   c. International Fisher effect
   d. Interest rate risk

8. A _____ is a normalized average (typically a weighted average) of prices for a given class of goods or services in a given region, during a given interval of time. It is a statistic designed to help to compare how these prices, taken as a whole, differ between time periods or geographical locations.
   a. Price discrimination
   b. Discounts and allowances
   c. Transfer pricing
   d. Price Index

9. In finance, the term _____ describes the amount in cash that returns to the owners of a security. Normally it does not include the price variations, at the difference of the total return. _____ applies to various stated rates of return on stocks (common and preferred, and convertible), fixed income instruments (bonds, notes, bills, strips, zero coupon), and some other investment type insurance products (e.g. annuities.)
   a. Yield
   b. Macaulay duration
   c. 4-4-5 Calendar
   d. Yield to maturity

10. In finance, the _____ is the relation between the interest rate (or cost of borrowing) and the time to maturity of the debt for a given borrower in a given currency. For example, the current U.S. dollar interest rates paid on U.S. Treasury securities for various maturities are closely watched by many traders, and are commonly plotted on a graph such as the one on the right which is informally called 'the _____.' More formal mathematical descriptions of this relation are often called the term structure of interest rates.

The yield of a debt instrument is the annualized percentage increase in the value of the investment.

   a. Yield curve
   b. 529 plan
   c. 7-Eleven
   d. 4-4-5 Calendar

11. A _____ is a unit that is equal to 1/100th of a percentage point. It is frequently used to express percentage point changes of less than 1%. It avoids the ambiguity between relative and absolute discussions about rates.
   a. 4-4-5 Calendar
   b. Bond market
   c. Basis point
   d. 529 plan

12. In finance and economics _____ refers to the rate of interest before adjustment for inflation (in contrast with the real interest rate); or, for interest balls stated' without adjustment for the full effect of compounding (also referred to as the nominal annual rate.) An interest rate is called nominal if the frequency of compounding (e.g. a month) is not identical to the basic time unit (normally a year.)

The real interest rate includes compensation for the lender's lost value due to inflation, whereas the _____ excludes inflation.

   a. SIBOR
   b. Shanghai Interbank Offered Rate
   c. Cash accumulation equation
   d. Nominal interest rate

Chapter 7. Inflation, Yield Curves, and Duration: Impact on Interest Rates and Asset Prices

13. The '_____' is approximately the nominal interest rate minus the inflation rate Since the inflation rate over the course of a loan is not known initially, volatility in inflation represents a risk to both the lender and the borrower.

In economics and finance, an individual who lends money for repayment at a later point in time expects to be compensated for the time value of money, or not having the use of that money while it is lent.

a. 529 plan
b. 4-4-5 Calendar
c. Real interest rate
d. 7-Eleven

14. In economics, the _____ is the proposition by Irving Fisher that the real interest rate is independent of monetary measures, especially the nominal interest rate. The Fisher equation is

$r_r = r_n >- >\pi^e$.

This means, the real interest rate (r_r) equals the nominal interest rate (r_n) minus expected rate of inflation ($>\pi^e$.) Here all the rates are continuously compounded.

a. 7-Eleven
b. 4-4-5 Calendar
c. 529 plan
d. Fisher hypothesis

15. _____ is a form of corporation equity ownership represented in the securities. It is dangerous in comparison to preferred shares and some other investment options, in that in the event of bankruptcy, _____ investors receive their funds after preferred stockholders, bondholders, creditors, etc. On the other hand, common shares on average perform better than preferred shares or bonds over time.

a. Stop-limit order
b. Stock market bubble
c. Common stock
d. Stock split

16. A _____ is the price of a single share of a no. of saleable stocks of the company. Once the stock is purchased, the owner becomes a shareholder of the company that issued the share.

a. Stock split
b. Trading curb
c. Share price
d. Whisper numbers

17. In business and finance, a _____ (also referred to as equity _____) of stock means a _____ of ownership in a corporation (company.) In the plural, stocks is often used as a synonym for _____s especially in the United States, but it is less commonly used that way outside of North America.

In the United Kingdom, South Africa, and Australia, stock can also refer to completely different financial instruments such as government bonds or, less commonly, to all kinds of marketable securities.

a. Margin
b. Share
c. Bucket shop
d. Procter ' Gamble

18. _____ is the difference between a lower selling price and a higher purchase price, resulting in a financial loss for the seller. Pursuant to IRS TAX TIP 2009-35 'If your _____ exceeds your capital gain, the excess can be deducted on your tax return, up to an annual limit of $3,000 ($1,500 if you are married filing separately.)'.

Chapter 7. Inflation, Yield Curves, and Duration: Impact on Interest Rates and Asset Prices   67

a. 7-Eleven
b. 4-4-5 Calendar
c. 529 plan
d. Capital loss

19. _____, refers to consumption opportunity gained by an entity within a specified time frame, which is generally expressed in monetary terms. However, for households and individuals, '_____ is the sum of all the wages, salaries, profits, interests payments, rents and other forms of earnings received... in a given period of time.' For firms, _____ generally refers to net-profit: what remains of revenue after expenses have been subtracted.
a. Annual report
b. Accrual
c. OIBDA
d. Income

20. An _____ is a tax levied on the financial income of people, corporations, or other legal entities. Various _____ systems exist, with varying degrees of tax incidence. Income taxation can be progressive, proportional, or regressive.
a. A Random Walk Down Wall Street
b. ABN Amro
c. Income tax
d. AAB

21. A _____ is a payment made by a corporation to its shareholder members. When a corporation earns a profit or surplus, that money can be put to two uses: it can either be re-invested in the business (called retained earnings), or it can be paid to the shareholders as a _____. Many corporations retain a portion of their earnings and pay the remainder as a _____.

a. Special dividend
b. Dividend
c. Dividend puzzle
d. Dividend yield

22. An _____ is a contract written by a seller that conveys to the buyer the right -- but not the obligation -- to buy (in the case of a call _____) or to sell (in the case of a put _____) a particular asset, such as a piece of property such as, among others, a futures contract. In return for granting the _____, the seller collects a payment (the premium) from the buyer.

For example, buying a call _____ provides the right to buy a specified quantity of a security at a set strike price at some time on or before expiration, while buying a put _____ provides the right to sell.

a. AT'T Mobility LLC
b. Amortization
c. Annuity
d. Option

23. A _____ is an exchange of promises between two or more parties to do an act which is enforceable in a court of law. It is where an unqualified offer meets a qualified acceptance and the parties reach Consensus ad Idem. The parties must have the necessary capacity to _____ and the _____ must not be either trifling, indeterminate, impossible or illegal.
a. 7-Eleven
b. Contract
c. 4-4-5 Calendar
d. 529 plan

24. A _____ is a fungible, negotiable instrument representing financial value. They are broadly categorized into debt securities (such as banknotes, bonds and debentures), and equity securities; e.g., common stocks. The company or other entity issuing the _____ is called the issuer.

a. Securities lending
b. Security
c. Tracking stock
d. Book entry

25. _____ is a mathematical science pertaining to the collection, analysis, interpretation or explanation, and presentation of data. It also provides tools for prediction and forecasting based on data. It is applicable to a wide variety of academic disciplines, from the natural and social sciences to the humanities, government and business.
a. Statistics
b. Covariance
c. Mean
d. Sample size

26. _____ are the inflation-indexed bonds issued by the U.S. Treasury. The principal is adjusted to the Consumer Price Index, the commonly used measure of inflation. The coupon rate is constant, but generates a different amount of interest when multiplied by the inflation-adjusted principal, thus protecting the holder against inflation. _____ are currently offered in 5-year, 10-year and 20-year maturities.
a. Treasury securities
b. Treasury Inflation-Protected Securities
c. Treasury Inflation Protected Securities
d. 4-4-5 Calendar

27. _____ is a life of security. It may also refer to the final payment date of a loan or other financial instrument, at which point all remaining interest and principal is due to be paid.

1, 3, 6 months _____ band can be calculated by using 30-day per month periods.

a. Primary market
b. False billing
c. Replacement cost
d. Maturity

28. In finance, the yield curve is the relation between the interest rate (or cost of borrowing) and the time to maturity of the debt for a given borrower in a given currency. For example, the current U.S. dollar interest rates paid on U.S. Treasury securities for various maturities are closely watched by many traders, and are commonly plotted on a graph such as the one on the right which is informally called 'the yield curve.' More formal mathematical descriptions of this relation are often called the _____.

The yield of a debt instrument is the annualized percentage increase in the value of the investment.

a. Term structure of interest rates
b. 7-Eleven
c. 4-4-5 Calendar
d. 529 plan

29. _____ are government bonds issued by the United States Department of the Treasury through the Bureau of the Public Debt. They are the debt financing instruments of the U.S. Federal government, and they are often referred to simply as Treasuries or Treasurys. There are four types of marketable _____: Treasury bills, Treasury notes, Treasury bonds, and Treasury Inflation Protected Securities (TIPS.)
a. Treasury Inflation-Protected Securities
b. Treasury Inflation Protected Securities
c. 4-4-5 Calendar
d. Treasury securities

30. The _____ on a portfolio of investments takes into account not only the capital appreciation on the portfolio, but also the income received on the portfolio. The income typically consists of interest, dividends, and securities lending fees. This contrasts with the price return, which takes into account only the capital gain on an investment.

Chapter 7. Inflation, Yield Curves, and Duration: Impact on Interest Rates and Asset Prices

a. Capitalization rate
c. Profitability index

b. Global tactical asset allocation
d. Total return

31. In economics and finance, _____ is the practice of taking advantage of a price differential between two or more markets: striking a combination of matching deals that capitalize upon the imbalance, the profit being the difference between the market prices. When used by academics, an _____ is a transaction that involves no negative cash flow at any probabilistic or temporal state and a positive cash flow in at least one state; in simple terms, a risk-free profit.
a. Initial margin
c. Issuer

b. Efficient-market hypothesis
d. Arbitrage

32. _____ is a measure of the ability of a debtor to pay their debts as and when they fall due. It is usually expressed as a ratio or a percentage of current liabilities.

For a corporation with a published balance sheet there are various ratios used to calculate a measure of liquidity.

a. Invested capital
c. Operating leverage

b. Operating profit margin
d. Accounting liquidity

33. _____ is a term used to explain a difference between two types of financial securities (e.g. stocks), that have all the same qualities except liquidity. For example:

_____ is a segment of a three-part theory that works to explain the behavior of yield curves for interest rates. The upwards-curving component of the interest yield can be explained by the _____.

a. Liquidity premium
c. 4-4-5 Calendar

b. 7-Eleven
d. 529 plan

34. _____, in bookkeeping, refers to assets, liabilities, income, and expenses recorded on individual pages of the so called book of final entry or ledger. Changes in _____ value are made by chronologically posting debit (DR) and credit (CR) entries to its page. Examples of _____s are cash, _____s receivable, mortgages, loans, land and buildings, common stock, sales, services provided, wages, and payroll overhead.
a. Account
c. Alpha

b. Option
d. Accretion

35. In economic models, the _____ time frame assumes no fixed factors of production. Firms can enter or leave the marketplace, and the cost (and availability) of land, labor, raw materials, and capital goods can be assumed to vary. In contrast, in the short-run time frame, certain factors are assumed to be fixed, because there is not sufficient time for them to change.
a. Long-run
c. 529 plan

b. 4-4-5 Calendar
d. Short-run

36. In statistics, _____ has two related meanings:

- the arithmetic _____
- the expected value of a random variable, which is also called the population _____.

It is sometimes stated that the '_____' is average. This is incorrect if '_____' is taken in the specific sense of 'arithmetic _____' as there are different types of averages: the _____, median, and mode. Other simple statistical analyses use measures of spread, such as range, interquartile range, or standard deviation. For a real-valued random variable X, the _____ is the expectation of X. Note that not every probability distribution has a defined _____; see the Cauchy distribution for an example.

- a. Mean
- b. Sample size
- c. Probability distribution
- d. Harmonic mean

37. The _____ or redemption yield is the yield promised to the bondholder on the assumption that the bond or other fixed-interest security such as gilts will be held to maturity, that all coupon and principal payments will be made and coupon payments are reinvested at the bond's promised yield at the same rate as invested. It is a measure of the return of the bond. This technique in theory allows investors to calculate the fair value of different financial instruments.
- a. Macaulay duration
- b. 4-4-5 Calendar
- c. Yield to maturity
- d. Yield

38. In business and accounting, _____s are everything of value that is owned by a person or company. The balance sheet of a firm records the monetary value of the _____s owned by the firm. The two major _____ classes are tangible _____s and intangible _____s.
- a. Accounts payable
- b. EBITDA
- c. Income
- d. Asset

39. In finance, a _____ is a debt security, in which the authorized issuer owes the holders a debt and, depending on the terms of the _____, is obliged to pay interest (the coupon) and/or to repay the principal at a later date, termed maturity.

Thus a _____ is a loan: the issuer is the borrower, the _____ holder is the lender, and the coupon is the interest. _____s provide the borrower with external funds to finance long-term investments, or, in the case of government _____s, to finance current expenditure.

- a. Catastrophe bonds
- b. Puttable bond
- c. Bond
- d. Convertible bond

40. _____ is that which is owed; usually referencing assets owed, but the term can cover other obligations. In the case of assets, _____ is a means of using future purchasing power in the present before a summation has been earned. Some companies and corporations use _____ as a part of their overall corporate finance strategy.
- a. Cross-collateralization
- b. Credit cycle
- c. Partial Payment
- d. Debt

41. A _____ is a situation that involves losing one quality or aspect of something in return for gaining another quality or aspect. It implies a decision to be made with full comprehension of both the upside and downside of a particular choice.

In economics the term is expressed as opportunity cost, referring the most preferred alternative given up.

Chapter 7. Inflation, Yield Curves, and Duration: Impact on Interest Rates and Asset Prices

a. Total revenue
c. Break-even point

b. Capital outflow
d. Trade-off

42. _____ is the difference between price and the costs of bringing to market whatever it is that is accounted as an enterprise (whether by harvest, extraction, manufacture, or purchase) in terms of the component costs of delivered goods and/or services and any operating or other expenses.

A key difficulty in measuring profit is in defining costs. Pure economic monetary profits can be zero or negative even in competitive equilibrium when accounted monetized costs exceed monetized price.

a. Accounting profit
c. AAB

b. A Random Walk Down Wall Street
d. Economic profit

43. The coupon or _____ of a bond is the amount of interest paid per year expressed as a percentage of the face value of the bond.

For example if you hold $10,000 nominal of a bond described as a 4.5% loan stock, you will receive $450 in interest each year (probably in two installments of $225 each.)

Not all bonds have coupons.

a. Puttable bond
c. Coupon rate

b. Revenue bonds
d. Zero-coupon bond

44. A _____ is the counterpart to a deterministic process (or deterministic system) in probability theory. Instead of dealing with only one possible 'reality' of how the process might evolve under time (as is the case, for example, for solutions of an ordinary differential equation), in a stochastic or random process there is some indeterminacy in its future evolution described by probability distributions. This means that even if the initial condition (or starting point) is known, there are many possibilities the process might go to, but some paths are more probable and others less.

a. 7-Eleven
c. 529 plan

b. 4-4-5 Calendar
d. Stochastic process

Chapter 8. The Risk Structure of Interest Rates

1. In finance, _____ occurs when a debtor has not met its legal obligations according to the debt contract, e.g. it has not made a scheduled payment, or has violated a loan covenant (condition) of the debt contract. _____ may occur if the debtor is either unwilling or unable to pay their debt. This can occur with all debt obligations including bonds, mortgages, loans, and promissory notes.

   a. Credit crunch
   b. Default
   c. Vendor finance
   d. Debt validation

2. _____ is the risk of loss due to a debtor's non-payment of a loan or other line of credit (either the principal or interest (coupon) or both)

Most lenders employ their own models (credit scorecards) to rank potential and existing customers according to risk, and then apply appropriate strategies. With products such as unsecured personal loans or mortgages, lenders charge a higher price for higher risk customers and vice versa. With revolving products such as credit cards and overdrafts, risk is controlled through careful setting of credit limits.

   a. Transaction risk
   b. Market risk
   c. Liquidity risk
   d. Credit risk

3. _____ is a fee paid on borrowed assets. It is the price paid for the use of borrowed money , or, money earned by deposited funds . Assets that are sometimes lent with _____ include money, shares, consumer goods through hire purchase, major assets such as aircraft, and even entire factories in finance lease arrangements.

   a. Insolvency
   b. AAB
   c. A Random Walk Down Wall Street
   d. Interest

4. An _____ is the price a borrower pays for the use of money they do not own, and the return a lender receives for deferring the use of funds, by lending it to the borrower. _____s are normally expressed as a percentage rate over the period of one year.

_____s targets are also a vital tool of monetary policy and are used to control variables like investment, inflation, and unemployment.

   a. ABN Amro
   b. Interest rate
   c. AAB
   d. A Random Walk Down Wall Street

5. _____ is the risk (variability in value) borne by an interest-bearing asset, such as a loan or a bond, due to variability of interest rates. In general, as rates rise, the price of a fixed rate bond will fall, and vice versa. _____ is commonly measured by the bond's duration.

   a. Official bank rate
   b. A Random Walk Down Wall Street
   c. Interest rate risk
   d. International Fisher effect

6. A _____ or market-based mechanism is any of a wide variety of ways to match up buyers and sellers.

An example of a _____ uses announced bid and ask prices. Generally speaking, when two parties wish to engage in a trade, the purchaser will announce a price he is willing to pay (the bid price) and seller will announce a price he is willing to accept (the ask price).

Chapter 8. The Risk Structure of Interest Rates

a. Price mechanism
c. 7-Eleven
b. 529 plan
d. 4-4-5 Calendar

7. The _____ for securities is the difference between the price quoted by a market maker for an immediate sale and an immediate purchase The size of the bid-offer spread in a given commodity is a measure of the liquidity of the market.

The trader initiating the transaction is said to demand liquidity, and the other party to the transaction supplies liquidity.

a. Trade-off
c. Capital outflow
b. Bid/offer spread
d. Defined contribution plan

8. _____ is a measure of the ability of a debtor to pay their debts as and when they fall due. It is usually expressed as a ratio or a percentage of current liabilities.

For a corporation with a published balance sheet there are various ratios used to calculate a measure of liquidity.

a. Operating leverage
c. Accounting liquidity
b. Operating profit margin
d. Invested capital

9. In business and accounting, _____s are everything of value that is owned by a person or company. The balance sheet of a firm records the monetary value of the _____s owned by the firm. The two major _____ classes are tangible _____s and intangible _____s.
a. Income
c. EBITDA
b. Accounts payable
d. Asset

10. _____ is the provision of resources (such as granting a loan) by one party to another party where that second party does not reimburse the first party immediately, thereby generating a debt, and instead arranges either to repay or return those resources (or material(s) of equal value) at a later date. The first party is called a creditor, also known as a lender, while the second party is called a debtor, also known as a borrower.

Movements of financial capital are normally dependent on either _____ or equity transfers.

a. Credit
c. Comparable
b. Warrant
d. Clearing house

11. In finance, a _____ is a derivative whose value derives from the credit risk on an underlying bond, loan or other financial asset. In this way, the credit risk is on an entity other than the counterparties to the transaction itself. This entity is known as the reference entity and may be a corporate, a sovereign or any other form of legal entity which has incurred debt.
a. Futures contract
c. Derivatives markets
b. STIRT
d. Credit derivative

12. A _____ is a financial contract whose value is derived from the value of something else (known as the underlying.) The underlying on which a _____ is based can be an asset, weather conditions bonds or other forms of credit.

a. 7-Eleven
b. Derivative
c. 529 plan
d. 4-4-5 Calendar

13. The institution most often referenced by the word '_____' is a public or publicly traded _____, the shares of which are traded on a public stock exchange (e.g., the New York Stock Exchange or Nasdaq in the United States) where shares of stock of _____s are bought and sold by and to the general public. Most of the largest businesses in the world are publicly traded _____s. However, the majority of _____s are said to be closely held, privately held or close _____s, meaning that no ready market exists for the trading of shares.

a. Depository Trust Company
b. Protect
c. Federal Home Loan Mortgage Corporation
d. Corporation

14. _____ is a legally declared inability or impairment of ability of an individual or organization to pay their creditors. Creditors may file a _____ petition against a debtor ('involuntary _____') in an effort to recoup a portion of what they are owed or initiate a restructuring. In the majority of cases, however, _____ is initiated by the debtor (a 'voluntary _____' that is filed by the bankrupt individual or organization.)

a. Debt settlement
b. Bankruptcy
c. 529 plan
d. 4-4-5 Calendar

15. In finance, the term _____ describes the amount in cash that returns to the owners of a security. Normally it does not include the price variations, at the difference of the total return. _____ applies to various stated rates of return on stocks (common and preferred, and convertible), fixed income instruments (bonds, notes, bills, strips, zero coupon), and some other investment type insurance products (e.g. annuities.)

a. 4-4-5 Calendar
b. Yield to maturity
c. Macaulay duration
d. Yield

16. A _____ is a bond issued by a corporation. The term is usually applied to longer-term debt instruments, generally with a maturity date falling at least a year after their issue date. (The term 'commercial paper' is sometimes used for instruments with a shorter maturity.)

a. Government bond
b. Brady bonds
c. Corporate bond
d. Serial bond

17. In finance, a _____ is a debt security, in which the authorized issuer owes the holders a debt and, depending on the terms of the _____, is obliged to pay interest (the coupon) and/or to repay the principal at a later date, termed maturity.

Thus a _____ is a loan: the issuer is the borrower, the _____ holder is the lender, and the coupon is the interest. _____s provide the borrower with external funds to finance long-term investments, or, in the case of government _____s, to finance current expenditure.

a. Puttable bond
b. Catastrophe bonds
c. Bond
d. Convertible bond

18. A _____ is a fungible, negotiable instrument representing financial value. They are broadly categorized into debt securities (such as banknotes, bonds and debentures), and equity securities; e.g., common stocks. The company or other entity issuing the _____ is called the issuer.

a. Tracking stock
b. Security
c. Securities lending
d. Book entry

19. A _____ assesses the credit worthiness of an individual, corporation, or even a country. _____s are calculated from financial history and current assets and liabilities. Typically, a _____ tells a lender or investor the probability of the subject being able to pay back a loan.
    a. Debenture
    b. Credit rating
    c. Credit report monitoring
    d. Credit cycle

20. In the global money market, _____ is an unsecured promissory note with a fixed maturity of one to 270 days. _____ is a money-market security issued (sold) by large banks and corporations to get money to meet short term debt obligations (for example, payroll), and is only backed by an issuing bank or corporation's promise to pay the face amount on the maturity date specified on the note. Since it is not backed by collateral, only firms with excellent credit ratings from a recognized rating agency will be able to sell their _____ at a reasonable price.
    a. Commercial paper
    b. Book building
    c. Trade-off theory
    d. Financial distress

21. In finance, a _____ (non-investment grade bond, speculative grade bond or junk bond) is a bond that is rated below investment grade at the time of purchase. These bonds have a higher risk of default or other adverse credit events, but typically pay higher yields than better quality bonds in order to make them attractive to investors.
    a. Volatility
    b. High yield bond
    c. Sharpe ratio
    d. Private equity

22. In economics, _____ is a rise in the general level of prices of goods and services in an economy over a period of time. The term '_____' once referred to increases in the money supply (monetary _____); however, economic debates about the relationship between money supply and price levels have led to its primary use today in describing price _____. _____ can also be described as a decline in the real value of money--a loss of purchasing power in the medium of exchange which is also the monetary unit of account.
    a. ABN Amro
    b. A Random Walk Down Wall Street
    c. AAB
    d. Inflation

23. The U.S. _____ is an independent agency of the United States government which holds primary responsibility for enforcing the federal securities laws and regulating the securities industry, the nation's stock and options exchanges, and other electronic securities markets. The SEC was created by section 4 of the SEC of 1934 (now codified as 15 U.S.C. Â§ 78d and commonly referred to as the 1934 Act.)
    a. Securities and Exchange Commission
    b. 7-Eleven
    c. 4-4-5 Calendar
    d. 529 plan

24. _____, in bookkeeping, refers to assets, liabilities, income, and expenses recorded on individual pages of the so called book of final entry or ledger. Changes in _____ value are made by chronologically posting debit (DR) and credit (CR) entries to its page. Examples of _____s are cash, _____s receivable, mortgages, loans, land and buildings, common stock, sales, services provided, wages, and payroll overhead.
    a. Alpha
    b. Account
    c. Accretion
    d. Option

Chapter 8. The Risk Structure of Interest Rates

25. The _____ , a component of the Federal Reserve System, is charged under United States law with overseeing the nation's open market operations. It is the Federal Reserve Committee that makes key decisions about interest rates and the growth jam of the United States money supply. It is the principal organ of United States national monetary policy.

   a. Fiscal policy
   b. Tax exemption
   c. Tax incidence
   d. Federal Open Market Committee

26. In finance, a _____ is a derivative in which two counterparties agree to exchange one stream of cash flows against another stream. These streams are called the legs of the _____.

The cash flows are calculated over a notional principal amount, which is usually not exchanged between counterparties.

   a. Volatility swap
   b. Volatility arbitrage
   c. Local volatility
   d. Swap

27. An _____ is a contract written by a seller that conveys to the buyer the right -- but not the obligation -- to buy (in the case of a call _____) or to sell (in the case of a put _____) a particular asset, such as a piece of property such as, among others, a futures contract. In return for granting the _____, the seller collects a payment (the premium) from the buyer.

For example, buying a call _____ provides the right to buy a specified quantity of a security at a set strike price at some time on or before expiration, while buying a put _____ provides the right to sell.

   a. AT'T Mobility LLC
   b. Annuity
   c. Option
   d. Amortization

28. The _____ on a portfolio of investments takes into account not only the capital appreciation on the portfolio, but also the income received on the portfolio. The income typically consists of interest, dividends, and securities lending fees. This contrasts with the price return, which takes into account only the capital gain on an investment.

   a. Total return
   b. Profitability index
   c. Global tactical asset allocation
   d. Capitalization rate

29. _____ or total rate of return swap is a financial contract which transfers both the credit risk and market risk of an underlying asset.

Let us assume that one bank (bank A) owns an asset (e.g. a bond) which periodically gives interest rate payments. Assume that bank A (the protection buyer) and bank B (the protection seller) has entered a Total rate swap contract.

   a. Constant maturity credit default swap
   b. Power reverse dual currency note
   c. Total return swap
   d. Correlation swap

30. In finance, the _____ of a financial asset measures the sensitivity of the asset's price to interest rate movements, expressed as a number of years. The reason for expressing this sensitivity in years is that the time that will elapse until a cash flow is received allows more interest to accumulate. Therefore the price of an asset with long term cashflows has more interest rate sensitivity than an asset with cashflows in the near future.

Chapter 8. The Risk Structure of Interest Rates

a. Macaulay duration
c. Yield to maturity
b. 4-4-5 Calendar
d. Duration

31. In finance, the _____ is the relation between the interest rate (or cost of borrowing) and the time to maturity of the debt for a given borrower in a given currency. For example, the current U.S. dollar interest rates paid on U.S. Treasury securities for various maturities are closely watched by many traders, and are commonly plotted on a graph such as the one on the right which is informally called 'the _____.' More formal mathematical descriptions of this relation are often called the term structure of interest rates.

The yield of a debt instrument is the annualized percentage increase in the value of the investment.

a. 7-Eleven
c. 4-4-5 Calendar
b. Yield curve
d. 529 plan

32. A _____ is a unit that is equal to 1/100th of a percentage point. It is frequently used to express percentage point changes of less than 1%. It avoids the ambiguity between relative and absolute discussions about rates.
a. 529 plan
c. Bond market
b. 4-4-5 Calendar
d. Basis point

33. The _____ (NYSE: FRE) is an insolvent government sponsored enterprise (GSE) of the United States federal government.

The _____ was created in 1970 to expand the secondary market for mortgages in the US. Along with other GSEs, Freddie Mac buys mortgages on the secondary market, pools them, and sells them as mortgage-backed securities to investors on the open market.

a. The Depository Trust ' Clearing Corporation
c. Governmental Accounting Standards Board
b. Federal Home Loan Mortgage Corporation
d. Public company

34. The _____ (NYSE: FNM), commonly known as Fannie Mae, is a stockholder-owned corporation chartered by Congress in 1968 as a government sponsored enterprise (GSE), but founded in 1938 during the Great Depression. The corporation's purpose is to purchase and securitize mortgages in order to ensure that funds are consistently available to the institutions that lend money to home buyers.

On September 7, 2008, James Lockhart, director of the Federal Housing Finance Agency (FHFA), announced that Fannie Mae and Freddie Mac were being placed into conservatorship of the FHFA.

a. The Depository Trust ' Clearing Corporation
c. General partnership
b. SPDR
d. Federal National Mortgage Association

35. _____ is early repayment of a loan by a borrower.

In the case of a mortgage-backed security (MBS), _____ is perceived as a risk, because mortgage debts are often paid off early in order to incur lower total interest payments through cheaper refinancing. The new financing may be cheaper because the borrower's credit rating has improved or because interest rates are lower, but in either case, the payments that would have been made to the MBS investor would be above market rates.

a. Prepayment
b. Disposal tax effect
c. Bankruptcy remote
d. Retention ratio

36. In structured finance, a _____ is one of a number of related securities offered as part of the same transaction. The word _____ is French for slice, section, series, or portion. In the financial sense of the word, each bond is a different slice of the deal's risk.
   a. 4-4-5 Calendar
   b. Tranche
   c. Yield curve spread
   d. Credit enhancement

37. _____ is that which is owed; usually referencing assets owed, but the term can cover other obligations. In the case of assets, _____ is a means of using future purchasing power in the present before a summation has been earned. Some companies and corporations use _____ as a part of their overall corporate finance strategy.
   a. Cross-collateralization
   b. Debt
   c. Credit cycle
   d. Partial Payment

38. _____ is the difference between a lower selling price and a higher purchase price, resulting in a financial loss for the seller. Pursuant to IRS TAX TIP 2009-35 'If your _____ exceeds your capital gain, the excess can be deducted on your tax return, up to an annual limit of $3,000 ($1,500 if you are married filing separately.)' .
   a. 7-Eleven
   b. 4-4-5 Calendar
   c. Capital loss
   d. 529 plan

39.

A _____ is a type of financial intermediary and a type of bank. Commercial banking is also known as business banking. It is a bank that provides checking accounts, savings accounts, and money market accounts and that accepts time deposits.

   a. 529 plan
   b. 4-4-5 Calendar
   c. 7-Eleven
   d. Commercial bank

40. _____, refers to consumption opportunity gained by an entity within a specified time frame, which is generally expressed in monetary terms. However, for households and individuals, '_____ is the sum of all the wages, salaries, profits, interests payments, rents and other forms of earnings received... in a given period of time.' For firms, _____ generally refers to net-profit: what remains of revenue after expenses have been subtracted.
   a. OIBDA
   b. Income
   c. Annual report
   d. Accrual

41. An _____ is a tax levied on the financial income of people, corporations, or other legal entities. Various _____ systems exist, with varying degrees of tax incidence. Income taxation can be progressive, proportional, or regressive.
   a. AAB
   b. Income Tax
   c. A Random Walk Down Wall Street
   d. ABN Amro

42. _____ refers to a tax levied by various jurisdictions on the profits made by companies or associations. It is a tax on the value of the corporation's profits.

The measure of taxable profits varies from country to country.

a. Proxy fight
b. Trade finance
c. First-mover advantage
d. Corporate tax

43. _____ is the quality of paper money substitutes which entitles the holder to redeem them on demand into money proper.

Historically, the banknote has followed a common or very similar pattern in the western nations. Originally decentralized and issued from various independent banks, it was gradually brought under state control and became a monopoly privilege of the central banks.

a. Petrodollar recycling
b. Functional currency
c. Devaluation
d. Convertibility

44. In finance, a _____ is a type of bond that can be converted into shares of stock in the issuing company, usually at some pre-announced ratio. It is a hybrid security with debt- and equity-like features. Although it typically has a low coupon rate, the holder is compensated with the ability to convert the bond to common stock, usually at a substantial discount to the stock's market value.

a. Convertible bond
b. Bond fund
c. Corporate bond
d. Gilts

45. _____ are government bonds issued by the United States Department of the Treasury through the Bureau of the Public Debt. They are the debt financing instruments of the U.S. Federal government, and they are often referred to simply as Treasuries or Treasurys. There are four types of marketable _____: Treasury bills, Treasury notes, Treasury bonds, and Treasury Inflation Protected Securities (TIPS.)

a. Treasury Inflation Protected Securities
b. Treasury Inflation-Protected Securities
c. Treasury securities
d. 4-4-5 Calendar

46. _____ is a form of corporation equity ownership represented in the securities. It is dangerous in comparison to preferred shares and some other investment options, in that in the event of bankruptcy, _____ investors receive their funds after preferred stockholders, bondholders, creditors, etc. On the other hand, common shares on average perform better than preferred shares or bonds over time.

a. Common stock
b. Stop-limit order
c. Stock market bubble
d. Stock split

47. A _____ is a payment made by a corporation to its shareholder members. When a corporation earns a profit or surplus, that money can be put to two uses: it can either be re-invested in the business (called retained earnings), or it can be paid to the shareholders as a _____. Many corporations retain a portion of their earnings and pay the remainder as a _____.

a. Dividend yield
b. Dividend puzzle
c. Special dividend
d. Dividend

48. A _____ is the price of a single share of a no. of saleable stocks of the company. Once the stock is purchased, the owner becomes a shareholder of the company that issued the share.

a. Trading curb
b. Stock split
c. Whisper numbers
d. Share price

49. In business and finance, a _____ (also referred to as equity _____) of stock means a _____ of ownership in a corporation (company.) In the plural, stocks is often used as a synonym for _____s especially in the United States, but it is less commonly used that way outside of North America.

In the United Kingdom, South Africa, and Australia, stock can also refer to completely different financial instruments such as government bonds or, less commonly, to all kinds of marketable securities.

a. Share
b. Procter ' Gamble
c. Bucket shop
d. Margin

50. _____ is the value of a property to a particular investor. In the U.S., it is equal to market value for the investor who has the capacity to put the property to good use -- its highest-and-best-use, its most valuable use. For other investors with limited capacity or vision, _____ is lower because they cannot put the property to use in a way that is maximally productive.

a. ABN Amro
b. Investment value
c. A Random Walk Down Wall Street
d. AAB

51. In finance, the _____ is the system that allows the transfer of money between savers and borrowers.

Put another way: the _____ is a set of complex and closely interconnected financial institutions, markets, instruments, services, practices, and transactions.

a. Passive income
b. Horizontal merger
c. 4-4-5 Calendar
d. Financial system

52. The _____ is the interest rate that it is assumed can be obtained by investing in financial instruments with no default risk. However, the financial instrument can carry other types of risk, e.g. market risk (the risk of changes in market interest rates), liquidity risk (the risk of being unable to sell the instrument for cash at short notice without significant costs) etc.

Though a truly risk-free asset exists only in theory, in practice most professionals and academics use short-dated government bonds of the currency in question.

a. London Interbank Bid Rate
b. Cash accumulation equation
c. London Interbank Offered Rate
d. Risk-free Interest rate

Chapter 9. Interest Rate Forecasting and Hedging: Swaps, Financial Futures, and Options

1. The term _____ or economic cycle refers to the fluctuations of economic activity (business fluctuations) around a long-term growth trend. The cycle involves shifts over time between periods of relatively rapid growth of output (recovery and prosperity), and periods of relative stagnation or decline (contraction or recession.) These fluctuations are often measured using the real gross domestic product.
   a. Fixed exchange rate
   b. Behavioral finance
   c. Business cycle
   d. Deflation

2. _____ is a fee paid on borrowed assets. It is the price paid for the use of borrowed money , or, money earned by deposited funds . Assets that are sometimes lent with _____ include money, shares, consumer goods through hire purchase, major assets such as aircraft, and even entire factories in finance lease arrangements.
   a. A Random Walk Down Wall Street
   b. AAB
   c. Insolvency
   d. Interest

3. An _____ is the price a borrower pays for the use of money they do not own, and the return a lender receives for deferring the use of funds, by lending it to the borrower. _____s are normally expressed as a percentage rate over the period of one year.

   _____s targets are also a vital tool of monetary policy and are used to control variables like investment, inflation, and unemployment.

   a. ABN Amro
   b. A Random Walk Down Wall Street
   c. Interest rate
   d. AAB

4. _____ is the risk (variability in value) borne by an interest-bearing asset, such as a loan or a bond, due to variability of interest rates. In general, as rates rise, the price of a fixed rate bond will fall, and vice versa. _____ is commonly measured by the bond's duration.
   a. International Fisher effect
   b. A Random Walk Down Wall Street
   c. Interest rate risk
   d. Official bank rate

5. In economic models, the _____ time frame assumes no fixed factors of production. Firms can enter or leave the marketplace, and the cost (and availability) of land, labor, raw materials, and capital goods can be assumed to vary. In contrast, in the short-run time frame, certain factors are assumed to be fixed, because there is not sufficient time for them to change.
   a. Long-run
   b. 4-4-5 Calendar
   c. Short-run
   d. 529 plan

6. In finance, a _____ is a debt security, in which the authorized issuer owes the holders a debt and, depending on the terms of the _____, is obliged to pay interest (the coupon) and/or to repay the principal at a later date, termed maturity.

   Thus a _____ is a loan: the issuer is the borrower, the _____ holder is the lender, and the coupon is the interest. _____s provide the borrower with external funds to finance long-term investments, or, in the case of government _____s, to finance current expenditure.

   a. Puttable bond
   b. Bond
   c. Convertible bond
   d. Catastrophe bonds

Chapter 9. Interest Rate Forecasting and Hedging: Swaps, Financial Futures, and Options

7. _____ is that which is owed; usually referencing assets owed, but the term can cover other obligations. In the case of assets, _____ is a means of using future purchasing power in the present before a summation has been earned. Some companies and corporations use _____ as a part of their overall corporate finance strategy.
   a. Credit cycle
   b. Debt
   c. Partial Payment
   d. Cross-collateralization

8. In statistics, _____ has two related meanings:

   - the arithmetic _____
   - the expected value of a random variable, which is also called the population _____.

   It is sometimes stated that the '_____' is average. This is incorrect if '_____' is taken in the specific sense of 'arithmetic _____' as there are different types of averages: the _____, median, and mode. Other simple statistical analyses use measures of spread, such as range, interquartile range, or standard deviation. For a real-valued random variable X, the _____ is the expectation of X. Note that not every probability distribution has a defined _____; see the Cauchy distribution for an example.

   a. Harmonic mean
   b. Sample size
   c. Mean
   d. Probability distribution

9. A _____ is a fungible, negotiable instrument representing financial value. They are broadly categorized into debt securities (such as banknotes, bonds and debentures), and equity securities; e.g., common stocks. The company or other entity issuing the _____ is called the issuer.
   a. Security
   b. Book entry
   c. Tracking stock
   d. Securities lending

10. The institution most often referenced by the word '_____' is a public or publicly traded _____, the shares of which are traded on a public stock exchange (e.g., the New York Stock Exchange or Nasdaq in the United States) where shares of stock of _____s are bought and sold by and to the general public. Most of the largest businesses in the world are publicly traded _____s. However, the majority of _____s are said to be closely held, privately held or close _____s, meaning that no ready market exists for the trading of shares.
    a. Federal Home Loan Mortgage Corporation
    b. Protect
    c. Depository Trust Company
    d. Corporation

11. In finance, a _____ is a derivative in which two counterparties agree to exchange one stream of cash flows against another stream. These streams are called the legs of the _____.

    The cash flows are calculated over a notional principal amount, which is usually not exchanged between counterparties.

    a. Swap
    b. Volatility arbitrage
    c. Local volatility
    d. Volatility swap

Chapter 9. Interest Rate Forecasting and Hedging: Swaps, Financial Futures, and Options

12. _____ is the provision of resources (such as granting a loan) by one party to another party where that second party does not reimburse the first party immediately, thereby generating a debt, and instead arranges either to repay or return those resources (or material(s) of equal value) at a later date. The first party is called a creditor, also known as a lender, while the second party is called a debtor, also known as a borrower.

Movements of financial capital are normally dependent on either _____ or equity transfers.

a. Clearing house
b. Comparable
c. Credit
d. Warrant

13. An _____ is a derivative in which one party exchanges a stream of interest payments for another party's stream of cash flows. _____s can be used by hedgers to manage their fixed or floating assets and liabilities. They can also be used by speculators to replicate unfunded bond exposures to profit from changes in interest rates.

a. International Swaps and Derivatives Association
b. Implied volatility
c. Equity swap
d. Interest rate Swap

14. A _____ or market-based mechanism is any of a wide variety of ways to match up buyers and sellers.

An example of a _____ uses announced bid and ask prices. Generally speaking, when two parties wish to engage in a trade, the purchaser will announce a price he is willing to pay (the bid price) and seller will announce a price he is willing to accept (the ask price).

a. 529 plan
b. 7-Eleven
c. 4-4-5 Calendar
d. Price mechanism

15. In finance, _____ occurs when a debtor has not met its legal obligations according to the debt contract, e.g. it has not made a scheduled payment, or has violated a loan covenant (condition) of the debt contract. _____ may occur if the debtor is either unwilling or unable to pay their debt. This can occur with all debt obligations including bonds, mortgages, loans, and promissory notes.

a. Default
b. Credit crunch
c. Vendor finance
d. Debt validation

16. _____ is the risk of loss due to a debtor's non-payment of a loan or other line of credit (either the principal or interest (coupon) or both)

Most lenders employ their own models (credit scorecards) to rank potential and existing customers according to risk, and then apply appropriate strategies. With products such as unsecured personal loans or mortgages, lenders charge a higher price for higher risk customers and vice versa. With revolving products such as credit cards and overdrafts, risk is controlled through careful setting of credit limits.

a. Transaction risk
b. Credit risk
c. Market risk
d. Liquidity risk

17. A _____ is a financial contract whose value is derived from the value of something else (known as the underlying.) The underlying on which a _____ is based can be an asset, weather conditions bonds or other forms of credit.

Chapter 9. Interest Rate Forecasting and Hedging: Swaps, Financial Futures, and Options

a. Derivative
b. 4-4-5 Calendar
c. 529 plan
d. 7-Eleven

18. A _____ is a futures contract on a short term interest rate (STIR.) Contracts vary, but are often defined on an interest rate index such as 3-month sterling or US dollar LIBOR.

They are traded across a wide range of currencies, including the G12 country currencies and many others.

a. Financial future
b. Dual currency deposit
c. Real estate derivatives
d. Notional amount

19. The _____ is a trade organization of participants in the market for over-the-counter derivatives. It is headquartered in New York, and has created a standardized contract (Master Agreement) to enter into derivatives transactions. There are currently two versions of the ISDA Master Agreement: the 1992 edition and the 2002 edition.

a. Interest rate derivative
b. Open interest
c. Equity swap
d. International Swaps and Derivatives Association

20. An _____ is a contract written by a seller that conveys to the buyer the right -- but not the obligation -- to buy (in the case of a call _____) or to sell (in the case of a put _____) a particular asset, such as a piece of property such as, among others, a futures contract. In return for granting the _____, the seller collects a payment (the premium) from the buyer.

For example, buying a call _____ provides the right to buy a specified quantity of a security at a set strike price at some time on or before expiration, while buying a put _____ provides the right to sell.

a. AT'T Mobility LLC
b. Option
c. Annuity
d. Amortization

21. An _____ is defined as 'a promise which meets the requirements for the formation of a contract and limits the promisor's power to revoke an offer.' Restatement (Second) of Contracts § 25 (1981.)

Quite simply, an _____ is a type of contract that protects an offeree from an offeror's ability to revoke the contract.

Consideration for the _____ is still required as it is still a form of contract.

a. AAB
b. A Random Walk Down Wall Street
c. Option contract
d. ABN Amro

22. _____ is a legally declared inability or impairment of ability of an individual or organization to pay their creditors. Creditors may file a _____ petition against a debtor ('involuntary _____') in an effort to recoup a portion of what they are owed or initiate a restructuring. In the majority of cases, however, _____ is initiated by the debtor (a 'voluntary _____' that is filed by the bankrupt individual or organization.)

a. Bankruptcy
b. 529 plan
c. Debt settlement
d. 4-4-5 Calendar

Chapter 9. Interest Rate Forecasting and Hedging: Swaps, Financial Futures, and Options

23. A _____ is an exchange of promises between two or more parties to do an act which is enforceable in a court of law. It is where an unqualified offer meets a qualified acceptance and the parties reach Consensus ad Idem. The parties must have the necessary capacity to _____ and the _____ must not be either trifling, indeterminate, impossible or illegal.

   a. 4-4-5 Calendar   b. 7-Eleven
   c. Contract   d. 529 plan

24. In finance, a _____ is a standardized contract, to buy or sell a specified commodity of standardized quality at a certain date in the future, at a market determined price (the futures price.)

The price is determined by the instantaneous equilibrium between the forces of supply and demand among competing buy and sell orders on the exchange at the time of the purchase or sale of the contract.

In many cases, the items may be such non-traditional 'commodities' as foreign currencies, commercial or government paper [e.g., bonds], or 'baskets' of corporate equity ['stock indices'] or other financial instruments.

   a. Futures contract   b. Heston model
   c. Financial future   d. Repurchase agreement

25. The role of the _____ is to issue accounting standards in the United Kingdom. It is recognised for that purpose under the Companies Act 1985. It took over the task of setting accounting standards from the Accounting Standards Committee (ASC) in 1990.

   a. A Random Walk Down Wall Street   b. ABN Amro
   c. Accounting Standards Board   d. AAB

26. The _____ is a private, not-for-profit organization whose primary purpose is to develop generally accepted accounting principles (GAAP) within the United States in the public's interest. The Securities and Exchange Commission (SEC) designated the _____ as the organization responsible for setting accounting standards for public companies in the U.S. It was created in 1973, replacing the Accounting Principles Board and the Committee on Accounting Procedure of the American Institute of Certified Public Accountants. The _____'s mission is 'to establish and improve standards of financial accounting and reporting for the guidance and education of the public, including issuers, auditors, and users of financial information.'

The _____ is not a governmental body.

   a. MRU Holdings   b. PlaNet Finance
   c. Credit karma   d. FASB

27. _____ is the field of accountancy concerned with the preparation of financial statements for decision makers, such as stockholders, suppliers, banks, employees, government agencies, owners, and other stakeholders. The fundamental need for _____ is to reduce principal-agent problem by measuring and monitoring agents' performance and reporting the results to interested users.

_____ is used to prepare accounting information for people outside the organization or not involved in the day to day running of the company.

Chapter 9. Interest Rate Forecasting and Hedging: Swaps, Financial Futures, and Options

a. 4-4-5 Calendar
c. 529 plan
b. 7-Eleven
d. Financial Accounting

28. The _____ is a private, not-for-profit organization whose primary purpose is to develop generally accepted accounting principles (GAAP) within the United States in the public's interest. The Securities and Exchange Commission (SEC) designated the _____ as the organization responsible for setting accounting standards for public companies in the U.S. It was created in 1973, replacing the Accounting Principles Board and the Committee on Accounting Procedure of the American Institute of Certified Public Accountants. The _____'s mission is 'to establish and improve standards of financial accounting and reporting for the guidance and education of the public, including issuers, auditors, and users of financial information.'

The _____ is not a governmental body.

a. World Congress of Accountants
c. Federal Deposit Insurance Corporation
b. KPMG
d. Financial Accounting Standards Board

29. _____ mature in one year or less. Like zero-coupon bonds, they do not pay interest prior to maturity; instead they are sold at a discount of the par value to create a positive yield to maturity. Many regard _____ as the least risky investment available to U.S. investors.

a. 4-4-5 Calendar
c. Treasury bills
b. Treasury securities
d. Treasury Inflation Protected Securities

30. _____ are government bonds issued by the United States Department of the Treasury through the Bureau of the Public Debt. They are the debt financing instruments of the U.S. Federal government, and they are often referred to simply as Treasuries or Treasurys. There are four types of marketable _____: Treasury bills, Treasury notes, Treasury bonds, and Treasury Inflation Protected Securities (TIPS.)

a. Treasury Inflation Protected Securities
c. Treasury securities
b. 4-4-5 Calendar
d. Treasury Inflation-Protected Securities

31. In finance, a _____ is collateral that the holder of a position in securities, options, or futures contracts has to deposit to cover the credit risk of his counterparty (most often his broker.) This risk can arise if the holder has done any of the following:

- borrowed cash from the counterparty to buy securities or options,
- sold securities or options short, or
- entered into a futures contract.

The collateral can be in the form of cash or securities, and it is deposited in a _____ account. On U.S. futures exchanges, '_____' was formally called performance bond.

_____ buying is buying securities with cash borrowed from a broker, using other securities as collateral.

a. Procter ' Gamble
c. Credit
b. Margin
d. Share

Chapter 9. Interest Rate Forecasting and Hedging: Swaps, Financial Futures, and Options 87

32. In finance, a _____ is a position established in one market in an attempt to offset exposure to the price risk of an equal but opposite obligation or position in another market -- usually, but not always, in the context of one's commercial activity. Hedging is a strategy designed to minimize exposure to such business risks as a sharp contraction in demand for one's inventory, while still allowing the business to profit from producing and maintaining that inventory. A typical hedger might be a farmer with 2000 acres of unharvested wheat in the ground, who would rather tend his crop without the distraction of uncertain prices.
   a. 529 plan
   b. 7-Eleven
   c. 4-4-5 Calendar
   d. Hedge

33. A _____ is a financial contract between two parties, the buyer and the seller of this type of option. Often it is simply labeled a 'call'. The buyer of the option has the right, but not the obligation to buy an agreed quantity of a particular commodity or financial instrument (the underlying instrument) from the seller of the option at a certain time (the expiration date) for a certain price (the strike price.)
   a. Bear call spread
   b. Bull spread
   c. Call option
   d. Bear spread

34. In options, the _____ is a key variable in a derivatives contract between two parties. Where the contract requires delivery of the underlying instrument, the trade will be at the _____, regardless of the spot price (market price) of the underlying instrument at that time.

Definition - The fixed price at which the owner of an option can purchase, in the case of a call in the case of a put, the underlying security or commodity.

   a. Strike price
   b. Swaption
   c. Naked put
   d. Moneyness

35. The _____ is an American financial and commodity derivative exchange based in Chicago. The _____ was founded in 1898 as the Chicago Butter and Egg Board. Originally, the exchange was a non-profit organization.
   a. Public Company Accounting Oversight Board
   b. Gamelan Council
   c. Financial Crimes Enforcement Network
   d. Chicago Mercantile Exchange

36. The _____ is the price the buyer of the options contract pays for the right to buy or sell a security at a specified price in the future.
   a. ABN Amro
   b. AAB
   c. A Random Walk Down Wall Street
   d. Option premium

37. A _____ is a financial contract between two parties, the seller (writer) and the buyer of the option. The put allows its buyer the right but not the obligation to sell a commodity or financial instrument (the underlying instrument) to the writer (seller) of the option at a certain time for a certain price (the strike price.) The writer (seller) has the obligation to purchase the underlying asset at that strike price, if the buyer exercises the option.
   a. Debit spread
   b. Put option
   c. Bear call spread
   d. Bear spread

38. A _____ is the price of a single share of a no. of saleable stocks of the company. Once the stock is purchased, the owner becomes a shareholder of the company that issued the share.

Chapter 9. Interest Rate Forecasting and Hedging: Swaps, Financial Futures, and Options

a. Whisper numbers
c. Trading curb
b. Stock split
d. Share price

39. A _____ is something for which there is demand, but which is supplied without qualitative differentiation across a market. It is a product that is the same no matter who produces it, such as petroleum, notebook paper, or milk. In other words, copper is copper.
   a. 529 plan
   c. 4-4-5 Calendar
   b. Commodity
   d. 7-Eleven

40. An _____ is an investment vehicle traded on stock exchanges, much like stocks. An ETF holds assets such as stocks or bonds and trades at approximately the same price as the net asset value of its underlying assets over the course of the trading day. Most ETFs track an index, such as the Dow Jones Industrial Average or the S'P 500.
   a. A Random Walk Down Wall Street
   c. ABN Amro
   b. Exchange-traded fund
   d. AAB

41. The U.S. _____ is an independent agency of the United States government which holds primary responsibility for enforcing the federal securities laws and regulating the securities industry, the nation's stock and options exchanges, and other electronic securities markets. The SEC was created by section 4 of the SEC of 1934 (now codified as 15 U.S.C. § 78d and commonly referred to as the 1934 Act.)
   a. 4-4-5 Calendar
   c. 529 plan
   b. 7-Eleven
   d. Securities and Exchange Commission

42. A _____ assesses the credit worthiness of an individual, corporation, or even a country. _____ s are calculated from financial history and current assets and liabilities. Typically, a _____ tells a lender or investor the probability of the subject being able to pay back a loan.
   a. Credit cycle
   c. Debenture
   b. Credit rating
   d. Credit report monitoring

43. A _____ is a central financial exchange where people can trade standardized futures contracts; that is, a contract to buy specific quantities of a commodity or financial instrument at a specified price with delivery set at a specified time in the future.

Though the origins of futures trading can supposedly be traced to Ancient Greek or Phoenician times, the first modern organized _____ began in 1710 at the Dojima Rice Exchange in Osaka, Japan.

The United States followed in the early 1800s.

   a. 4-4-5 Calendar
   c. 7-Eleven
   b. 529 plan
   d. Futures exchange

44. _____ in finance is the risk associated with imperfect hedging using futures. It could arise because of the difference between the asset whose price is to be hedged and the asset underlying the derivative, or because of a mismatch between the expiration date of the futures and the actual selling date of the asset.

Under these conditions, the spot price of the asset, and the futures price, do not converge on the expiration date of the future.

Chapter 9. Interest Rate Forecasting and Hedging: Swaps, Financial Futures, and Options

a. Liquidity risk
b. Basis risk
c. Credit risk
d. Currency risk

45. In economics, business, and accounting, a _____ is the value of money that has been used up to produce something, and hence is not available for use anymore. In business, the _____ may be one of acquisition, in which case the amount of money expended to acquire it is counted as _____. In this case, money is the input that is gone in order to acquire the thing.

a. Marginal cost
b. Fixed costs
c. Sliding scale fees
d. Cost

46. _____ is a major futures and options exchange for European benchmark derivatives featuring open and low-cost electronic access globally. Its electronic trading and clearing platform offers a broad range of products and amongst other, operates the most liquid fixed income markets. _____ was established in 1998 with the merger of Deutsche Terminbörse and SOFFEX (Swiss Options and Financial Futures.)

a. EUREX
b. A Random Walk Down Wall Street
c. AAB
d. ABN Amro

47. _____ N.V. is a pan-European stock exchange based in Paris and with subsidiaries in Belgium, France, Netherlands, Luxembourg, Portugal and the United Kingdom. In addition to equities and derivatives markets, the _____ group provides clearing and information services. As of 31 January 2006, markets run by _____ had a market capitalization of US$2.9 trillion, making it the 5th largest exchange on the planet.

a. A Random Walk Down Wall Street
b. AAB
c. Euronext
d. ABN Amro

48. The _____ Options Exchange is a futures exchange based in London. _____ is now part of NYSE Euronext following its takeover by Euronext in January 2002 and Euronext's merger with New York Stock Exchange in April 2007.

The _____ started life on September 30, 1982, to take advantage of the removal of currency controls in the UK in 1979.

a. 529 plan
b. LIFFE
c. 7-Eleven
d. 4-4-5 Calendar

49. _____ is a measure of the ability of a debtor to pay their debts as and when they fall due. It is usually expressed as a ratio or a percentage of current liabilities.

For a corporation with a published balance sheet there are various ratios used to calculate a measure of liquidity.

a. Operating profit margin
b. Accounting liquidity
c. Invested capital
d. Operating leverage

50. _____ arises from situations in which a party interested in trading an asset cannot do it because nobody in the market wants to trade that asset. _____ becomes particularly important to parties who are about to hold or currently hold an asset, since it affects their ability to trade.

Manifestation of _____ is very different from a drop of price to zero.

Chapter 9. Interest Rate Forecasting and Hedging: Swaps, Financial Futures, and Options

a. Credit risk
c. Tracking error
b. Liquidity risk
d. Currency risk

51. The _____ started life on September 30, 1982, to take advantage of the removal of currency controls in the UK in 1979. The exchange modelled itself after the Chicago Board of Trade and the Chicago Mercantile Exchange. It initially offered futures contracts and options linked to short term interest rates.

a. 529 plan
c. 4-4-5 Calendar
b. 7-Eleven
d. London International Financial Futures Exchange

52. _____, also called fair price (in a commonplace conflation of the two distinct concepts), is a concept used in finance and economics, defined as a rational and unbiased estimate of the potential market price of a good, service, or asset, taking into account such objective factors as:

- acquisition/production/distribution costs, replacement costs, or costs of close substitutes
- actual utility at a given level of development of social productive capability
- supply vs. demand

and subjective factors such as

- risk characteristics
- cost of capital
- individually perceived utility

In accounting, _____ is used as an estimate of the market value of an asset (or liability) for which a market price cannot be determined (usually because there is no established market for the asset.) Under GAAP (FAS 157), _____ is the amount at which the asset could be bought or sold in a current transaction between willing parties, or transferred to an equivalent party, other than in a liquidation sale. This is used for assets whose carrying value is based on mark-to-market valuations; for assets carried at historical cost, the _____ of the asset is not used. One example of where _____ is an issue is a College kitchen with a cost of $2 million which was built 5 years ago.

a. 4-4-5 Calendar
c. 529 plan
b. 7-Eleven
d. Fair value

53. _____ is one of the authors of the Black-Scholes equation. In 1997 he was awarded the Nobel Memorial Prize in Economic Sciences for 'a new method to determine the value of derivatives'. The model provides the fundamental conceptual framework for valuing options, such as calls or puts, and is referred to as the Black-Scholes model, which has become the standard in financial markets globally.

a. Robert James Shiller
c. Andrew Tobias
b. Adolph Coors
d. Myron Samuel Scholes

Chapter 9. Interest Rate Forecasting and Hedging: Swaps, Financial Futures, and Options

54. The term _____ refers to three closely related concepts:

    - The _____ model is a mathematical model of the market for an equity, in which the equity's price is a stochastic process.
    - The _____ PDE is a partial differential equation which (in the model) must be satisfied by the price of a derivative on the equity.
    - The _____ formula is the result obtained by solving the _____ PDE for a European call option.

Fischer Black and Myron Scholes first articulated the _____ formula in their 1973 paper, 'The Pricing of Options and Corporate Liabilities.' The foundation for their research relied on work developed by scholars such as Jack L. Treynor, Paul Samuelson, A. James Boness, Sheen T. Kassouf, and Edward O. Thorp. The fundamental insight of _____ is that the option is implicitly priced if the stock is traded.

Robert C. Merton was the first to publish a paper expanding the mathematical understanding of the options pricing model and coined the term '_____' options pricing model.

a. Black-Scholes
b. Modified Internal Rate of Return
c. Stochastic volatility
d. Perpetuity

1. In the global money market, _____ is an unsecured promissory note with a fixed maturity of one to 270 days. _____ is a money-market security issued (sold) by large banks and corporations to get money to meet short term debt obligations (for example, payroll), and is only backed by an issuing bank or corporation's promise to pay the face amount on the maturity date specified on the note. Since it is not backed by collateral, only firms with excellent credit ratings from a recognized rating agency will be able to sell their _____ at a reasonable price.
   a. Financial distress
   b. Commercial paper
   c. Book building
   d. Trade-off theory

2. _____ is the term used to describe deposits residing in banks that are located outside the borders of the country that issues the currency the deposit is denominated in. For example a deposit denominated in US dollars residing in a Japanese bank is a _____ deposit, or more specifically a Eurodollar deposit.

Key points are the location of the bank and the denomination of the currency, not the nationality of the bank or the owner of the deposit/loan.

   a. ABN Amro
   b. AAB
   c. Eurocurrency
   d. A Random Walk Down Wall Street

3. In finance, the _____ is the global financial market for short-term borrowing and lending. It provides short-term liquidity funding for the global financial system. The _____ is where short-term obligations such as Treasury bills, commercial paper and bankers' acceptances are bought and sold.
   a. Consumer debt
   b. Debt-for-equity swap
   c. Money market
   d. Cramdown

4. In finance, a _____ is the party in a loan agreement which receives money or other instrument from a lender and promises to repay the lender in a specified time.
   a. Cash credit
   b. Borrower
   c. Line of credit
   d. Debt management plan

5. _____, in bookkeeping, refers to assets, liabilities, income, and expenses recorded on individual pages of the so called book of final entry or ledger. Changes in _____ value are made by chronologically posting debit (DR) and credit (CR) entries to its page. Examples of _____s are cash, _____s receivable, mortgages, loans, land and buildings, common stock, sales, services provided, wages, and payroll overhead.
   a. Alpha
   b. Accretion
   c. Option
   d. Account

6. A _____, reserve bank, or monetary authority is the entity responsible for the monetary policy of a country or of a group of member states. It is a bank that can lend money to other banks in times of need. Its primary responsibility is to maintain the stability of the national currency and money supply, but more active duties include controlling subsidized-loan interest rates, and acting as a lender of last resort to the banking sector during times of financial crisis (private banks often being integral to the national financial system.)
   a. 7-Eleven
   b. 529 plan
   c. 4-4-5 Calendar
   d. Central Bank

7. _____ is a fee paid on borrowed assets. It is the price paid for the use of borrowed money , or, money earned by deposited funds . Assets that are sometimes lent with _____ include money, shares, consumer goods through hire purchase, major assets such as aircraft, and even entire factories in finance lease arrangements.

Chapter 10. Introduction to the Money Market and the Roles Played

a. AAB
b. A Random Walk Down Wall Street
c. Insolvency
d. Interest

8. An _____ is the price a borrower pays for the use of money they do not own, and the return a lender receives for deferring the use of funds, by lending it to the borrower. _____s are normally expressed as a percentage rate over the period of one year.

_____s targets are also a vital tool of monetary policy and are used to control variables like investment, inflation, and unemployment.

a. Interest rate
b. AAB
c. ABN Amro
d. A Random Walk Down Wall Street

9. _____ is the risk (variability in value) borne by an interest-bearing asset, such as a loan or a bond, due to variability of interest rates. In general, as rates rise, the price of a fixed rate bond will fall, and vice versa. _____ is commonly measured by the bond's duration.

a. Interest rate risk
b. A Random Walk Down Wall Street
c. International Fisher effect
d. Official bank rate

10. _____ is a measure of the ability of a debtor to pay their debts as and when they fall due. It is usually expressed as a ratio or a percentage of current liabilities.

For a corporation with a published balance sheet there are various ratios used to calculate a measure of liquidity.

a. Invested capital
b. Operating leverage
c. Operating profit margin
d. Accounting liquidity

11. In business and accounting, _____s are everything of value that is owned by a person or company. The balance sheet of a firm records the monetary value of the _____s owned by the firm. The two major _____ classes are tangible _____s and intangible _____s.

a. EBITDA
b. Accounts payable
c. Income
d. Asset

12. A _____ is a fungible, negotiable instrument representing financial value. They are broadly categorized into debt securities (such as banknotes, bonds and debentures), and equity securities; e.g., common stocks. The company or other entity issuing the _____ is called the issuer.

a. Security
b. Tracking stock
c. Securities lending
d. Book entry

13. The institution most often referenced by the word '_____' is a public or publicly traded _____, the shares of which are traded on a public stock exchange (e.g., the New York Stock Exchange or Nasdaq in the United States) where shares of stock of _____s are bought and sold by and to the general public. Most of the largest businesses in the world are publicly traded _____s. However, the majority of _____s are said to be closely held, privately held or close _____s, meaning that no ready market exists for the trading of shares.

a. Protect
c. Depository Trust Company

b. Corporation
d. Federal Home Loan Mortgage Corporation

14. _____ is a form of risk that arises from the change in price of one currency against another. Whenever investors or companies have assets or business operations across national borders, they face _____ if their positions are not hedged.

- Transaction risk is the risk that exchange rates will change unfavourably over time. It can be hedged against using forward currency contracts;
- Translation risk is an accounting risk, proportional to the amount of assets held in foreign currencies. Changes in the exchange rate over time will render a report inaccurate, and so assets are usually balanced by borrowings in that currency.

The exchange risk associated with a foreign denominated instrument is a key element in foreign investment. This risk flows from differential monetary policy and growth in real productivity, which results in differential inflation rates.

a. Market risk
c. Tracking error

b. Currency risk
d. Credit risk

15. In economics, _____ is a rise in the general level of prices of goods and services in an economy over a period of time. The term '_____' once referred to increases in the money supply (monetary _____); however, economic debates about the relationship between money supply and price levels have led to its primary use today in describing price _____. _____ can also be described as a decline in the real value of money--a loss of purchasing power in the medium of exchange which is also the monetary unit of account.

a. ABN Amro
c. A Random Walk Down Wall Street

b. AAB
d. Inflation

16. _____ is the risk that the value of an investment will decrease due to moves in market factors. The five standard _____ factors are:

- Equity risk, the risk that stock prices will change.
- Interest rate risk, the risk that interest rates will change.
- Currency risk, the risk that foreign exchange rates will change.
- Commodity risk, the risk that commodity prices (e.g. grains, metals) will change.

As with other forms of risk, _____ may be measured in a number of ways. Traditionally, this is done using a Value at Risk methodology. Value at risk is well established as a risk management technique, but it contains a number of limiting assumptions that constrain its accuracy.

a. Market risk
c. Currency risk

b. Tracking error
d. Transaction risk

17. _____ is a type of risk faced by investors, corporations, and governments. It is a risk that can be understood and managed with proper aforethought and investment.

Broadly, _____ refers to the complications businesses and governments may face as a result of what are commonly referred to as political decisions--or 'any political change that alters the expected outcome and value of a given economic action by changing the probability of achieving business objectives.' .

a. Political risk
b. Mid price
c. Capital asset
d. Single-index model

18. _____ refers to a business or organization attempting to acquire goods or services to accomplish the goals of the enterprise. Though there are several organizations that attempt to set standards in the _____ process, processes can vary greatly between organizations. Typically the word '_____' is not used interchangeably with the word 'procurement', since procurement typically includes Expediting, Supplier Quality, and Traffic and Logistics (T'L) in addition to _____.

a. Purchasing
b. 529 plan
c. 4-4-5 Calendar
d. 7-Eleven

19. _____ is the value of goods/services compared to the amount paid with a currency. Currency can be either a commodity money, like gold or silver, or fiat currency like US dollars which are the world reserve currency. As Adam Smith noted, having money gives one the ability to 'command' others' labor, so _____ to some extent is power over other people, to the extent that they are willing to trade their labor or goods for money or currency.

a. Purchasing power
b. 4-4-5 Calendar
c. 529 plan
d. 7-Eleven

20. _____ is one of the main genres of financial risk. The term describes the risk that a particular investment might be canceled or stopped somehow, that one may have to find a new place to invest that money with the risk being there might not be a similarly attractive investment available. This primarily occurs if bonds (which are portions of loans to entities) are paid back earlier then expected.

a. Standard of deferred payment
b. Reinvestment risk
c. Biweekly Mortgage
d. Debt cash flow

21. _____ is a legally declared inability or impairment of ability of an individual or organization to pay their creditors. Creditors may file a _____ petition against a debtor ('involuntary _____') in an effort to recoup a portion of what they are owed or initiate a restructuring. In the majority of cases, however, _____ is initiated by the debtor (a 'voluntary _____' that is filed by the bankrupt individual or organization.)

a. 4-4-5 Calendar
b. Debt settlement
c. 529 plan
d. Bankruptcy

22. In finance, _____ occurs when a debtor has not met its legal obligations according to the debt contract, e.g. it has not made a scheduled payment, or has violated a loan covenant (condition) of the debt contract. _____ may occur if the debtor is either unwilling or unable to pay their debt. This can occur with all debt obligations including bonds, mortgages, loans, and promissory notes.

a. Credit crunch
b. Debt validation
c. Vendor finance
d. Default

23. In the United States, _____ are overnight borrowings by banks to maintain their bank reserves at the Federal Reserve. Banks keep reserves at Federal Reserve Banks to meet their reserve requirements and to clear financial transactions. Transactions in the _____ market enable depository institutions with reserve balances in excess of reserve requirements to lend reserves to institutions with reserve deficiencies.

- a. 4-4-5 Calendar
- b. Regulation T
- c. Federal funds rate
- d. Federal funds

24. _____ is a life of security. It may also refer to the final payment date of a loan or other financial instrument, at which point all remaining interest and principal is due to be paid.

1, 3, 6 months _____ band can be calculated by using 30-day per month periods.

- a. Primary market
- b. Replacement cost
- c. False billing
- d. Maturity

25. A _____ is a financial services company that provides clearing and settlement services for financial transactions, usually on a futures exchange, and often acts as central counterparty (the payor actually pays the _____, which then pays the payee). A _____ may also offer novation, the substitution of a new contract or debt for an old, or other credit enhancement services to its members.

The term is also used for banks like Suffolk Bank that acted as a restraint on the over-issuance of private bank notes.

- a. Clearing house
- b. Valuation
- c. Bucket shop
- d. Warrant

26. _____ consists of the sale of goods or merchandise from a fixed location, such as a department store, boutique or kiosk in small or individual lots for direct consumption by the purchaser. _____ may include subordinated services, such as delivery. Purchasers may be individuals or businesses.

- a. 4-4-5 Calendar
- b. 529 plan
- c. 7-Eleven
- d. Retailing

27. _____ mature in one year or less. Like zero-coupon bonds, they do not pay interest prior to maturity; instead they are sold at a discount of the par value to create a positive yield to maturity. Many regard _____ as the least risky investment available to U.S. investors.

- a. 4-4-5 Calendar
- b. Treasury Inflation Protected Securities
- c. Treasury securities
- d. Treasury bills

28. In United States banking, _____ is a marketing term for certain services offered primarily to larger business customers. It may be used to describe all bank accounts (such as checking accounts) provided to businesses of a certain size, but it is more often used to describe specific services such as cash concentration, zero balance accounting, and automated clearing house facilities. Sometimes, private banking customers are given _____ services.

- a. Cash management
- b. Global tactical asset allocation
- c. Capitalization rate
- d. Profitability index

Chapter 10. Introduction to the Money Market and the Roles Played

29. _____ are government bonds issued by the United States Department of the Treasury through the Bureau of the Public Debt. They are the debt financing instruments of the U.S. Federal government, and they are often referred to simply as Treasuries or Treasurys. There are four types of marketable _____: Treasury bills, Treasury notes, Treasury bonds, and Treasury Inflation Protected Securities (TIPS.)
  a. Treasury Inflation Protected Securities
  b. Treasury securities
  c. 4-4-5 Calendar
  d. Treasury Inflation-Protected Securities

30. In finance, the term _____ describes the amount in cash that returns to the owners of a security. Normally it does not include the price variations, at the difference of the total return. _____ applies to various stated rates of return on stocks (common and preferred, and convertible), fixed income instruments (bonds, notes, bills, strips, zero coupon), and some other investment type insurance products (e.g. annuities.)
  a. 4-4-5 Calendar
  b. Macaulay duration
  c. Yield to maturity
  d. Yield

31. A _____ is a bond issued by a corporation. The term is usually applied to longer-term debt instruments, generally with a maturity date falling at least a year after their issue date. (The term 'commercial paper' is sometimes used for instruments with a shorter maturity.)
  a. Corporate bond
  b. Brady bonds
  c. Government bond
  d. Serial bond

32. _____ is that which is owed; usually referencing assets owed, but the term can cover other obligations. In the case of assets, _____ is a means of using future purchasing power in the present before a summation has been earned. Some companies and corporations use _____ as a part of their overall corporate finance strategy.
  a. Partial Payment
  b. Cross-collateralization
  c. Credit cycle
  d. Debt

33. A _____ is a bank or securities broker-dealer that may trade directly with the Federal Reserve System of the United States ('the Fed'.) Such firms are required to make bids or offers when the Fed conducts open market operations, provide information to the Fed's open market trading desk, and to participate actively in U.S. Treasury securities auctions. They consult with both the U.S. Treasury and the Fed about funding the budget deficit and implementing monetary policy.
  a. 529 plan
  b. 4-4-5 Calendar
  c. 7-Eleven
  d. Primary dealer

34. In financial accounting, the term _____ is most commonly used to describe any part of shareholders' equity, except for basic share capital. Sometimes, the term is used instead of the term provision; such a use, however, is inconsistent with the terminology suggested by International Accounting Standards Board. For more information about provisions, see provision (accounting.)
  a. FIFO and LIFO accounting
  b. Treasury stock
  c. Reserve
  d. Closing entries

35. In finance, a _____ is a debt security, in which the authorized issuer owes the holders a debt and, depending on the terms of the _____, is obliged to pay interest (the coupon) and/or to repay the principal at a later date, termed maturity.

Thus a _____ is a loan: the issuer is the borrower, the _____ holder is the lender, and the coupon is the interest. _____s provide the borrower with external funds to finance long-term investments, or, in the case of government _____s, to finance current expenditure.

a. Convertible bond
b. Puttable bond
c. Catastrophe bonds
d. Bond

36. A _____ is a type of auction where the auctioneer begins with a high asking price which is lowered until some participant is willing to accept the auctioneer's price, or a predetermined reserve price (the seller's minimum acceptable price) is reached. The winning participant pays the last announced price. This is also known as a 'clock auction' or an open-outcry descending-price auction.

a. 4-4-5 Calendar
b. 7-Eleven
c. 529 plan
d. Dutch auction

37. A _____ allows a borrower to use a financial security as collateral for a cash loan at a fixed rate of interest. In a repo, the borrower agrees to immediately sell a security to a lender and also agrees to buy the same security from the lender at a fixed price at some later date. A repo is equivalent to a cash transaction combined with a forward contract.

a. Repurchase agreement
b. Volatility arbitrage
c. Total return swap
d. Contango

38. A _____ is an exchange of promises between two or more parties to do an act which is enforceable in a court of law. It is where an unqualified offer meets a qualified acceptance and the parties reach Consensus ad Idem. The parties must have the necessary capacity to _____ and the _____ must not be either trifling, indeterminate, impossible or illegal.

a. Contract
b. 7-Eleven
c. 4-4-5 Calendar
d. 529 plan

39. In banking and finance, _____ denotes all activities from the time a commitment is made for a transaction until it is settled. _____ is necessary because the speed of trades is much faster than the cycle time for completing the underlying transaction.

In its widest sense _____ involves the management of post-trading, pre-settlement credit exposures, to ensure that trades are settled in accordance with market rules, even if a buyer or seller should become insolvent prior to settlement.

a. Clearing
b. Clearing house
c. Share
d. Procter ' Gamble

40. In lending agreements, _____ is a borrower's pledge of specific property to a lender, to secure repayment of a loan. The _____ serves as protection for a lender against a borrower's risk of default - that is, a borrower failing to pay the principal and interest under the terms of a loan obligation. If a borrower does default on a loan (due to insolvency or other event), that borrower forfeits (gives up) the property pledged as _____ *ollateral* - and the lender then becomes the owner of the _____.

Chapter 10. Introduction to the Money Market and the Roles Played

a. Refinancing risk
b. Nominal value
c. Future-oriented
d. Collateral

41. A _____ is a futures contract on a short term interest rate (STIR.) Contracts vary, but are often defined on an interest rate index such as 3-month sterling or US dollar LIBOR.

They are traded across a wide range of currencies, including the G12 country currencies and many others.

a. Dual currency deposit
b. Notional amount
c. Financial future
d. Real estate derivatives

42. _____ refers to any type of investment that yields a regular (or fixed) return.

For example, if you lend money to a borrower and the borrower has to pay interest once a month, you have been issued a fixed-income security. When a company does this, it is often called a bond or corporate bank debt (although preferred stock is also sometimes considered to be _____).

a. 529 plan
b. 4-4-5 Calendar
c. Bond market
d. Fixed Income

43. _____, refers to consumption opportunity gained by an entity within a specified time frame, which is generally expressed in monetary terms. However, for households and individuals, '_____ is the sum of all the wages, salaries, profits, interests payments, rents and other forms of earnings received... in a given period of time.' For firms, _____ generally refers to net-profit: what remains of revenue after expenses have been subtracted.

a. OIBDA
b. Income
c. Accrual
d. Annual report

44. In finance, a _____ is a standardized contract, to buy or sell a specified commodity of standardized quality at a certain date in the future, at a market determined price (the futures price.)

The price is determined by the instantaneous equilibrium between the forces of supply and demand among competing buy and sell orders on the exchange at the time of the purchase or sale of the contract.

In many cases, the items may be such non-traditional 'commodities' as foreign currencies, commercial or government paper [e.g., bonds], or 'baskets' of corporate equity ['stock indices'] or other financial instruments.

a. Financial future
b. Heston model
c. Repurchase agreement
d. Futures contract

45. In finance, _____ is that risk which is common to an entire market and not to any individual entity or component thereof. It should be distinguished from systemic risk which is the risk that the entire financial system will collapse as a result of some catastrophic event.

Risks can be reduced in four main ways: Avoidance, Reduction, Retention and Transfer.

a. Primary market
b. Capital surplus
c. Conglomerate merger
d. Systematic risk

46. The _____ of an asset is the return obtained from holding it (if positive), or the cost of holding it (if negative)

For instance, commodities are usually negative _____ assets, as they incur storage costs, but in some circumstances, commodities can be positive _____ assets as the market is willing to pay a premium for availability.

This can also refer to a trade with more than one leg, where you earn the spread between borrowing a low _____ asset and lending a high _____ one.

a. Carry
b. Bankruptcy remote
c. Financial assistance
d. Cramdown

47. In finance, a _____ in a security, such as a stock or a bond means the holder of the position owns the security and will profit if the price of the security goes up.

Similarly, a _____ in a futures contract or similar derivative, means the holder of the position will profit if the price of the underlying security goes up. Going long is the more conventional practice of investing and is contrasted with going short

- Short (finance)

a. Forward market
b. Central Securities Depository
c. Delta hedging
d. Long position

48. Days to Cover (DTC) is a numerical term that describes the relationship between the amount of shares in a given equity that have been short sold and the number of days of typical trading that it would require to 'cover' all _____ outstanding. For example, if there are ten million shares of XYZ Inc. that are currently short sold and the average daily volume of XYZ shares traded each day is one million, it would require ten days of trading for all _____ to be covered (10 million / 1 million.)

a. Short positions
b. Cash budget
c. Stock or scrip dividends
d. Guaranteed investment contracts

49. _____ is the difference between price and the costs of bringing to market whatever it is that is accounted as an enterprise (whether by harvest, extraction, manufacture, or purchase) in terms of the component costs of delivered goods and/or services and any operating or other expenses.

A key difficulty in measuring profit is in defining costs. Pure economic monetary profits can be zero or negative even in competitive equilibrium when accounted monetized costs exceed monetized price.

Chapter 10. Introduction to the Money Market and the Roles Played

a. AAB
b. A Random Walk Down Wall Street
c. Economic profit
d. Accounting profit

50. In finance, a _____ is collateral that the holder of a position in securities, options, or futures contracts has to deposit to cover the credit risk of his counterparty (most often his broker.) This risk can arise if the holder has done any of the following:

- borrowed cash from the counterparty to buy securities or options,
- sold securities or options short, or
- entered into a futures contract.

The collateral can be in the form of cash or securities, and it is deposited in a _____ account. On U.S. futures exchanges, '_____' was formally called performance bond.

_____ buying is buying securities with cash borrowed from a broker, using other securities as collateral.

a. Margin
b. Procter ' Gamble
c. Credit
d. Share

51. The term _____ is often used to refer to the investment management of collective investments, (not necessarily) whilst the more generic fund management may refer to all forms of institutional investment as well as investment management for private investors. Investment managers who specialize in advisory or discretionary management on behalf of (normally wealthy) private investors may often refer to their services as wealth management or portfolio management often within the context of so-called 'private banking'.

The provision of 'investment management services' includes elements of financial analysis, asset selection, stock selection, plan implementation and ongoing monitoring of investments.

a. ABN Amro
b. A Random Walk Down Wall Street
c. AAB
d. Asset Management

Chapter 11. Commercial Banks, Major Corporations, and Credit Agencies in the Money Market

1. In the global money market, _____ is an unsecured promissory note with a fixed maturity of one to 270 days. _____ is a money-market security issued (sold) by large banks and corporations to get money to meet short term debt obligations (for example, payroll), and is only backed by an issuing bank or corporation's promise to pay the face amount on the maturity date specified on the note. Since it is not backed by collateral, only firms with excellent credit ratings from a recognized rating agency will be able to sell their _____ at a reasonable price.
   - a. Financial distress
   - b. Book building
   - c. Trade-off theory
   - d. Commercial paper

2. In finance, the _____ is the global financial market for short-term borrowing and lending. It provides short-term liquidity funding for the global financial system. The _____ is where short-term obligations such as Treasury bills, commercial paper and bankers' acceptances are bought and sold.
   - a. Consumer debt
   - b. Debt-for-equity swap
   - c. Money market
   - d. Cramdown

3.

   A _____ is a type of financial intermediary and a type of bank. Commercial banking is also known as business banking. It is a bank that provides checking accounts, savings accounts, and money market accounts and that accepts time deposits.

   - a. 7-Eleven
   - b. 529 plan
   - c. Commercial bank
   - d. 4-4-5 Calendar

4. _____ is the term used to describe deposits residing in banks that are located outside the borders of the country that issues the currency the deposit is denominated in. For example a deposit denominated in US dollars residing in a Japanese bank is a _____ deposit, or more specifically a Eurodollar deposit.

   Key points are the location of the bank and the denomination of the currency, not the nationality of the bank or the owner of the deposit/loan.

   - a. ABN Amro
   - b. Eurocurrency
   - c. AAB
   - d. A Random Walk Down Wall Street

5. In the United States, _____ are overnight borrowings by banks to maintain their bank reserves at the Federal Reserve. Banks keep reserves at Federal Reserve Banks to meet their reserve requirements and to clear financial transactions. Transactions in the _____ market enable depository institutions with reserve balances in excess of reserve requirements to lend reserves to institutions with reserve deficiencies.
   - a. Federal funds rate
   - b. Federal funds
   - c. Regulation T
   - d. 4-4-5 Calendar

6. _____ are the means of implementing monetary policy by which a central bank controls its national money supply by buying and selling government securities, or other financial instruments. Monetary targets, such as interest rates or exchange rates, are used to guide this implementation.

Chapter 11. Commercial Banks, Major Corporations, and Credit Agencies in the Money Market

Since most money is now in the form of electronic records, rather than paper records such as banknotes, _____ are conducted simply by electronically increasing or decreasing ('crediting' or 'debiting') the amount of money that a bank has, e.g., in its reserve account at the central bank, in exchange for a bank selling or buying a financial instrument.

a. ABN Amro
c. AAB
b. A Random Walk Down Wall Street
d. Open market operations

7. In financial accounting, the term _____ is most commonly used to describe any part of shareholders' equity, except for basic share capital. Sometimes, the term is used instead of the term provision; such a use, however, is inconsistent with the terminology suggested by International Accounting Standards Board. For more information about provisions, see provision (accounting.)

a. FIFO and LIFO accounting
c. Closing entries
b. Treasury stock
d. Reserve

8. A _____, reserve bank, or monetary authority is the entity responsible for the monetary policy of a country or of a group of member states. It is a bank that can lend money to other banks in times of need. Its primary responsibility is to maintain the stability of the national currency and money supply, but more active duties include controlling subsidized-loan interest rates, and acting as a lender of last resort to the banking sector during times of financial crisis (private banks often being integral to the national financial system.)

a. 529 plan
c. 4-4-5 Calendar
b. 7-Eleven
d. Central bank

9. The _____ is a bank regulation that sets the minimum reserves each bank must hold to customer deposits and notes. These reserves are designed to satisfy withdrawal demands, and would normally be in the form of fiat currency stored in a bank vault (vault cash), or with a central bank.

The reserve ratio is sometimes used as a tool in the monetary policy, influencing the country's economy, borrowing, and interest rates.

a. Variable rate mortgage
c. Wall Street Journal prime rate
b. Prime rate
d. Reserve requirement

10. _____ is the provision of resources (such as granting a loan) by one party to another party where that second party does not reimburse the first party immediately, thereby generating a debt, and instead arranges either to repay or return those resources (or material(s) of equal value) at a later date. The first party is called a creditor, also known as a lender, while the second party is called a debtor, also known as a borrower.

Movements of financial capital are normally dependent on either _____ or equity transfers.

a. Clearing house
c. Comparable
b. Warrant
d. Credit

Chapter 11. Commercial Banks, Major Corporations, and Credit Agencies in the Money Market

11. _____, in bookkeeping, refers to assets, liabilities, income, and expenses recorded on individual pages of the so called book of final entry or ledger. Changes in _____ value are made by chronologically posting debit (DR) and credit (CR) entries to its page. Examples of _____s are cash, _____s receivable, mortgages, loans, land and buildings, common stock, sales, services provided, wages, and payroll overhead.
   a. Accretion
   b. Alpha
   c. Account
   d. Option

12. In the United States, the _____ is the interest rate at which private depository institutions (mostly banks) lend balances (federal funds) at the Federal Reserve to other depository institutions, usually overnight. Changing the target rate is one form of open market operations that the Chairman of the Federal Reserve uses to regulate the supply of money in the U.S. economy.

    U.S. banks and thrift institutions are obligated by law to maintain certain levels of reserves, either as reserves with the Fed or as vault cash.

   a. Taylor rule
   b. Regulation T
   c. 4-4-5 Calendar
   d. Federal funds rate

13. _____ is a fee paid on borrowed assets. It is the price paid for the use of borrowed money, or, money earned by deposited funds. Assets that are sometimes lent with _____ include money, shares, consumer goods through hire purchase, major assets such as aircraft, and even entire factories in finance lease arrangements.
   a. Insolvency
   b. A Random Walk Down Wall Street
   c. AAB
   d. Interest

14. An _____ is the price a borrower pays for the use of money they do not own, and the return a lender receives for deferring the use of funds, by lending it to the borrower. _____s are normally expressed as a percentage rate over the period of one year.

    _____s targets are also a vital tool of monetary policy and are used to control variables like investment, inflation, and unemployment.

   a. ABN Amro
   b. AAB
   c. A Random Walk Down Wall Street
   d. Interest rate

15. _____ is the process by which the government, or monetary authority of a country controls (i) the supply of money central bank (ii) availability of money, and (iii) cost of money or rate of interest, in order to attain a set of objectives oriented towards the growth and stability of the economy. Monetary theory provides insight into how to craft optimal _____.

    _____ is referred to as either being an expansionary policy where an expansionary policy increases the total supply of money in the economy, and a contractionary policy decreases the total money supply.

   a. Monetary policy
   b. Tax exemption
   c. Natural resources consumption tax
   d. Federal Open Market Committee

16. A _____ s a time deposit, a financial product commonly offered to consumers by banks, thrift institutions, and credit unions.

Chapter 11. Commercial Banks, Major Corporations, and Credit Agencies in the Money Market

They are similar to savings accounts in that they are insured and thus virtually risk-free; they are 'money in the bank'. They are different from savings accounts in that they have a specific, fixed term (often three months, six months, or one to five years), and, usually, a fixed interest rate.

- a. Reserve requirement
- b. Variable rate mortgage
- c. Time deposit
- d. Certificate of deposit

17. _____ or amalgamation is the act of merging many things into one. In business, it often refers to the mergers or acquisitions of many smaller companies into much larger ones. The financial accounting term of _____ refers to the aggregated financial statements of a group company as consolidated account.
- a. Retained earnings
- b. Write-off
- c. Consolidation
- d. Cost of goods sold

18. _____ is the removal or simplification of government rules and regulations that constrain the operation of market forces. _____ does not mean elimination of laws against fraud, but eliminating or reducing government control of how business is done, thereby moving toward a more free market.

The stated rationale for '_____' is often that fewer and simpler regulations will lead to a raised level of competitiveness, therefore higher productivity, more efficiency and lower prices overall.

- a. Demand shock
- b. Supply shock
- c. Value added
- d. Deregulation

19. In economics and finance, _____ is the practice of taking advantage of a price differential between two or more markets: striking a combination of matching deals that capitalize upon the imbalance, the profit being the difference between the market prices. When used by academics, an _____ is a transaction that involves no negative cash flow at any probabilistic or temporal state and a positive cash flow in at least one state; in simple terms, a risk-free profit.
- a. Efficient-market hypothesis
- b. Issuer
- c. Initial margin
- d. Arbitrage

20. In finance, a _____ is a debt security, in which the authorized issuer owes the holders a debt and, depending on the terms of the _____, is obliged to pay interest (the coupon) and/or to repay the principal at a later date, termed maturity.

Thus a _____ is a loan: the issuer is the borrower, the _____ holder is the lender, and the coupon is the interest. _____s provide the borrower with external funds to finance long-term investments, or, in the case of government _____s, to finance current expenditure.

- a. Convertible bond
- b. Bond
- c. Catastrophe bonds
- d. Puttable bond

21. _____ is that which is owed; usually referencing assets owed, but the term can cover other obligations. In the case of assets, _____ is a means of using future purchasing power in the present before a summation has been earned. Some companies and corporations use _____ as a part of their overall corporate finance strategy.

a. Partial Payment
b. Credit cycle
c. Debt
d. Cross-collateralization

22. A _____ is a fungible, negotiable instrument representing financial value. They are broadly categorized into debt securities (such as banknotes, bonds and debentures), and equity securities; e.g., common stocks. The company or other entity issuing the _____ is called the issuer.
   a. Security
   b. Tracking stock
   c. Book entry
   d. Securities lending

23. _____s are deposits denominated in United States dollars at banks outside the United States, and thus are not under the jurisdiction of the Federal Reserve. Consequently, such deposits are subject to much less regulation than similar deposits within the United States, allowing for higher margins. There is nothing 'European' about _____ deposits; a US dollar-denominated deposit in Tokyo or Caracas would likewise be deemed _____ deposits.
   a. A Random Walk Down Wall Street
   b. AAB
   c. Eurodollar
   d. ABN Amro

24. _____ is the risk (variability in value) borne by an interest-bearing asset, such as a loan or a bond, due to variability of interest rates. In general, as rates rise, the price of a fixed rate bond will fall, and vice versa. _____ is commonly measured by the bond's duration.
   a. Official bank rate
   b. International Fisher effect
   c. A Random Walk Down Wall Street
   d. Interest rate risk

25. _____ is a type of risk faced by investors, corporations, and governments. It is a risk that can be understood and managed with proper aforethought and investment.

Broadly, _____ refers to the complications businesses and governments may face as a result of what are commonly referred to as political decisions--or 'any political change that alters the expected outcome and value of a given economic action by changing the probability of achieving business objectives.' .

   a. Mid price
   b. Capital asset
   c. Political risk
   d. Single-index model

26. _____ is a legally declared inability or impairment of ability of an individual or organization to pay their creditors. Creditors may file a _____ petition against a debtor ('involuntary _____') in an effort to recoup a portion of what they are owed or initiate a restructuring. In the majority of cases, however, _____ is initiated by the debtor (a 'voluntary _____' that is filed by the bankrupt individual or organization.)
   a. Bankruptcy
   b. 529 plan
   c. 4-4-5 Calendar
   d. Debt settlement

27. In finance, _____ occurs when a debtor has not met its legal obligations according to the debt contract, e.g. it has not made a scheduled payment, or has violated a loan covenant (condition) of the debt contract. _____ may occur if the debtor is either unwilling or unable to pay their debt. This can occur with all debt obligations including bonds, mortgages, loans, and promissory notes.
   a. Vendor finance
   b. Credit crunch
   c. Debt validation
   d. Default

Chapter 11. Commercial Banks, Major Corporations, and Credit Agencies in the Money Market

28. _____ is the risk of loss due to a debtor's non-payment of a loan or other line of credit (either the principal or interest (coupon) or both)

Most lenders employ their own models (credit scorecards) to rank potential and existing customers according to risk, and then apply appropriate strategies. With products such as unsecured personal loans or mortgages, lenders charge a higher price for higher risk customers and vice versa. With revolving products such as credit cards and overdrafts, risk is controlled through careful setting of credit limits.

a. Liquidity risk
c. Market risk
b. Transaction risk
d. Credit risk

29. In economics, business, and accounting, a _____ is the value of money that has been used up to produce something, and hence is not available for use anymore. In business, the _____ may be one of acquisition, in which case the amount of money expended to acquire it is counted as _____. In this case, money is the input that is gone in order to acquire the thing.

a. Fixed costs
c. Sliding scale fees
b. Marginal cost
d. Cost

30. A _____ can require immediate payment by the second party to the third upon presentation of the _____. This is called a sight _____. A Cheques is a sight _____. An importer might write a _____ promising payment to an exporter for delivery of goods with payment to occur 60 days after the goods are delivered. Such a _____ is called a time _____.

a. Cashflow matching
c. Gross profit margin
b. Second lien loan
d. Draft

31. In the most general sense, a _____ is anything that is a hindrance, or puts individuals at a disadvantage.

Before we discuss the financial terms, we should note that a _____ can also have a much more important slang meaning.

This is best described in an example.

a. Liability
c. Covenant
b. Limited liability
d. McFadden Act

32. In the _____ contract the underwriter agrees to sell as many shares as possible at the agreed-upon price.

Under the all-or-none contract the underwriter agrees either to sell the entire offering or to cancel the deal.

Stand-by underwriting, also known as strict underwriting or old-fashioned underwriting is a form of stock insurance: the issuer contracts the underwriter for the latter to purchase the shares the issuer failed to sell under stockholders' subscription and applications.

a. Book building
b. Follow-on offering
c. Real option
d. Best efforts

33. The institution most often referenced by the word '_____' is a public or publicly traded _____, the shares of which are traded on a public stock exchange (e.g., the New York Stock Exchange or Nasdaq in the United States) where shares of stock of _____s are bought and sold by and to the general public. Most of the largest businesses in the world are publicly traded _____s. However, the majority of _____s are said to be closely held, privately held or close _____s, meaning that no ready market exists for the trading of shares.

a. Federal Home Loan Mortgage Corporation
b. Depository Trust Company
c. Corporation
d. Protect

34. _____ is a key part of the securitization transaction in structured finance, and is important for credit rating agencies when rating a securitization. The credit crisis of 2007-2008 has discredited the process of _____ of structured securities as a legitimate financial practice.

There are two primary types of _____: Internal and External.

a. 4-4-5 Calendar
b. Credit enhancement
c. Tranche
d. Yield curve spread

35. A '_____' is a 'Charge' that is paid to obtain the right to delay a payment. Essentially, the payer purchases the right to make a given payment in the future instead of in the Present. The '_____', or 'Charge' that must be paid to delay the payment, is simply the difference between what the payment amount would be if it were paid in the present and what the payment amount would be paid if it were paid in the future.

a. Risk aversion
b. Risk modeling
c. Value at risk
d. Discount

36. The _____ is an interest rate a central bank charges depository institutions that borrow reserves from it.

The term _____ has two meanings:

- the same as interest rate; the term 'discount' does not refer to the meaning of the word, but to the purpose of using the quantity, such as computations of present value, e.g. net present value / discounted cash flow

- the annual effective _____, which is the annual interest divided by the capital including that interest; this rate is lower than the interest rate; it corresponds to using the value after a year as the nominal value, and seeing the initial value as the nominal value minus a discount; it is used for Treasury Bills and similar financial instruments

The annual effective _____ is the annual interest divided by the capital including that interest, which is the interest rate divided by 100% plus the interest rate. It is the annual discount factor to be applied to the future cash flow, to find the discount, subtracted from a future value to find the value one year earlier.

For example, suppose there is a government bond that sells for $95 and pays $100 in a year's time.

Chapter 11. Commercial Banks, Major Corporations, and Credit Agencies in the Money Market

a. Discount rate
b. Stochastic volatility
c. Fisher equation
d. Black-Scholes

37. In economics, _____ refers to the ability of a person or a country to produce a particular good at a lower marginal cost and opportunity cost than another person or country. It is the ability to produce a product most efficiently given all the other products that could be produced. It can be contrasted with absolute advantage which refers to the ability of a person or a country to produce a particular good at a lower absolute cost than another.
   a. Reputational risk
   b. Loans and interest, in Judaism
   c. Case-Shiller Home Price Indices
   d. Comparative advantage

38. The U.S. _____ is an independent agency of the United States government which holds primary responsibility for enforcing the federal securities laws and regulating the securities industry, the nation's stock and options exchanges, and other electronic securities markets. The SEC was created by section 4 of the SEC of 1934 (now codified as 15 U.S.C. § 78d and commonly referred to as the 1934 Act.)
   a. Securities and Exchange Commission
   b. 4-4-5 Calendar
   c. 529 plan
   d. 7-Eleven

39. A _____ assesses the credit worthiness of an individual, corporation, or even a country. _____ s are calculated from financial history and current assets and liabilities. Typically, a _____ tells a lender or investor the probability of the subject being able to pay back a loan.
   a. Credit cycle
   b. Credit rating
   c. Debenture
   d. Credit report monitoring

40. _____ is a form of commercial paper that is collateralised by other financial assets. ABCPs are typically short-term investments that mature between 90 and 180 days and are typically issued by a bank or other financial institution. They are designed to be used for short-term financing needs.
   a. Earmark
   b. Asset-liability mismatch
   c. Amortizing loan
   d. Asset-backed commercial paper

41. _____ is a financial transaction whereby a business sells its accounts receivable (i.e., invoices) at a discount. _____ differs from a bank loan in three main ways. First, the emphasis is on the value of the receivables (essentially a financial asset), not the firm's credit worthiness.
   a. Debt-for-equity swap
   b. Factoring
   c. Financial Literacy Month
   d. Credit card balance transfer

42. _____ is a structured finance process that involves pooling and repackaging of cash-flow-producing financial assets into securities, which are then sold to investors. The term '_____' is derived from the fact that the form of financial instruments used to obtain funds from the investors are securities. As a portfolio risk backed by amortizing cash flows - and unlike general corporate debt - the credit quality of securitized debt is non-stationary due to changes in volatility that are time- and structure-dependent.
   a. Special journals
   b. Reputational risk
   c. The Glass-Steagall Act of 1933
   d. Securitization

43. _____ refer to services provided by the finance industry.

Chapter 11. Commercial Banks, Major Corporations, and Credit Agencies in the Money Market

The finance industry encompasses a broad range of organizations that deal with the management of money. Among these organizations are banks, credit card companies, insurance companies, consumer finance companies, stock brokerages, investment funds and some government sponsored enterprises.

- a. Cost of carry
- b. Delta hedging
- c. Financial Services
- d. Financial instruments

44. The _____ Act is an Act of the 106th United States Congress which repealed part of the Glass-Steagall Act of 1933, opening up competition among banks, securities companies and insurance companies. The Glass-Steagall Act prohibited any one institution from acting as both an investment bank and a commercial bank, or as both a bank and an insurer.

The _____ Act (GLBA) allowed commercial and investment banks to consolidate.

- a. Gramm-Leach-Bliley
- b. 4-4-5 Calendar
- c. 7-Eleven
- d. 529 plan

45. The _____ is a federally chartered network of borrower-owned lending institutions composed of cooperatives and related service organizations. Cooperatives are organizations that are owned and controlled by their members who use the cooperative'e;s products, supplies or services. The U.S. Congress authorized the creation of the first System institutions in 1916.

- a. 7-Eleven
- b. 4-4-5 Calendar
- c. 529 plan
- d. Farm Credit System

46. The _____ (NYSE: FRE) is an insolvent government sponsored enterprise (GSE) of the United States federal government.

The _____ was created in 1970 to expand the secondary market for mortgages in the US. Along with other GSEs, Freddie Mac buys mortgages on the secondary market, pools them, and sells them as mortgage-backed securities to investors on the open market.

- a. The Depository Trust ' Clearing Corporation
- b. Federal Home Loan Mortgage Corporation
- c. Governmental Accounting Standards Board
- d. Public company

47. The _____ (NYSE: FNM), commonly known as Fannie Mae, is a stockholder-owned corporation chartered by Congress in 1968 as a government sponsored enterprise (GSE), but founded in 1938 during the Great Depression. The corporation's purpose is to purchase and securitize mortgages in order to ensure that funds are consistently available to the institutions that lend money to home buyers.

On September 7, 2008, James Lockhart, director of the Federal Housing Finance Agency (FHFA), announced that Fannie Mae and Freddie Mac were being placed into conservatorship of the FHFA.

- a. Federal National Mortgage Association
- b. The Depository Trust ' Clearing Corporation
- c. SPDR
- d. General partnership

Chapter 11. Commercial Banks, Major Corporations, and Credit Agencies in the Money Market

48. _____ mature in one year or less. Like zero-coupon bonds, they do not pay interest prior to maturity; instead they are sold at a discount of the par value to create a positive yield to maturity. Many regard _____ as the least risky investment available to U.S. investors.
   a. Treasury Inflation Protected Securities
   b. Treasury securities
   c. 4-4-5 Calendar
   d. Treasury bills

49. _____ are government bonds issued by the United States Department of the Treasury through the Bureau of the Public Debt. They are the debt financing instruments of the U.S. Federal government, and they are often referred to simply as Treasuries or Treasurys. There are four types of marketable _____: Treasury bills, Treasury notes, Treasury bonds, and Treasury Inflation Protected Securities (TIPS.)
   a. Treasury Inflation-Protected Securities
   b. Treasury Inflation Protected Securities
   c. 4-4-5 Calendar
   d. Treasury securities

50. _____ or financing is to provide capital (funds), which means money for a project, a person, a business or any other private or public institutions.

Those funds can be allocated for either short term or long term purposes. The health fund is a new way of _____ private healthcare centers.

   a. Synthetic CDO
   b. Proxy fight
   c. Product life cycle
   d. Funding

51. The _____ provide stable, on-demand, low-cost funding to American financial institutions for home mortgage loans, small business, rural, agricultural, and economic development lending. With their members, the _____ank System represents the largest collective source of home mortgage and community credit in the United States. The banks do not provide loans directly to individuals, only to other banks.
   a. 529 plan
   b. Federal Home Loan Banks
   c. 7-Eleven
   d. 4-4-5 Calendar

Chapter 12. Roles and Services of the Federal Reserve and Other Central Banks

1. A _____, reserve bank, or monetary authority is the entity responsible for the monetary policy of a country or of a group of member states. It is a bank that can lend money to other banks in times of need. Its primary responsibility is to maintain the stability of the national currency and money supply, but more active duties include controlling subsidized-loan interest rates, and acting as a lender of last resort to the banking sector during times of financial crisis (private banks often being integral to the national financial system.)
   a. 529 plan
   b. 4-4-5 Calendar
   c. 7-Eleven
   d. Central Bank

2. In the United States, _____ are overnight borrowings by banks to maintain their bank reserves at the Federal Reserve. Banks keep reserves at Federal Reserve Banks to meet their reserve requirements and to clear financial transactions. Transactions in the _____ market enable depository institutions with reserve balances in excess of reserve requirements to lend reserves to institutions with reserve deficiencies.
   a. 4-4-5 Calendar
   b. Federal funds
   c. Federal funds rate
   d. Regulation T

3. In economics, _____ is a rise in the general level of prices of goods and services in an economy over a period of time. The term '_____' once referred to increases in the money supply (monetary _____); however, economic debates about the relationship between money supply and price levels have led to its primary use today in describing price _____. _____ can also be described as a decline in the real value of money--a loss of purchasing power in the medium of exchange which is also the monetary unit of account.
   a. AAB
   b. Inflation
   c. ABN Amro
   d. A Random Walk Down Wall Street

4. _____ is the process by which the government, or monetary authority of a country controls (i) the supply of money central bank (ii) availability of money, and (iii) cost of money or rate of interest, in order to attain a set of objectives oriented towards the growth and stability of the economy. Monetary theory provides insight into how to craft optimal _____.

   _____ is referred to as either being an expansionary policy where an expansionary policy increases the total supply of money in the economy, and a contractionary policy decreases the total money supply.

   a. Tax exemption
   b. Natural resources consumption tax
   c. Federal Open Market Committee
   d. Monetary policy

5. In economics, _____ is the total amount of money available in an economy at a particular point in time. There are several ways to define 'money', but each includes currency in circulation and demand deposits.

   _____ data are recorded and published.

   a. 529 plan
   b. 4-4-5 Calendar
   c. 7-Eleven
   d. Money supply

6. In financial accounting, the term _____ is most commonly used to describe any part of shareholders' equity, except for basic share capital. Sometimes, the term is used instead of the term provision; such a use, however, is inconsistent with the terminology suggested by International Accounting Standards Board. For more information about provisions, see provision (accounting.)

Chapter 12. Roles and Services of the Federal Reserve and Other Central Banks 113

a. Closing entries
c. Treasury stock
b. FIFO and LIFO accounting
d. Reserve

7. The _____ is the market for securities, where companies and governments can raise longterm funds. The _____ includes the stock market and the bond market. Financial regulators, such as the U.S. Securities and Exchange Commission, oversee the _____s in their designated countries to ensure that investors are protected against fraud.
   a. Delta neutral
   c. Capital market
   b. Forward market
   d. Spot rate

8. In the global money market, _____ is an unsecured promissory note with a fixed maturity of one to 270 days. _____ is a money-market security issued (sold) by large banks and corporations to get money to meet short term debt obligations (for example, payroll), and is only backed by an issuing bank or corporation's promise to pay the face amount on the maturity date specified on the note. Since it is not backed by collateral, only firms with excellent credit ratings from a recognized rating agency will be able to sell their _____ at a reasonable price.
   a. Financial distress
   c. Book building
   b. Trade-off theory
   d. Commercial paper

9. In economics, a _____ is a mechanism that allows people to easily buy and sell (trade) financial securities (such as stocks and bonds), commodities (such as precious metals or agricultural goods), and other fungible items of value at low transaction costs and at prices that reflect the efficient-market hypothesis.

   _____s have evolved significantly over several hundred years and are undergoing constant innovation to improve liquidity.

   Both general markets (where many commodities are traded) and specialized markets (where only one commodity is traded) exist.

   a. Delta hedging
   c. Cost of carry
   b. Financial market
   d. Secondary market

10. In finance, the _____ is the global financial market for short-term borrowing and lending. It provides short-term liquidity funding for the global financial system. The _____ is where short-term obligations such as Treasury bills, commercial paper and bankers' acceptances are bought and sold.
    a. Debt-for-equity swap
    c. Cramdown
    b. Consumer debt
    d. Money market

11. _____ in economics is a persistent decrease in the general price level of goods and services - a negative inflation rate. When the inflation rate slows down (decreases, but remains positive), this is known as disinflation.

    Inflation destroys real value in money.

    a. Deflation
    c. Recession
    b. Mercantilism
    d. Fixed exchange rate

Chapter 12. Roles and Services of the Federal Reserve and Other Central Banks

12. _____, in bookkeeping, refers to assets, liabilities, income, and expenses recorded on individual pages of the so called book of final entry or ledger. Changes in _____ value are made by chronologically posting debit (DR) and credit (CR) entries to its page. Examples of _____s are cash, _____s receivable, mortgages, loans, land and buildings, common stock, sales, services provided, wages, and payroll overhead.
- a. Alpha
- b. Option
- c. Accretion
- d. Account

13. A '_____' is a 'Charge' that is paid to obtain the right to delay a payment. Essentially, the payer purchases the right to make a given payment in the future instead of in the Present. The '_____', or 'Charge' that must be paid to delay the payment, is simply the difference between what the payment amount would be if it were paid in the present and what the payment amount would be paid if it were paid in the future.
- a. Risk modeling
- b. Value at risk
- c. Risk aversion
- d. Discount

14. The _____ is an interest rate a central bank charges depository institutions that borrow reserves from it.

The term _____ has two meanings:

- the same as interest rate; the term 'discount' does not refer to the meaning of the word, but to the purpose of using the quantity, such as computations of present value, e.g. net present value / discounted cash flow

- the annual effective _____, which is the annual interest divided by the capital including that interest; this rate is lower than the interest rate; it corresponds to using the value after a year as the nominal value, and seeing the initial value as the nominal value minus a discount; it is used for Treasury Bills and similar financial instruments

The annual effective _____ is the annual interest divided by the capital including that interest, which is the interest rate divided by 100% plus the interest rate. It is the annual discount factor to be applied to the future cash flow, to find the discount, subtracted from a future value to find the value one year earlier.

For example, suppose there is a government bond that sells for $95 and pays $100 in a year's time.

- a. Black-Scholes
- b. Stochastic volatility
- c. Fisher equation
- d. Discount rate

15. A _____ is a fungible, negotiable instrument representing financial value. They are broadly categorized into debt securities (such as banknotes, bonds and debentures), and equity securities; e.g., common stocks. The company or other entity issuing the _____ is called the issuer.
- a. Tracking stock
- b. Securities lending
- c. Book entry
- d. Security

16. The _____ , a component of the Federal Reserve System, is charged under United States law with overseeing the nation's open market operations. It is the Federal Reserve Committee that makes key decisions about interest rates and the growth jam of the United States money supply. It is the principal organ of United States national monetary policy.

Chapter 12. Roles and Services of the Federal Reserve and Other Central Banks 115

a. Tax incidence
b. Tax exemption
c. Fiscal policy
d. Federal Open Market Committee

17. In finance, a _____ is a debt security, in which the authorized issuer owes the holders a debt and, depending on the terms of the _____, is obliged to pay interest (the coupon) and/or to repay the principal at a later date, termed maturity.

Thus a _____ is a loan: the issuer is the borrower, the _____ holder is the lender, and the coupon is the interest. _____s provide the borrower with external funds to finance long-term investments, or, in the case of government _____s, to finance current expenditure.

a. Bond
b. Puttable bond
c. Catastrophe bonds
d. Convertible bond

18. A _____ is a financial services company that provides clearing and settlement services for financial transactions, usually on a futures exchange, and often acts as central counterparty (the payor actually pays the _____, which then pays the payee). A _____ may also offer novation, the substitution of a new contract or debt for an old, or other credit enhancement services to its members.

The term is also used for banks like Suffolk Bank that acted as a restraint on the over-issuance of private bank notes.

a. Clearing house
b. Bucket shop
c. Valuation
d. Warrant

19. _____ is a fee paid on borrowed assets. It is the price paid for the use of borrowed money, or, money earned by deposited funds. Assets that are sometimes lent with _____ include money, shares, consumer goods through hire purchase, major assets such as aircraft, and even entire factories in finance lease arrangements.
a. Interest
b. AAB
c. Insolvency
d. A Random Walk Down Wall Street

20. An _____ is the price a borrower pays for the use of money they do not own, and the return a lender receives for deferring the use of funds, by lending it to the borrower. _____s are normally expressed as a percentage rate over the period of one year.

_____s targets are also a vital tool of monetary policy and are used to control variables like investment, inflation, and unemployment.

a. ABN Amro
b. A Random Walk Down Wall Street
c. AAB
d. Interest rate

21. _____ is the provision of resources (such as granting a loan) by one party to another party where that second party does not reimburse the first party immediately, thereby generating a debt, and instead arranges either to repay or return those resources (or material(s) of equal value) at a later date. The first party is called a creditor, also known as a lender, while the second party is called a debtor, also known as a borrower.

Movements of financial capital are normally dependent on either _____ or equity transfers.

a. Warrant
b. Comparable
c. Credit
d. Clearing house

22. _____ is the removal or simplification of government rules and regulations that constrain the operation of market forces. _____ does not mean elimination of laws against fraud, but eliminating or reducing government control of how business is done, thereby moving toward a more free market.

The stated rationale for '_____' is often that fewer and simpler regulations will lead to a raised level of competitiveness, therefore higher productivity, more efficiency and lower prices overall.

a. Value added
b. Supply shock
c. Demand shock
d. Deregulation

23. In economics and contract theory, _____ deals with the study of decisions in transactions where one party has more or better information than the other. This creates an imbalance of power in transactions which can sometimes cause the transactions to go awry. Examples of this problem are adverse selection and moral hazard.

a. AAB
b. A Random Walk Down Wall Street
c. ABN Amro
d. Information asymmetry

24. In finance, the _____ of a financial asset measures the sensitivity of the asset's price to interest rate movements, expressed as a number of years. The reason for expressing this sensitivity in years is that the time that will elapse until a cash flow is received allows more interest to accumulate. Therefore the price of an asset with long term cashflows has more interest rate sensitivity than an asset with cashflows in the near future.

a. Macaulay duration
b. Yield to maturity
c. 4-4-5 Calendar
d. Duration

25. _____ is the risk (variability in value) borne by an interest-bearing asset, such as a loan or a bond, due to variability of interest rates. In general, as rates rise, the price of a fixed rate bond will fall, and vice versa. _____ is commonly measured by the bond's duration.

a. International Fisher effect
b. A Random Walk Down Wall Street
c. Official bank rate
d. Interest rate risk

26. _____ are the means of implementing monetary policy by which a central bank controls its national money supply by buying and selling government securities, or other financial instruments. Monetary targets, such as interest rates or exchange rates, are used to guide this implementation.

Since most money is now in the form of electronic records, rather than paper records such as banknotes, _____ are conducted simply by electronically increasing or decreasing ('crediting' or 'debiting') the amount of money that a bank has, e.g., in its reserve account at the central bank, in exchange for a bank selling or buying a financial instrument.

Chapter 12. Roles and Services of the Federal Reserve and Other Central Banks

a. A Random Walk Down Wall Street
b. Open market operations
c. ABN Amro
d. AAB

27. The _____ is a bank regulation that sets the minimum reserves each bank must hold to customer deposits and notes. These reserves are designed to satisfy withdrawal demands, and would normally be in the form of fiat currency stored in a bank vault (vault cash), or with a central bank.

The reserve ratio is sometimes used as a tool in the monetary policy, influencing the country's economy, borrowing, and interest rates.

a. Variable rate mortgage
b. Prime rate
c. Wall Street Journal prime rate
d. Reserve requirement

28. In finance, the term _____ describes the amount in cash that returns to the owners of a security. Normally it does not include the price variations, at the difference of the total return. _____ applies to various stated rates of return on stocks (common and preferred, and convertible), fixed income instruments (bonds, notes, bills, strips, zero coupon), and some other investment type insurance products (e.g. annuities.)

a. Yield to maturity
b. Yield
c. Macaulay duration
d. 4-4-5 Calendar

29. In finance, the _____ is the relation between the interest rate (or cost of borrowing) and the time to maturity of the debt for a given borrower in a given currency. For example, the current U.S. dollar interest rates paid on U.S. Treasury securities for various maturities are closely watched by many traders, and are commonly plotted on a graph such as the one on the right which is informally called 'the _____.' More formal mathematical descriptions of this relation are often called the term structure of interest rates.

The yield of a debt instrument is the annualized percentage increase in the value of the investment.

a. 529 plan
b. 4-4-5 Calendar
c. 7-Eleven
d. Yield curve

30. A _____ is a unit that is equal to 1/100th of a percentage point. It is frequently used to express percentage point changes of less than 1%. It avoids the ambiguity between relative and absolute discussions about rates.

a. Bond market
b. 4-4-5 Calendar
c. 529 plan
d. Basis point

Chapter 13. The Tools and Goals of Central Bank Monetary Policy

1. _____ is the provision of resources (such as granting a loan) by one party to another party where that second party does not reimburse the first party immediately, thereby generating a debt, and instead arranges either to repay or return those resources (or material(s) of equal value) at a later date. The first party is called a creditor, also known as a lender, while the second party is called a debtor, also known as a borrower.

Movements of financial capital are normally dependent on either _____ or equity transfers.

   a. Comparable
   b. Credit
   c. Clearing house
   d. Warrant

2. _____ is a fee paid on borrowed assets. It is the price paid for the use of borrowed money, or, money earned by deposited funds. Assets that are sometimes lent with _____ include money, shares, consumer goods through hire purchase, major assets such as aircraft, and even entire factories in finance lease arrangements.
   a. Insolvency
   b. AAB
   c. A Random Walk Down Wall Street
   d. Interest

3. An _____ is the price a borrower pays for the use of money they do not own, and the return a lender receives for deferring the use of funds, by lending it to the borrower. _____s are normally expressed as a percentage rate over the period of one year.

_____s targets are also a vital tool of monetary policy and are used to control variables like investment, inflation, and unemployment.

   a. AAB
   b. A Random Walk Down Wall Street
   c. Interest rate
   d. ABN Amro

4. _____ is the process by which the government, or monetary authority of a country controls (i) the supply of money central bank (ii) availability of money, and (iii) cost of money or rate of interest, in order to attain a set of objectives oriented towards the growth and stability of the economy. Monetary theory provides insight into how to craft optimal _____.

_____ is referred to as either being an expansionary policy where an expansionary policy increases the total supply of money in the economy, and a contractionary policy decreases the total money supply.

   a. Natural resources consumption tax
   b. Monetary policy
   c. Tax exemption
   d. Federal Open Market Committee

5. _____ are the means of implementing monetary policy by which a central bank controls its national money supply by buying and selling government securities, or other financial instruments. Monetary targets, such as interest rates or exchange rates, are used to guide this implementation.

Since most money is now in the form of electronic records, rather than paper records such as banknotes, _____ are conducted simply by electronically increasing or decreasing ('crediting' or 'debiting') the amount of money that a bank has, e.g., in its reserve account at the central bank, in exchange for a bank selling or buying a financial instrument.

Chapter 13. The Tools and Goals of Central Bank Monetary Policy

a. ABN Amro
c. AAB
b. A Random Walk Down Wall Street
d. Open market operations

6. A _____, reserve bank, or monetary authority is the entity responsible for the monetary policy of a country or of a group of member states. It is a bank that can lend money to other banks in times of need. Its primary responsibility is to maintain the stability of the national currency and money supply, but more active duties include controlling subsidized-loan interest rates, and acting as a lender of last resort to the banking sector during times of financial crisis (private banks often being integral to the national financial system.)
   a. 529 plan
   c. 7-Eleven
   b. 4-4-5 Calendar
   d. Central bank

7. In financial accounting, the term _____ is most commonly used to describe any part of shareholders' equity, except for basic share capital. Sometimes, the term is used instead of the term provision; such a use, however, is inconsistent with the terminology suggested by International Accounting Standards Board. For more information about provisions, see provision (accounting.)
   a. FIFO and LIFO accounting
   c. Treasury stock
   b. Reserve
   d. Closing entries

8. _____ refers to a business or organization attempting to acquire goods or services to accomplish the goals of the enterprise. Though there are several organizations that attempt to set standards in the _____ process, processes can vary greatly between organizations. Typically the word '_____' is not used interchangeably with the word 'procurement', since procurement typically includes Expediting, Supplier Quality, and Traffic and Logistics (T'L) in addition to _____.
   a. 4-4-5 Calendar
   c. Purchasing
   b. 7-Eleven
   d. 529 plan

9. A _____ is a fungible, negotiable instrument representing financial value. They are broadly categorized into debt securities (such as banknotes, bonds and debentures), and equity securities; e.g., common stocks. The company or other entity issuing the _____ is called the issuer.
   a. Book entry
   c. Securities lending
   b. Security
   d. Tracking stock

10. _____, in bookkeeping, refers to assets, liabilities, income, and expenses recorded on individual pages of the so called book of final entry or ledger. Changes in _____ value are made by chronologically posting debit (DR) and credit (CR) entries to its page. Examples of _____s are cash, _____s receivable, mortgages, loans, land and buildings, common stock, sales, services provided, wages, and payroll overhead.
    a. Account
    c. Accretion
    b. Alpha
    d. Option

11. In the global money market, _____ is an unsecured promissory note with a fixed maturity of one to 270 days. _____ is a money-market security issued (sold) by large banks and corporations to get money to meet short term debt obligations (for example, payroll), and is only backed by an issuing bank or corporation's promise to pay the face amount on the maturity date specified on the note. Since it is not backed by collateral, only firms with excellent credit ratings from a recognized rating agency will be able to sell their _____ at a reasonable price.
    a. Financial distress
    c. Trade-off theory
    b. Commercial paper
    d. Book building

12. In the United States, _____ are overnight borrowings by banks to maintain their bank reserves at the Federal Reserve. Banks keep reserves at Federal Reserve Banks to meet their reserve requirements and to clear financial transactions. Transactions in the _____ market enable depository institutions with reserve balances in excess of reserve requirements to lend reserves to institutions with reserve deficiencies.
   a. Federal funds rate
   b. 4-4-5 Calendar
   c. Regulation T
   d. Federal funds

13. In the United States, the _____ is the interest rate at which private depository institutions (mostly banks) lend balances (federal funds) at the Federal Reserve to other depository institutions, usually overnight. Changing the target rate is one form of open market operations that the Chairman of the Federal Reserve uses to regulate the supply of money in the U.S. economy.

U.S. banks and thrift institutions are obligated by law to maintain certain levels of reserves, either as reserves with the Fed or as vault cash.

   a. 4-4-5 Calendar
   b. Regulation T
   c. Taylor rule
   d. Federal funds rate

14. In finance, the _____ is the global financial market for short-term borrowing and lending. It provides short-term liquidity funding for the global financial system. The _____ is where short-term obligations such as Treasury bills, commercial paper and bankers' acceptances are bought and sold.
   a. Consumer debt
   b. Money market
   c. Cramdown
   d. Debt-for-equity swap

15. A _____ allows a borrower to use a financial security as collateral for a cash loan at a fixed rate of interest. In a repo, the borrower agrees to immediately sell a security to a lender and also agrees to buy the same security from the lender at a fixed price at some later date. A repo is equivalent to a cash transaction combined with a forward contract.
   a. Total return swap
   b. Volatility arbitrage
   c. Repurchase agreement
   d. Contango

16. A '_____' is a 'Charge' that is paid to obtain the right to delay a payment. Essentially, the payer purchases the right to make a given payment in the future instead of in the Present. The '_____', or 'Charge' that must be paid to delay the payment, is simply the difference between what the payment amount would be if it were paid in the present and what the payment amount would be paid if it were paid in the future.
   a. Discount
   b. Risk aversion
   c. Value at risk
   d. Risk modeling

17. The _____ is an interest rate a central bank charges depository institutions that borrow reserves from it.

Chapter 13. The Tools and Goals of Central Bank Monetary Policy

The term _____ has two meanings:

- the same as interest rate; the term 'discount' does not refer to the meaning of the word, but to the purpose of using the quantity, such as computations of present value, e.g. net present value / discounted cash flow

- the annual effective _____, which is the annual interest divided by the capital including that interest; this rate is lower than the interest rate; it corresponds to using the value after a year as the nominal value, and seeing the initial value as the nominal value minus a discount; it is used for Treasury Bills and similar financial instruments

The annual effective _____ is the annual interest divided by the capital including that interest, which is the interest rate divided by 100% plus the interest rate. It is the annual discount factor to be applied to the future cash flow, to find the discount, subtracted from a future value to find the value one year earlier.

For example, suppose there is a government bond that sells for $95 and pays $100 in a year's time.

a. Stochastic volatility
c. Discount rate
b. Fisher equation
d. Black-Scholes

18. In economics, business, and accounting, a _____ is the value of money that has been used up to produce something, and hence is not available for use anymore. In business, the _____ may be one of acquisition, in which case the amount of money expended to acquire it is counted as _____. In this case, money is the input that is gone in order to acquire the thing.

a. Fixed costs
c. Sliding scale fees
b. Marginal cost
d. Cost

19. _____ is the removal or simplification of government rules and regulations that constrain the operation of market forces. _____ does not mean elimination of laws against fraud, but eliminating or reducing government control of how business is done, thereby moving toward a more free market.

The stated rationale for '_____' is often that fewer and simpler regulations will lead to a raised level of competitiveness, therefore higher productivity, more efficiency and lower prices overall.

a. Demand shock
c. Value added
b. Deregulation
d. Supply shock

20. The _____ is a bank regulation that sets the minimum reserves each bank must hold to customer deposits and notes. These reserves are designed to satisfy withdrawal demands, and would normally be in the form of fiat currency stored in a bank vault (vault cash), or with a central bank.

The reserve ratio is sometimes used as a tool in the monetary policy, influencing the country's economy, borrowing, and interest rates.

Chapter 13. The Tools and Goals of Central Bank Monetary Policy

a. Variable rate mortgage
c. Wall Street Journal prime rate
b. Reserve requirement
d. Prime rate

21. _____ refer to services provided by the finance industry.

The finance industry encompasses a broad range of organizations that deal with the management of money. Among these organizations are banks, credit card companies, insurance companies, consumer finance companies, stock brokerages, investment funds and some government sponsored enterprises.

a. Cost of carry
c. Financial Services
b. Financial instruments
d. Delta hedging

22. Unemployment occurs when a person is available to work and currently seeking work, but the person is without work. The prevalence of unemployment is usually measured using the _____, which is defined as the percentage of those in the labor force who are unemployed. The _____ is also used in economic studies and economic indexes such as the United States' Conference Board's Index of Leading Indicators as a measure of the state of the macroeconomics.

a. ABN Amro
c. AAB
b. A Random Walk Down Wall Street
d. Unemployment rate

23. In finance, the _____ of a financial asset measures the sensitivity of the asset's price to interest rate movements, expressed as a number of years. The reason for expressing this sensitivity in years is that the time that will elapse until a cash flow is received allows more interest to accumulate. Therefore the price of an asset with long term cashflows has more interest rate sensitivity than an asset with cashflows in the near future.

a. Yield to maturity
c. Macaulay duration
b. 4-4-5 Calendar
d. Duration

24. _____ is the term used to describe deposits residing in banks that are located outside the borders of the country that issues the currency the deposit is denominated in. For example a deposit denominated in US dollars residing in a Japanese bank is a _____ deposit, or more specifically a Eurodollar deposit.

Key points are the location of the bank and the denomination of the currency, not the nationality of the bank or the owner of the deposit/loan.

a. A Random Walk Down Wall Street
c. AAB
b. ABN Amro
d. Eurocurrency

25. In economics, _____ is a rise in the general level of prices of goods and services in an economy over a period of time. The term '_____' once referred to increases in the money supply (monetary _____); however, economic debates about the relationship between money supply and price levels have led to its primary use today in describing price _____.
_____ can also be described as a decline in the real value of money--a loss of purchasing power in the medium of exchange which is also the monetary unit of account.

a. ABN Amro
c. A Random Walk Down Wall Street
b. Inflation
d. AAB

Chapter 13. The Tools and Goals of Central Bank Monetary Policy

26. _____ is the risk (variability in value) borne by an interest-bearing asset, such as a loan or a bond, due to variability of interest rates. In general, as rates rise, the price of a fixed rate bond will fall, and vice versa. _____ is commonly measured by the bond's duration.
   a. Official bank rate
   b. International Fisher effect
   c. A Random Walk Down Wall Street
   d. Interest rate risk

27. A _____ is a money deposit at a banking institution that cannot be withdrawn for a certain 'term' or period of time. When the term is over it can be withdrawn or it can be held for another term. Generally speaking, the longer the term the better the yield on the money.
   a. Certificate of deposit
   b. Private money
   c. Basel Accord
   d. Time deposit

28. In finance, the term _____ describes the amount in cash that returns to the owners of a security. Normally it does not include the price variations, at the difference of the total return. _____ applies to various stated rates of return on stocks (common and preferred, and convertible), fixed income instruments (bonds, notes, bills, strips, zero coupon), and some other investment type insurance products (e.g. annuities.)
   a. Yield
   b. 4-4-5 Calendar
   c. Yield to maturity
   d. Macaulay duration

29. In finance, the _____ is the relation between the interest rate (or cost of borrowing) and the time to maturity of the debt for a given borrower in a given currency. For example, the current U.S. dollar interest rates paid on U.S. Treasury securities for various maturities are closely watched by many traders, and are commonly plotted on a graph such as the one on the right which is informally called 'the _____.' More formal mathematical descriptions of this relation are often called the term structure of interest rates.

The yield of a debt instrument is the annualized percentage increase in the value of the investment.

   a. 4-4-5 Calendar
   b. Yield curve
   c. 7-Eleven
   d. 529 plan

30. A _____ is a unit that is equal to 1/100th of a percentage point. It is frequently used to express percentage point changes of less than 1%. It avoids the ambiguity between relative and absolute discussions about rates.
   a. Bond market
   b. 529 plan
   c. 4-4-5 Calendar
   d. Basis point

31. In finance, a _____ is collateral that the holder of a position in securities, options, or futures contracts has to deposit to cover the credit risk of his counterparty (most often his broker.) This risk can arise if the holder has done any of the following:

   - borrowed cash from the counterparty to buy securities or options,
   - sold securities or options short, or
   - entered into a futures contract.

The collateral can be in the form of cash or securities, and it is deposited in a _____ account. On U.S. futures exchanges, '_____' was formally called performance bond.

_____ buying is buying securities with cash borrowed from a broker, using other securities as collateral.

a. Credit
b. Margin
c. Share
d. Procter ' Gamble

32. In economic models, the _____ time frame assumes no fixed factors of production. Firms can enter or leave the marketplace, and the cost (and availability) of land, labor, raw materials, and capital goods can be assumed to vary. In contrast, in the short-run time frame, certain factors are assumed to be fixed, because there is not sufficient time for them to change.

a. Short-run
b. Long-run
c. 529 plan
d. 4-4-5 Calendar

33. A _____ is a futures contract on a short term interest rate (STIR.) Contracts vary, but are often defined on an interest rate index such as 3-month sterling or US dollar LIBOR.

They are traded across a wide range of currencies, including the G12 country currencies and many others.

a. Dual currency deposit
b. Real estate derivatives
c. Notional amount
d. Financial future

34. A _____ is an exchange of promises between two or more parties to do an act which is enforceable in a court of law. It is where an unqualified offer meets a qualified acceptance and the parties reach Consensus ad Idem. The parties must have the necessary capacity to _____ and the _____ must not be either trifling, indeterminate, impossible or illegal.

a. 529 plan
b. 4-4-5 Calendar
c. Contract
d. 7-Eleven

35. In finance, a _____ is a standardized contract, to buy or sell a specified commodity of standardized quality at a certain date in the future, at a market determined price (the futures price.)

The price is determined by the instantaneous equilibrium between the forces of supply and demand among competing buy and sell orders on the exchange at the time of the purchase or sale of the contract.

In many cases, the items may be such non-traditional 'commodities' as foreign currencies, commercial or government paper [e.g., bonds], or 'baskets' of corporate equity ['stock indices'] or other financial instruments.

a. Heston model
b. Repurchase agreement
c. Financial future
d. Futures contract

36. A _____ is a measure of the average price of consumer goods and services purchased by households. The _____ can be used to index (i.e., adjust for the effects of inflation) wages, salaries, pensions, or regulated or contracted prices. The _____ is, along with the population census and the National Income and Product Accounts, one of the most closely watched national economic statistics.

Chapter 13. The Tools and Goals of Central Bank Monetary Policy

a. Divisia index
b. Consumer price index
c. 529 plan
d. 4-4-5 Calendar

37. _____ in economics is a persistent decrease in the general price level of goods and services - a negative inflation rate. When the inflation rate slows down (decreases, but remains positive), this is known as disinflation.

Inflation destroys real value in money.

a. Fixed exchange rate
b. Recession
c. Mercantilism
d. Deflation

38. In economics, _____ is inflation that is very high or 'out of control', a condition in which prices increase rapidly as a currency loses its value. Definitions used by the media vary from a cumulative inflation rate over three years approaching 100% to 'inflation exceeding 50% a month.' In informal usage the term is often applied to much lower rates. As a rule of thumb, normal inflation is reported per year, but _____ is often reported for much shorter intervals, often per month.

a. 4-4-5 Calendar
b. 7-Eleven
c. 529 plan
d. Hyperinflation

39. A _____ is a normalized average (typically a weighted average) of prices for a given class of goods or services in a given region, during a given interval of time. It is a statistic designed to help to compare how these prices, taken as a whole, differ between time periods or geographical locations.

a. Price Index
b. Price discrimination
c. Transfer pricing
d. Discounts and allowances

40. The _____ (NYSE: FRE) is an insolvent government sponsored enterprise (GSE) of the United States federal government.

The _____ was created in 1970 to expand the secondary market for mortgages in the US. Along with other GSEs, Freddie Mac buys mortgages on the secondary market, pools them, and sells them as mortgage-backed securities to investors on the open market.

a. Governmental Accounting Standards Board
b. Public company
c. The Depository Trust ' Clearing Corporation
d. Federal Home Loan Mortgage Corporation

41. The _____ is one of the measures of national income and input for a given country's economy. _____ is defined as the total cost of all finished goods and services produced within the country in a stipulated period of time (usually a 365-day year.) It is sometimes regarded as the sum of profits added at every level of production (the intermediate stages) of all final goods and services produced within a country in a stipulated timeframe, and it is rarely given a monetary value.

a. Behavioral finance
b. Macroeconomics
c. Gross domestic product
d. Recession

Chapter 14. The Commercial Banking Industry: Structure, Products, and Management

1. _____ or amalgamation is the act of merging many things into one. In business, it often refers to the mergers or acquisitions of many smaller companies into much larger ones. The financial accounting term of _____ refers to the aggregated financial statements of a group company as consolidated account.

   a. Consolidation
   b. Write-off
   c. Cost of goods sold
   d. Retained earnings

2. _____, in bookkeeping, refers to assets, liabilities, income, and expenses recorded on individual pages of the so called book of final entry or ledger. Changes in _____ value are made by chronologically posting debit (DR) and credit (CR) entries to its page. Examples of _____s are cash, _____s receivable, mortgages, loans, land and buildings, common stock, sales, services provided, wages, and payroll overhead.

   a. Alpha
   b. Option
   c. Accretion
   d. Account

3. _____ is the removal or simplification of government rules and regulations that constrain the operation of market forces. _____ does not mean elimination of laws against fraud, but eliminating or reducing government control of how business is done, thereby moving toward a more free market.

   The stated rationale for '_____' is often that fewer and simpler regulations will lead to a raised level of competitiveness, therefore higher productivity, more efficiency and lower prices overall.

   a. Demand shock
   b. Supply shock
   c. Value added
   d. Deregulation

4.

   A _____ is a type of financial intermediary and a type of bank. Commercial banking is also known as business banking. It is a bank that provides checking accounts, savings accounts, and money market accounts and that accepts time deposits.

   a. 4-4-5 Calendar
   b. 7-Eleven
   c. Commercial bank
   d. 529 plan

5. A _____ is a company that owns other companies' outstanding stock. It usually refers to a company which does not produce goods or services itself, rather its only purpose is owning shares of other companies. They allow the reduction of risk for the owners and can allow the ownership and control of a number of different companies.

   a. MRU Holdings
   b. Federal National Mortgage Association
   c. Privately held company
   d. Holding company

6. _____ refer to services provided by the finance industry.

   The finance industry encompasses a broad range of organizations that deal with the management of money. Among these organizations are banks, credit card companies, insurance companies, consumer finance companies, stock brokerages, investment funds and some government sponsored enterprises.

   a. Financial Services
   b. Delta hedging
   c. Financial instruments
   d. Cost of carry

Chapter 14. The Commercial Banking Industry: Structure, Products, and Management   127

7. The _____ Act is an Act of the 106th United States Congress which repealed part of the Glass-Steagall Act of 1933, opening up competition among banks, securities companies and insurance companies. The Glass-Steagall Act prohibited any one institution from acting as both an investment bank and a commercial bank, or as both a bank and an insurer.

The _____ Act (GLBA) allowed commercial and investment banks to consolidate.

  a. 529 plan
  b. 7-Eleven
  c. Gramm-Leach-Bliley
  d. 4-4-5 Calendar

8. A _____ is an entity formed between two or more parties to undertake economic activity together. The parties agree to create a new entity by both contributing equity, and they then share in the revenues, expenses, and control of the enterprise. The venture can be for one specific project only, or a continuing business relationship such as the Sony Ericsson _____.
  a. Pre-emption right
  b. Fair Debt Collection Practices Act
  c. Lien
  d. Joint venture

9. A _____, in business matters, is an entity that is controlled by a bigger and more powerful entity. The controlled entity is called a company, corporation, or limited liability company, and the controlling entity is called its parent (or the parent company.) The reason for this distinction is that a lone company cannot be a _____ of any organization; only an entity representing a legal fiction as a separate entity can be a _____.
  a. Joint stock company
  b. 529 plan
  c. 4-4-5 Calendar
  d. Subsidiary

10. The institution most often referenced by the word '_____' is a public or publicly traded _____, the shares of which are traded on a public stock exchange (e.g., the New York Stock Exchange or Nasdaq in the United States) where shares of stock of _____s are bought and sold by and to the general public. Most of the largest businesses in the world are publicly traded _____s. However, the majority of _____s are said to be closely held, privately held or close _____s, meaning that no ready market exists for the trading of shares.
  a. Protect
  b. Corporation
  c. Federal Home Loan Mortgage Corporation
  d. Depository Trust Company

11. Explicit _____ is a measure implemented in many countries to protect bank depositors, in full or in part, from losses caused by a bank's inability to pay its debts when due. _____ systems are one component of a financial system safety net that promotes financial stability.
  a. Banking panic
  b. Reserve requirement
  c. Time deposit
  d. Deposit Insurance

12. The _____ is a United States government corporation created by the Glass-Steagall Act of 1933. It provides deposit insurance, which guarantees the safety of checking and savings deposits in member banks, currently up to $250,000 per depositor per bank. Insured deposits are backed by the full faith and credit of the United States.
  a. FASB
  b. Ford Foundation
  c. NYSE Group
  d. Federal Deposit Insurance Corporation

13. _____ is that which is owed; usually referencing assets owed, but the term can cover other obligations. In the case of assets, _____ is a means of using future purchasing power in the present before a summation has been earned. Some companies and corporations use _____ as a part of their overall corporate finance strategy.

a. Credit cycle
b. Debt
c. Cross-collateralization
d. Partial Payment

14. In finance, a _____ is a debt security, in which the authorized issuer owes the holders a debt and, depending on the terms of the _____, is obliged to pay interest (the coupon) and/or to repay the principal at a later date, termed maturity.

Thus a _____ is a loan: the issuer is the borrower, the _____ holder is the lender, and the coupon is the interest. _____s provide the borrower with external funds to finance long-term investments, or, in the case of government _____s, to finance current expenditure.

a. Catastrophe bonds
b. Puttable bond
c. Bond
d. Convertible bond

15. A _____ is a financial services company that provides clearing and settlement services for financial transactions, usually on a futures exchange, and often acts as central counterparty (the payor actually pays the _____, which then pays the payee). A _____ may also offer novation, the substitution of a new contract or debt for an old, or other credit enhancement services to its members.

The term is also used for banks like Suffolk Bank that acted as a restraint on the over-issuance of private bank notes.

a. Valuation
b. Warrant
c. Bucket shop
d. Clearing house

16. In financial accounting, a _____ or statement of financial position is a summary of a person's or organization's balances. Assets, liabilities and ownership equity are listed as of a specific date, such as the end of its financial year. A _____ is often described as a snapshot of a company's financial condition.

a. Statement on Auditing Standards No. 70: Service Organizations
b. Balance sheet
c. Financial statements
d. Statement of retained earnings

17. The _____ is a private, not-for-profit organization whose primary purpose is to develop generally accepted accounting principles (GAAP) within the United States in the public's interest. The Securities and Exchange Commission (SEC) designated the _____ as the organization responsible for setting accounting standards for public companies in the U.S. It was created in 1973, replacing the Accounting Principles Board and the Committee on Accounting Procedure of the American Institute of Certified Public Accountants. The _____'s mission is 'to establish and improve standards of financial accounting and reporting for the guidance and education of the public, including issuers, auditors, and users of financial information.'

The _____ is not a governmental body.

a. MRU Holdings
b. Credit karma
c. FASB
d. PlaNet Finance

18. _____ are formal records of a business' financial activities.

Chapter 14. The Commercial Banking Industry: Structure, Products, and Management

_____ provide an overview of a business' financial condition in both short and long term. There are four basic _____:

1. **Balance sheet**: also referred to as statement of financial position or condition, reports on a company's assets, liabilities, and net equity as of a given point in time.
2. **Income statement**: also referred to as Profit and Loss statement (or a 'P'L'), reports on a company's income, expenses, and profits over a period of time.
3. **Statement of retained earnings**: explains the changes in a company's retained earnings over the reporting period.
4. **Statement of cash flows**: reports on a company's cash flow activities, particularly its operating, investing and financing activities.

a. Notes to the Financial Statements

b. Statement on Auditing Standards No. 70: Service Organizations

c. Statement of retained earnings

d. Financial statements

19. In financial accounting, the term _____ is most commonly used to describe any part of shareholders' equity, except for basic share capital. Sometimes, the term is used instead of the term provision; such a use, however, is inconsistent with the terminology suggested by International Accounting Standards Board. For more information about provisions, see provision (accounting.)

a. FIFO and LIFO accounting

b. Closing entries

c. Treasury stock

d. Reserve

20. A _____ is a bond issued by a corporation. The term is usually applied to longer-term debt instruments, generally with a maturity date falling at least a year after their issue date. (The term 'commercial paper' is sometimes used for instruments with a shorter maturity.)

a. Corporate bond

b. Serial bond

c. Brady bonds

d. Government bond

21. In the United States, _____ are overnight borrowings by banks to maintain their bank reserves at the Federal Reserve. Banks keep reserves at Federal Reserve Banks to meet their reserve requirements and to clear financial transactions. Transactions in the _____ market enable depository institutions with reserve balances in excess of reserve requirements to lend reserves to institutions with reserve deficiencies.

a. 4-4-5 Calendar

b. Federal funds rate

c. Regulation T

d. Federal funds

22. A _____ allows a borrower to use a financial security as collateral for a cash loan at a fixed rate of interest. In a repo, the borrower agrees to immediately sell a security to a lender and also agrees to buy the same security from the lender at a fixed price at some later date. A repo is equivalent to a cash transaction combined with a forward contract.

a. Contango

b. Volatility arbitrage

c. Total return swap

d. Repurchase agreement

Chapter 14. The Commercial Banking Industry: Structure, Products, and Management

23. An _____ is a security whose value and income payments are derived from and collateralized (or 'backed') by a specified pool of underlying assets. The pool of assets is typically a group of small and illiquid assets that are unable to be sold individually. Pooling the assets allows them to be sold to general investors, a process called securitization, and allows the risk of investing in the underlying assets to be diversified because each security will represent a fraction of the total value of the diverse pool of underlying assets.
    - a. AAB
    - b. ABN Amro
    - c. A Random Walk Down Wall Street
    - d. Asset-backed security

24. A _____ is a fungible, negotiable instrument representing financial value. They are broadly categorized into debt securities (such as banknotes, bonds and debentures), and equity securities; e.g., common stocks. The company or other entity issuing the _____ is called the issuer.
    - a. Securities lending
    - b. Security
    - c. Book entry
    - d. Tracking stock

25. _____ refers to making a wide range of secured and unsecured loans to consumers for consumable items such as a car, boat, manufactured home, home equity loan, home equity line of credit, signature loan, signature line of credit, recreational vehicle, or share or certificate of deposit or Stocks and Mutual Funds secured loans.

    _____ does not include mortgage loans, typically used for home purchases, which follow some different regulations than consumer loans. Also, consumer loans are different from commercial loans, which can be calculated on a daily basis, rather than 12 monthly payments, and include interest for leap day, such as in Actual/366 loan calculations.
    - a. Primary market
    - b. Sogflation
    - c. Coupon leverage
    - d. Consumer lending

26. _____ is the value of a homeowner's unencumbered interest in their property, i.e. the difference between the home's fair market value and the unpaid balance of the mortgage and any outstanding debt over the home. _____ increases as the mortgage is paid or as the property enjoys appreciation. This is sometimes called real property value in economics.
    - a. Real Estate Investment Trust
    - b. Liquidation value
    - c. REIT
    - d. Home equity

27. _____ is a fee paid on borrowed assets. It is the price paid for the use of borrowed money, or, money earned by deposited funds. Assets that are sometimes lent with _____ include money, shares, consumer goods through hire purchase, major assets such as aircraft, and even entire factories in finance lease arrangements.
    - a. AAB
    - b. A Random Walk Down Wall Street
    - c. Insolvency
    - d. Interest

28. An _____ is the price a borrower pays for the use of money they do not own, and the return a lender receives for deferring the use of funds, by lending it to the borrower. _____s are normally expressed as a percentage rate over the period of one year.

    _____s targets are also a vital tool of monetary policy and are used to control variables like investment, inflation, and unemployment.

Chapter 14. The Commercial Banking Industry: Structure, Products, and Management

a. AAB
c. ABN Amro

b. A Random Walk Down Wall Street
d. Interest rate

29. _____ is the risk (variability in value) borne by an interest-bearing asset, such as a loan or a bond, due to variability of interest rates. In general, as rates rise, the price of a fixed rate bond will fall, and vice versa. _____ is commonly measured by the bond's duration.
   a. International Fisher effect
   c. Official bank rate
   b. A Random Walk Down Wall Street
   d. Interest rate risk

30. In economics, the concept of the _____ refers to the decision-making time frame of a firm in which at least one factor of production is fixed. Costs which are fixed in the _____ have no impact on a firms decisions. For example a firm can raise output by increasing the amount of labour through overtime.
   a. 529 plan
   c. Long-run
   b. 4-4-5 Calendar
   d. Short-run

31. _____ is a legally declared inability or impairment of ability of an individual or organization to pay their creditors. Creditors may file a _____ petition against a debtor ('involuntary _____') in an effort to recoup a portion of what they are owed or initiate a restructuring. In the majority of cases, however, _____ is initiated by the debtor (a 'voluntary _____' that is filed by the bankrupt individual or organization.)
   a. Bankruptcy
   c. Debt settlement
   b. 529 plan
   d. 4-4-5 Calendar

32. _____ is a type of bank account where the money in the account is legally able to be withdrawn immediately upon demand (or 'at call'.) This type of bank account can also be referred to as a 'cheque' or 'checking' or transactional account.

This type of bank account, allowing immediate conversion of the account balance into cash or withdrawal to another account, can be contrasted with a time deposit (also known as a certificate of deposit or term deposit), where the funds are not legally available for immediate withdrawal by the depositor.

   a. 4-4-5 Calendar
   c. Synthetic lease
   b. 529 plan
   d. Demand deposit

33. In finance, the _____ is the global financial market for short-term borrowing and lending. It provides short-term liquidity funding for the global financial system. The _____ is where short-term obligations such as Treasury bills, commercial paper and bankers' acceptances are bought and sold.
   a. Debt-for-equity swap
   c. Consumer debt
   b. Money market
   d. Cramdown

34. A _____ is a money deposit at a banking institution that cannot be withdrawn for a certain 'term' or period of time. When the term is over it can be withdrawn or it can be held for another term. Generally speaking, the longer the term the better the yield on the money.
   a. Basel Accord
   c. Certificate of deposit
   b. Private money
   d. Time deposit

Chapter 14. The Commercial Banking Industry: Structure, Products, and Management

35. A _____ is a current account at a banking institution that allows money to be deposited and withdrawn by the account holder, with the transactions and resulting balance being recorded on the bank's books. Some banks charge a fee for this service, while others may pay the customer interest on the funds deposited.

Although restrictions placed on access depend upon the terms and conditions of the account and the provider, the account holder retains rights to have their funds repaid on demand.

 a. 4-4-5 Calendar
 b. Deposit account
 c. Contractum trinius
 d. Bilateral netting

36. Leasing is a process by which a firm can obtain the use of a certain fixed assets for which it must pay a series of contractual, periodic, tax deductable payments. The lessee is the receiver of the services or the assets under the lease contract and the lessor is the owner of the assets. The relationship between the tenant and the landlord is called a _____, and can be for a fixed or an indefinite period of time (called the term of the lease.)
 a. REIT
 b. Real Estate Investment Trust
 c. Real estate investing
 d. Tenancy

37. _____, consists of the buying and selling of products or services over electronic systems such as the Internet and other computer networks. The amount of trade conducted electronically has grown extraordinarily with widespread Internet usage. The use of commerce is conducted in this way, spurring and drawing on innovations in electronic funds transfer, supply chain management, Internet marketing, online transaction processing, electronic data interchange (EDI), inventory management systems, and automated data collection systems.
 a. AAB
 b. ABN Amro
 c. Electronic commerce
 d. A Random Walk Down Wall Street

38. _____ is a structured finance process that involves pooling and repackaging of cash-flow-producing financial assets into securities, which are then sold to investors. The term '_____' is derived from the fact that the form of financial instruments used to obtain funds from the investors are securities. As a portfolio risk backed by amortizing cash flows - and unlike general corporate debt - the credit quality of securitized debt is non-stationary due to changes in volatility that are time- and structure-dependent.
 a. The Glass-Steagall Act of 1933
 b. Special journals
 c. Reputational risk
 d. Securitization

39. In business and accounting, _____s are everything of value that is owned by a person or company. The balance sheet of a firm records the monetary value of the _____s owned by the firm. The two major _____ classes are tangible _____s and intangible _____s.
 a. Income
 b. Accounts payable
 c. EBITDA
 d. Asset

40. _____ is the provision of resources (such as granting a loan) by one party to another party where that second party does not reimburse the first party immediately, thereby generating a debt, and instead arranges either to repay or return those resources (or material(s) of equal value) at a later date. The first party is called a creditor, also known as a lender, while the second party is called a debtor, also known as a borrower.

Movements of financial capital are normally dependent on either _____ or equity transfers.

Chapter 14. The Commercial Banking Industry: Structure, Products, and Management

a. Credit
c. Clearing house
b. Comparable
d. Warrant

41. A standard, commercial _____ is a document issued mostly by a financial institution, used primarily in trade finance, which usually provides an irrevocable payment undertaking.

The _____ can also be the source of payment for a transaction, meaning that redeeming the _____ will pay an exporter. Letters of credit are used primarily in international trade transactions of significant value, for deals between a supplier in one country and a customer in another.

a. Letter of credit
c. McFadden Act
b. Bond indenture
d. Duty of loyalty

42. _____, refers to consumption opportunity gained by an entity within a specified time frame, which is generally expressed in monetary terms. However, for households and individuals, '_____ is the sum of all the wages, salaries, profits, interests payments, rents and other forms of earnings received... in a given period of time.' For firms, _____ generally refers to net-profit: what remains of revenue after expenses have been subtracted.

a. Accrual
c. Annual report
b. OIBDA
d. Income

43. An _____ is a financial statement for companies that indicates how Revenue is transformed into net income The purpose of the _____ is to show managers and investors whether the company made or lost money during the period being reported.

The important thing to remember about an _____ is that it represents a period of time.

a. ABN Amro
c. A Random Walk Down Wall Street
b. Income statement
d. AAB

44. In business, _____ is income that a company receives from its normal business activities, usually from the sale of goods and services to customers. Some companies also receive _____ from interest, dividends or royalties paid to them by other companies. _____ may refer to business income in general, or it may refer to the amount, in a monetary unit, received during a period of time, as in 'Last year, Company X had _____ of $32 million.'

In many countries, including the UK, _____ is referred to as turnover.

a. Revenue
c. Furniture, Fixtures and Equipment
b. Matching principle
d. Bottom line

Chapter 14. The Commercial Banking Industry: Structure, Products, and Management

45. In finance, a _____ is collateral that the holder of a position in securities, options, or futures contracts has to deposit to cover the credit risk of his counterparty (most often his broker.) This risk can arise if the holder has done any of the following:

- borrowed cash from the counterparty to buy securities or options,
- sold securities or options short, or
- entered into a futures contract.

The collateral can be in the form of cash or securities, and it is deposited in a _____ account. On U.S. futures exchanges, '_____' was formally called performance bond.

_____ buying is buying securities with cash borrowed from a broker, using other securities as collateral.

a. Margin
c. Credit

b. Procter ' Gamble
d. Share

46. _____ is a measure of the ability of a debtor to pay their debts as and when they fall due. It is usually expressed as a ratio or a percentage of current liabilities.

For a corporation with a published balance sheet there are various ratios used to calculate a measure of liquidity.

a. Invested capital
c. Accounting liquidity

b. Operating profit margin
d. Operating leverage

47. In the most general sense, a _____ is anything that is a hindrance, or puts individuals at a disadvantage.

Before we discuss the financial terms, we should note that a _____ can also have a much more important slang meaning.

This is best described in an example.

a. Liability
c. McFadden Act

b. Covenant
d. Limited liability

48. An _____ is a contract written by a seller that conveys to the buyer the right -- but not the obligation -- to buy (in the case of a call _____) or to sell (in the case of a put _____) a particular asset, such as a piece of property such as, among others, a futures contract. In return for granting the _____, the seller collects a payment (the premium) from the buyer.

For example, buying a call _____ provides the right to buy a specified quantity of a security at a set strike price at some time on or before expiration, while buying a put _____ provides the right to sell.

a. Amortization
c. AT'T Mobility LLC

b. Annuity
d. Option

Chapter 14. The Commercial Banking Industry: Structure, Products, and Management

49. In business, _____ is the total assets minus total outside liabilities of an individual or a company. For a company, this is called shareholders' equity and may be referred to as book value. _____ is stated as at a particular point in time.
   a. Certified International Investment Analyst
   b. Net worth
   c. Restructuring
   d. Moneylender

50. A _____ is a pool of assets forming an independent legal entity that are bought with the contributions to a pension plan for the exclusive purpose of financing pension plan benefits.

   _____s are important shareholders of listed and private companies. They are especially important to the stock market where large institutional investors like the Ontario Teachers' Pension Plan dominate.

   a. Leveraged buyout
   b. Limited liability company
   c. Leverage
   d. Pension fund

51. _____ measures the rate of return on the ownership interest (shareholders' equity) of the common stock owners. _____ is viewed as one of the most important financial ratios. It measures a firm's efficiency at generating profits from every dollar of shareholders' equity (also known as net assets or assets minus liabilities.)
   a. Return of capital
   b. Return on sales
   c. Return on equity
   d. Diluted Earnings Per Share

52. The _____ percentage shows how profitable a company's assets are in generating revenue.

   _____ can be computed as:

   $$ROA = \frac{\text{Net Income}}{\text{Total Assets}}$$

   This number tells you 'what the company can do with what it's got', i.e. how many dollars of earnings they derive from each dollar of assets they control. It's a useful number for comparing competing companies in the same industry.

   a. Return on assets
   b. P/E ratio
   c. Return on sales
   d. Receivables turnover ratio

53. In economics, a _____ is a mechanism that allows people to easily buy and sell (trade) financial securities (such as stocks and bonds), commodities (such as precious metals or agricultural goods), and other fungible items of value at low transaction costs and at prices that reflect the efficient-market hypothesis.

   _____s have evolved significantly over several hundred years and are undergoing constant innovation to improve liquidity.

   Both general markets (where many commodities are traded) and specialized markets (where only one commodity is traded) exist.

a. Delta hedging
b. Cost of carry
c. Secondary market
d. Financial market

Chapter 15. Nonbank Thrift Institutions

1. A _____ is a financial institution that specializes in accepting savings deposits and making mortgage and other loans. The S'L or thrift term is mainly used in the United States; similar institutions in the United Kingdom, Ireland and some Commonwealth countries include building societies and trustee savings banks.

They are often mutually held, meaning that the depositors and borrowers are members with voting rights, and have the ability to direct the financial and managerial goals of the organization, not unlike the poliyholders of a mutual insurance company.

    a. Net asset value
    b. Savings and loan association
    c. Mutual fund
    d. Person-to-person lending

2. The _____ is the market for securities, where companies and governments can raise longterm funds. The _____ includes the stock market and the bond market. Financial regulators, such as the U.S. Securities and Exchange Commission, oversee the _____s in their designated countries to ensure that investors are protected against fraud.

    a. Delta neutral
    b. Spot rate
    c. Capital market
    d. Forward market

3.

A _____ is a type of financial intermediary and a type of bank. Commercial banking is also known as business banking. It is a bank that provides checking accounts, savings accounts, and money market accounts and that accepts time deposits.

    a. 529 plan
    b. 4-4-5 Calendar
    c. 7-Eleven
    d. Commercial bank

4. _____ is the provision of resources (such as granting a loan) by one party to another party where that second party does not reimburse the first party immediately, thereby generating a debt, and instead arranges either to repay or return those resources (or material(s) of equal value) at a later date. The first party is called a creditor, also known as a lender, while the second party is called a debtor, also known as a borrower.

Movements of financial capital are normally dependent on either _____ or equity transfers.

    a. Clearing house
    b. Comparable
    c. Warrant
    d. Credit

5. A _____ is a cooperative financial institution that is owned and controlled by its members, and operated for the purpose of promoting thrift, providing credit at reasonable rates, and providing other financial services to its members. Many _____s exist to further community development or sustainable international development on a local level. Worldwide, _____ systems vary significantly in terms of total system assets and average institution asset size since _____s exist in a wide range of sizes, ranging from volunteer operations with a handful of members to institutions with several billion dollars in assets and hundreds of thousands of members.

    a. Corporate credit union
    b. Credit union
    c. Fi-linx
    d. Credit Union Service Organization

Chapter 15. Nonbank Thrift Institutions

6. A _____ is a financial debt vehicle that was first created in June 1983 by investment banks Salomon Brothers and First Boston for Freddie Mac. (The First Boston team was led by Dexter Senft.) Legally, a _____ is a special purpose entity that is wholly separate from the institution(s) that create it.

    a. Yield curve spread
    b. Tranche
    c. 4-4-5 Calendar
    d. Collateralized mortgage obligation

7. A _____ is a bond issued by a corporation. The term is usually applied to longer-term debt instruments, generally with a maturity date falling at least a year after their issue date. (The term 'commercial paper' is sometimes used for instruments with a shorter maturity.)

    a. Serial bond
    b. Government bond
    c. Brady bonds
    d. Corporate bond

8. The institution most often referenced by the word '_____' is a public or publicly traded _____, the shares of which are traded on a public stock exchange (e.g., the New York Stock Exchange or Nasdaq in the United States) where shares of stock of _____s are bought and sold by and to the general public. Most of the largest businesses in the world are publicly traded _____s. However, the majority of _____s are said to be closely held, privately held or close _____s, meaning that no ready market exists for the trading of shares.

    a. Protect
    b. Corporation
    c. Federal Home Loan Mortgage Corporation
    d. Depository Trust Company

9. _____ is that which is owed; usually referencing assets owed, but the term can cover other obligations. In the case of assets, _____ is a means of using future purchasing power in the present before a summation has been earned. Some companies and corporations use _____ as a part of their overall corporate finance strategy.

    a. Partial Payment
    b. Debt
    c. Credit cycle
    d. Cross-collateralization

10. The _____ (NYSE: FRE) is an insolvent government sponsored enterprise (GSE) of the United States federal government.

    The _____ was created in 1970 to expand the secondary market for mortgages in the US. Along with other GSEs, Freddie Mac buys mortgages on the secondary market, pools them, and sells them as mortgage-backed securities to investors on the open market.

    a. Governmental Accounting Standards Board
    b. The Depository Trust ' Clearing Corporation
    c. Public company
    d. Federal Home Loan Mortgage Corporation

11. The _____ is a U.S. government-owned corporation within the Department of Housing and Urban Development

    Ginnie Mae provides guarantees on mortgage-backed securities backed by federally insured or guaranteed loans, mainly loans issued by the Federal Housing Administration, Department of Veterans Affairs, Rural Housing Service, and Office of Public and Indian Housing. Ginnie Mae securities are the only MBS that are guaranteed by the United States government.

    a. Case-Shiller Home Price Indices
    b. GNMA
    c. Cash budget
    d. Certified Emission Reductions

Chapter 15. Nonbank Thrift Institutions

12. The _____ is a U.S. government-owned corporation within the Department of Housing and Urban Development

Ginnie Mae provides guarantees on mortgage-backed securities backed by federally insured or guaranteed loans, mainly loans issued by the Federal Housing Administration, Department of Veterans Affairs, Rural Housing Service, and Office of Public and Indian Housing. Ginnie Mae securities are the only MBS that are guaranteed by the United States government.

- a. Jumbo mortgage
- b. 4-4-5 Calendar
- c. Graduated payment mortgage
- d. Government National Mortgage Association

13. A _____ is an asset-backed security whose cash flows are backed by the principal and interest payments of a set of mortgage loans. Payments are typically made monthly over the lifetime of the underlying loans.
- a. Shared appreciation mortgage
- b. Conforming loan
- c. Home equity line of credit
- d. Mortgage-backed security

14. In finance, 'participation' is an ownership interest in a mortgage or other loan. In particular, _____ is a cooperation of multiple lenders to issue a loan (known as participation loan) to one borrower. This is usually done in order to reduce individual risks of the lenders.
- a. Doctrine of the Proper Law
- b. Securitization
- c. Short positions
- d. Loan participation

15. _____ are government bonds issued by the United States Department of the Treasury through the Bureau of the Public Debt. They are the debt financing instruments of the U.S. Federal government, and they are often referred to simply as Treasuries or Treasurys. There are four types of marketable _____: Treasury bills, Treasury notes, Treasury bonds, and Treasury Inflation Protected Securities (TIPS.)
- a. Treasury securities
- b. Treasury Inflation-Protected Securities
- c. Treasury Inflation Protected Securities
- d. 4-4-5 Calendar

16. In finance, a _____ is a debt security, in which the authorized issuer owes the holders a debt and, depending on the terms of the _____, is obliged to pay interest (the coupon) and/or to repay the principal at a later date, termed maturity.

Thus a _____ is a loan: the issuer is the borrower, the _____ holder is the lender, and the coupon is the interest. _____s provide the borrower with external funds to finance long-term investments, or, in the case of government _____s, to finance current expenditure.

- a. Catastrophe bonds
- b. Convertible bond
- c. Bond
- d. Puttable bond

17. A _____ is a fungible, negotiable instrument representing financial value. They are broadly categorized into debt securities (such as banknotes, bonds and debentures), and equity securities; e.g., common stocks. The company or other entity issuing the _____ is called the issuer.
- a. Tracking stock
- b. Book entry
- c. Securities lending
- d. Security

Chapter 15. Nonbank Thrift Institutions

18. _____ is a structured finance process that involves pooling and repackaging of cash-flow-producing financial assets into securities, which are then sold to investors. The term '_____' is derived from the fact that the form of financial instruments used to obtain funds from the investors are securities. As a portfolio risk backed by amortizing cash flows - and unlike general corporate debt - the credit quality of securitized debt is non-stationary due to changes in volatility that are time- and structure-dependent.

    a. Reputational risk
    b. Special journals
    c. The Glass-Steagall Act of 1933
    d. Securitization

19. An _____ is a retirement plan account that provides some tax advantages for retirement savings in the United States.

    a. AAB
    b. ABN Amro
    c. A Random Walk Down Wall Street
    d. Individual Retirement Arrangement

20. _____s are full-fledged pension plans for self-employed people in the United States. They are sometimes called HR10 plans and are not Individual Retirement Accounts (IRA.)

Since a _____ is a full-fledged pension, there is a Keogh for every employer-sponsored pension-plan design.

    a. 529 plan
    b. 4-4-5 Calendar
    c. 7-Eleven
    d. Keogh plan

21. In finance, the _____ is the global financial market for short-term borrowing and lending. It provides short-term liquidity funding for the global financial system. The _____ is where short-term obligations such as Treasury bills, commercial paper and bankers' acceptances are bought and sold.

    a. Consumer debt
    b. Debt-for-equity swap
    c. Cramdown
    d. Money market

22. _____, in bookkeeping, refers to assets, liabilities, income, and expenses recorded on individual pages of the so called book of final entry or ledger. Changes in _____ value are made by chronologically posting debit (DR) and credit (CR) entries to its page. Examples of _____s are cash, _____s receivable, mortgages, loans, land and buildings, common stock, sales, services provided, wages, and payroll overhead.

    a. Option
    b. Accretion
    c. Account
    d. Alpha

23. A _____ is a current account at a banking institution that allows money to be deposited and withdrawn by the account holder, with the transactions and resulting balance being recorded on the bank's books. Some banks charge a fee for this service, while others may pay the customer interest on the funds deposited.

Although restrictions placed on access depend upon the terms and conditions of the account and the provider, the account holder retains rights to have their funds repaid on demand.

    a. 4-4-5 Calendar
    b. Contractum trinius
    c. Bilateral netting
    d. Deposit account

Chapter 15. Nonbank Thrift Institutions

24. In economics, business, and accounting, a _____ is the value of money that has been used up to produce something, and hence is not available for use anymore. In business, the _____ may be one of acquisition, in which case the amount of money expended to acquire it is counted as _____. In this case, money is the input that is gone in order to acquire the thing.

    a. Marginal cost
    b. Sliding scale fees
    c. Fixed costs
    d. Cost

25. The _____ (FSLIC) was an institution that administered deposit insurance for savings and loan institutions in the United States. It was abolished in 1989 by the Financial Institutions Reform, Recovery and Enforcement Act, which passed responsibility for savings and loan deposit insurance to the Federal Deposit Insurance Corporation (FDIC.)

    The FSLIC was created as part of the National Housing Act of 1934 in order to insure deposits in savings and loans, a year after the FDIC was created to insure deposits in commercial banks.

    a. Prudent man rule
    b. SIPC
    c. Securities Investor Protection Corporation
    d. Federal Savings and Loan Insurance Corporation

26. The _____ provide stable, on-demand, low-cost funding to American financial institutions for home mortgage loans, small business, rural, agricultural, and economic development lending. With their members, the _____ank System represents the largest collective source of home mortgage and community credit in the United States. The banks do not provide loans directly to individuals, only to other banks.

    a. Federal Home Loan Banks
    b. 7-Eleven
    c. 529 plan
    d. 4-4-5 Calendar

27. In business and accounting, _____s are everything of value that is owned by a person or company. The balance sheet of a firm records the monetary value of the _____s owned by the firm. The two major _____ classes are tangible _____s and intangible _____s.

    a. Accounts payable
    b. EBITDA
    c. Income
    d. Asset

28. In business, _____ is income that a company receives from its normal business activities, usually from the sale of goods and services to customers. Some companies also receive _____ from interest, dividends or royalties paid to them by other companies. _____ may refer to business income in general, or it may refer to the amount, in a monetary unit, received during a period of time, as in 'Last year, Company X had _____ of $32 million.'

    In many countries, including the UK, _____ is referred to as turnover.

    a. Bottom line
    b. Furniture, Fixtures and Equipment
    c. Matching principle
    d. Revenue

29. _____ is a life of security. It may also refer to the final payment date of a loan or other financial instrument, at which point all remaining interest and principal is due to be paid.

    1, 3, 6 months _____ band can be calculated by using 30-day per month periods.

a. Primary market
b. False billing
c. Replacement cost
d. Maturity

30. The _____, an agency of the United States Department of the Treasury, is the primary regulator of federal savings associations (sometimes referred to as federal thrifts.) Federal savings associations include both federal savings banks and federal savings and loans. The OTS is also responsible for supervising savings and loan holding companies (SLHCs) and some state-chartered institutions.

a. ABN Amro
b. Office of Thrift Supervision
c. A Random Walk Down Wall Street
d. AAB

31. _____ or amalgamation is the act of merging many things into one. In business, it often refers to the mergers or acquisitions of many smaller companies into much larger ones. The financial accounting term of _____ refers to the aggregated financial statements of a group company as consolidated account.

a. Write-off
b. Cost of goods sold
c. Consolidation
d. Retained earnings

32. _____ is the removal or simplification of government rules and regulations that constrain the operation of market forces. _____ does not mean elimination of laws against fraud, but eliminating or reducing government control of how business is done, thereby moving toward a more free market.

The stated rationale for '_____' is often that fewer and simpler regulations will lead to a raised level of competitiveness, therefore higher productivity, more efficiency and lower prices overall.

a. Demand shock
b. Value added
c. Supply shock
d. Deregulation

33. _____ is a financial term that was popularized by the media during the 'credit crunch' of 2007 and involves financial institutions lending in ways which do not meet 'prime' standards to an extent which puts the loans into the riskiest category of consumer loans typically sold in the secondary market. These standards refer to the size of the loan, 'traditional' or 'nontraditional' structure of the loan, borrower credit rating, ratio of borrower debt to income or assets, ratio of loan to value or collateral, documentation provided on those loans which do not meet Fannie Mae or Freddie Mac underwriting guidelines for prime mortgages (are 'non-conforming'.) Although there is no single, standard definition, in the US subprime loans are usually classified as those where the borrower has a FICO score below 640.

a. Negative equity
b. Cash-out
c. Fixed rate mortgage
d. Subprime lending

34. _____ refer to services provided by the finance industry.

The finance industry encompasses a broad range of organizations that deal with the management of money. Among these organizations are banks, credit card companies, insurance companies, consumer finance companies, stock brokerages, investment funds and some government sponsored enterprises.

a. Financial instruments
b. Delta hedging
c. Financial Services
d. Cost of carry

Chapter 15. Nonbank Thrift Institutions

35. In business and finance, a _____ (also referred to as equity _____) of stock means a _____ of ownership in a corporation (company.) In the plural, stocks is often used as a synonym for _____s especially in the United States, but it is less commonly used that way outside of North America.

In the United Kingdom, South Africa, and Australia, stock can also refer to completely different financial instruments such as government bonds or, less commonly, to all kinds of marketable securities.

a. Bucket shop
b. Margin
c. Procter ' Gamble
d. Share

36. A _____ can require immediate payment by the second party to the third upon presentation of the _____. This is called a sight _____. A Cheques is a sight _____. An importer might write a _____ promising payment to an exporter for delivery of goods with payment to occur 60 days after the goods are delivered. Such a _____ is called a time _____.

a. Draft
b. Cashflow matching
c. Gross profit margin
d. Second lien loan

37. The _____ is a free-trade and professional association that promotes and advocates issues important to the banking industry in the United States. The _____'s national headquarters are in Washington, D.C. In addition to its trade association mission, the _____ also performs educational components for consumers through its Educational Foundation affiliate.

While the _____ works on a national level, it also is supported by state operated offices (sometimes referred to as 'Leagues') which focus attention on state level support.

a. ABN Amro
b. A Random Walk Down Wall Street
c. AAB
d. American Bankers Association

38. A _____ or bank is a financial institution whose primary activity is to act as a payment agent for customers and to borrow and lend money.

The first modern bank was founded in Italy in Genoa in 1406, its name was Banco di San Giorgio (Bank of St. George.)

Many other financial activities were added over time.

a. Banker
b. 4-4-5 Calendar
c. Bought deal
d. Black Sea Trade and Development Bank

39. Money funds (or _____, money market mutual funds) are mutual funds that invest in short-term debt instruments.

_____, also known as principal stability funds, seek to limit exposure to losses due to credit, market and liquidity risks.
_____, in the United States, are regulated by the Securities and Exchange Commission's (SEC) Investment Company Act of 1940.

a. Mutual fund fees and expenses
b. Stock fund
c. Closed-end fund
d. Money market funds

40. A _____ is a professionally managed type of collective investment scheme that pools money from many investors and invests it in stocks, bonds, short-term money market instruments, and/or other securities. The _____ will have a fund manager that trades the pooled money on a regular basis. Currently, the worldwide value of all _____s totals more than $26 trillion.

Since 1940, there have been three basic types of investment companies in the United States: open-end funds, also known in the US as _____s; unit investment trusts (UITs); and closed-end funds.

a. Financial intermediary
b. Net asset value
c. Trust company
d. Mutual fund

41. _____ or financing is to provide capital (funds), which means money for a project, a person, a business or any other private or public institutions.

Those funds can be allocated for either short term or long term purposes. The health fund is a new way of _____ private healthcare centers.

a. Product life cycle
b. Proxy fight
c. Funding
d. Synthetic CDO

42. In financial accounting, the term _____ is most commonly used to describe any part of shareholders' equity, except for basic share capital. Sometimes, the term is used instead of the term provision; such a use, however, is inconsistent with the terminology suggested by International Accounting Standards Board. For more information about provisions, see provision (accounting.)
a. Treasury stock
b. Reserve
c. Closing entries
d. FIFO and LIFO accounting

43. The U.S. _____ is an independent agency of the United States government which holds primary responsibility for enforcing the federal securities laws and regulating the securities industry, the nation's stock and options exchanges, and other electronic securities markets. The SEC was created by section 4 of the SEC of 1934 (now codified as 15 U.S.C. § 78d and commonly referred to as the 1934 Act.)
a. 529 plan
b. 7-Eleven
c. 4-4-5 Calendar
d. Securities and Exchange Commission

44. In the global money market, _____ is an unsecured promissory note with a fixed maturity of one to 270 days. _____ is a money-market security issued (sold) by large banks and corporations to get money to meet short term debt obligations (for example, payroll), and is only backed by an issuing bank or corporation's promise to pay the face amount on the maturity date specified on the note. Since it is not backed by collateral, only firms with excellent credit ratings from a recognized rating agency will be able to sell their _____ at a reasonable price.
a. Book building
b. Trade-off theory
c. Financial distress
d. Commercial paper

45. A _____ assesses the credit worthiness of an individual, corporation, or even a country. _____s are calculated from financial history and current assets and liabilities. Typically, a _____ tells a lender or investor the probability of the subject being able to pay back a loan.
   a. Credit cycle
   b. Debenture
   c. Credit rating
   d. Credit report monitoring

46. _____, consists of the buying and selling of products or services over electronic systems such as the Internet and other computer networks. The amount of trade conducted electronically has grown extraordinarily with widespread Internet usage. The use of commerce is conducted in this way, spurring and drawing on innovations in electronic funds transfer, supply chain management, Internet marketing, online transaction processing, electronic data interchange (EDI), inventory management systems, and automated data collection systems.
   a. Electronic commerce
   b. AAB
   c. A Random Walk Down Wall Street
   d. ABN Amro

47. In economics and related disciplines, a _____ is a cost incurred in making an economic exchange. For example, most people, when buying or selling a stock, must pay a commission to their broker; that commission is a _____ of doing the stock deal. Or consider buying a banana from a store; to purchase the banana, your costs will be not only the price of the banana itself, but also the energy and effort it requires to find out which of the various banana products you prefer, where to get them and at what price, the cost of traveling from your house to the store and back, the time waiting in line, and the effort of the paying itself; the costs above and beyond the cost of the banana are the _____s.
   a. Fixed costs
   b. Marginal cost
   c. Variable costs
   d. Transaction cost

Chapter 16. Mutual Funds, Insurance Companies, Investment Banks, and Other Financial Firms

1. In finance, a _____ is a debt security, in which the authorized issuer owes the holders a debt and, depending on the terms of the _____, is obliged to pay interest (the coupon) and/or to repay the principal at a later date, termed maturity.

Thus a _____ is a loan: the issuer is the borrower, the _____ holder is the lender, and the coupon is the interest. _____s provide the borrower with external funds to finance long-term investments, or, in the case of government _____s, to finance current expenditure.

   a. Bond
   b. Puttable bond
   c. Catastrophe bonds
   d. Convertible bond

2. A _____ is a collective investment scheme that invests in bonds and other debt securities. _____s yield monthly dividends that include interest payments on the fund's underlying securities plus any capital appreciation in the prices of the portfolio's bonds. _____s tend to pay higher dividends than CDs and money market accounts, and they generally pay out dividends more frequently and regularly than individual bonds.
   a. Premium bond
   b. Gilts
   c. Bond fund
   d. Private activity bond

3. _____ in finance is a risk management technique, related to hedging, that mixes a wide variety of investments within a portfolio. Because the fluctuations of a single security have less impact on a diverse portfolio, _____ minimizes the risk from any one investment.

A simple example of _____ is the following: On a particular island the entire economy consists of two companies: one that sells umbrellas and another that sells sunscreen.

   a. 7-Eleven
   b. 529 plan
   c. 4-4-5 Calendar
   d. Diversification

4. An _____ is a company whose main business is holding securities of other companies purely for investment purposes. The _____ invests money on behalf of its shareholders who in turn share in the profits and losses.
   a. AAB
   b. Unit investment trust
   c. A Random Walk Down Wall Street
   d. Investment company

5. A _____ is a professionally managed type of collective investment scheme that pools money from many investors and invests it in stocks, bonds, short-term money market instruments, and/or other securities. The _____ will have a fund manager that trades the pooled money on a regular basis. Currently, the worldwide value of all _____s totals more than $26 trillion.

Since 1940, there have been three basic types of investment companies in the United States: open-end funds, also known in the US as _____s; unit investment trusts (UITs); and closed-end funds.

   a. Net asset value
   b. Trust company
   c. Financial intermediary
   d. Mutual fund

Chapter 16. Mutual Funds, Insurance Companies, Investment Banks, and Other Financial Firms

6. In financial accounting, the term _____ is most commonly used to describe any part of shareholders' equity, except for basic share capital. Sometimes, the term is used instead of the term provision; such a use, however, is inconsistent with the terminology suggested by International Accounting Standards Board. For more information about provisions, see provision (accounting.)

   a. FIFO and LIFO accounting
   b. Reserve
   c. Closing entries
   d. Treasury stock

7. _____ refer to services provided by the finance industry.

   The finance industry encompasses a broad range of organizations that deal with the management of money. Among these organizations are banks, credit card companies, insurance companies, consumer finance companies, stock brokerages, investment funds and some government sponsored enterprises.

   a. Delta hedging
   b. Financial instruments
   c. Financial services
   d. Cost of carry

8. An _____ or index tracker is a collective investment scheme (usually a mutual fund or exchange-traded fund) that aims to replicate the movements of an index of a specific financial market regardless of market conditions.

   Tracking can be achieved by trying to hold all of the securities in the index, in the same proportions as the index. Other methods include statistically sampling the market and holding 'representative' securities.

   a. A Random Walk Down Wall Street
   b. AAB
   c. Investment company
   d. Index fund

9. In finance, the _____ is the global financial market for short-term borrowing and lending. It provides short-term liquidity funding for the global financial system. The _____ is where short-term obligations such as Treasury bills, commercial paper and bankers' acceptances are bought and sold.

   a. Money market
   b. Debt-for-equity swap
   c. Consumer debt
   d. Cramdown

10. Money funds (or _____, money market mutual funds) are mutual funds that invest in short-term debt instruments.

    _____, also known as principal stability funds, seek to limit exposure to losses due to credit, market and liquidity risks.
    _____, in the United States, are regulated by the Securities and Exchange Commission's (SEC) Investment Company Act of 1940.

    a. Closed-end fund
    b. Stock fund
    c. Mutual fund fees and expenses
    d. Money market funds

11. A _____ is a method of measuring a section of the stock market. Many indices are cited by news or financial services firms and are used to benchmark the performance of portfolios such as mutual funds.

    a. Stop order
    b. Program trading
    c. Trading curb
    d. Stock market index

Chapter 16. Mutual Funds, Insurance Companies, Investment Banks, and Other Financial Firms

12. A _____ or equity fund is a fund that invests in Equities more commonly known as stocks. Such funds are typically held either in stock or cash, as opposed to Bonds, notes, or other securities. This may be a mutual fund or exchange-traded fund.
    a. Money market funds
    b. Mutual fund fees and expenses
    c. Stock fund
    d. Closed-end fund

13. _____ also known as Deferred Sales Charge, is a fee paid when shares are sold. This fee typically goes to the brokers that sell the fund's shares. The amount of this type of load will depend on how long the investor holds his or her shares and typically decreases to zero if the investor holds his or her shares long enough.
    a. Closed-end fund
    b. Money market funds
    c. Mutual fund fees and expenses
    d. Back-end load

14. In economics, business, and accounting, a _____ is the value of money that has been used up to produce something, and hence is not available for use anymore. In business, the _____ may be one of acquisition, in which case the amount of money expended to acquire it is counted as _____. In this case, money is the input that is gone in order to acquire the thing.
    a. Sliding scale fees
    b. Marginal cost
    c. Cost
    d. Fixed costs

15. An _____ is an investment vehicle traded on stock exchanges, much like stocks. An ETF holds assets such as stocks or bonds and trades at approximately the same price as the net asset value of its underlying assets over the course of the trading day. Most ETFs track an index, such as the Dow Jones Industrial Average or the S'P 500.
    a. AAB
    b. A Random Walk Down Wall Street
    c. ABN Amro
    d. Exchange-traded fund

16. In business and finance, a _____ (also referred to as equity _____) of stock means a _____ of ownership in a corporation (company.) In the plural, stocks is often used as a synonym for _____s especially in the United States, but it is less commonly used that way outside of North America.

    In the United Kingdom, South Africa, and Australia, stock can also refer to completely different financial instruments such as government bonds or, less commonly, to all kinds of marketable securities.

    a. Margin
    b. Bucket shop
    c. Procter ' Gamble
    d. Share

17. A _____, securities exchange or (in Europe) bourse is a corporation or mutual organization which provides 'trading' facilities for stock brokers and traders, to trade stocks and other securities. _____s also provide facilities for the issue and redemption of securities as well as other financial instruments and capital events including the payment of income and dividends. The securities traded on a _____ include: shares issued by companies, unit trusts and other pooled investment products and bonds.
    a. 529 plan
    b. 7-Eleven
    c. 4-4-5 Calendar
    d. Stock Exchange

18. The _____ of an asset is the return obtained from holding it (if positive), or the cost of holding it (if negative)

Chapter 16. Mutual Funds, Insurance Companies, Investment Banks, and Other Financial Firms

For instance, commodities are usually negative _____ assets, as they incur storage costs, but in some circumstances, commodities can be positive _____ assets as the market is willing to pay a premium for availability.

This can also refer to a trade with more than one leg, where you earn the spread between borrowing a low _____ asset and lending a high _____ one.

a. Financial assistance
c. Cramdown
b. Bankruptcy remote
d. Carry

19. In finance, a _____ is a position established in one market in an attempt to offset exposure to the price risk of an equal but opposite obligation or position in another market -- usually, but not always, in the context of one's commercial activity. Hedging is a strategy designed to minimize exposure to such business risks as a sharp contraction in demand for one's inventory, while still allowing the business to profit from producing and maintaining that inventory. A typical hedger might be a farmer with 2000 acres of unharvested wheat in the ground, who would rather tend his crop without the distraction of uncertain prices.

a. 7-Eleven
c. Hedge
b. 529 plan
d. 4-4-5 Calendar

20. A _____ is a private investment fund open to a limited range of investors that is permitted by regulators to undertake a wider range of activities than other investment funds and also pays a performance fee to its investment manager. Each fund will have its own strategy which determines the type of investments and the methods of investment it undertakes. _____s as a class invest in a broad range of investments extending over shares, debt, commodities and beyond.

a. 7-Eleven
c. 4-4-5 Calendar
b. 529 plan
d. Hedge fund

21. _____ is the difference between a lower selling price and a higher purchase price, resulting in a financial loss for the seller. Pursuant to IRS TAX TIP 2009-35 'If your _____ exceeds your capital gain, the excess can be deducted on your tax return, up to an annual limit of $3,000 ($1,500 if you are married filing separately.)' .

a. 7-Eleven
c. 4-4-5 Calendar
b. 529 plan
d. Capital loss

22. A _____ is a financial contract whose value is derived from the value of something else (known as the underlying.) The underlying on which a _____ is based can be an asset, weather conditions bonds or other forms of credit.

a. 529 plan
c. Derivative
b. 4-4-5 Calendar
d. 7-Eleven

23. A _____ is a futures contract on a short term interest rate (STIR.) Contracts vary, but are often defined on an interest rate index such as 3-month sterling or US dollar LIBOR.

They are traded across a wide range of currencies, including the G12 country currencies and many others.

a. Financial future
b. Real estate derivatives
c. Notional amount
d. Dual currency deposit

24. _____, refers to consumption opportunity gained by an entity within a specified time frame, which is generally expressed in monetary terms. However, for households and individuals, '_____ is the sum of all the wages, salaries, profits, interests payments, rents and other forms of earnings received... in a given period of time.' For firms, _____ generally refers to net-profit: what remains of revenue after expenses have been subtracted.

a. Income
b. Accrual
c. OIBDA
d. Annual report

25. An _____ is a contract written by a seller that conveys to the buyer the right -- but not the obligation -- to buy (in the case of a call _____) or to sell (in the case of a put _____) a particular asset, such as a piece of property such as, among others, a futures contract. In return for granting the _____, the seller collects a payment (the premium) from the buyer.

For example, buying a call _____ provides the right to buy a specified quantity of a security at a set strike price at some time on or before expiration, while buying a put _____ provides the right to sell.

a. Amortization
b. AT'T Mobility LLC
c. Annuity
d. Option

26. An _____ is defined as 'a promise which meets the requirements for the formation of a contract and limits the promisor's power to revoke an offer.' Restatement (Second) of Contracts § 25 (1981.)

Quite simply, an _____ is a type of contract that protects an offeree from an offeror's ability to revoke the contract.

Consideration for the _____ is still required as it is still a form of contract.

a. AAB
b. Option contract
c. ABN Amro
d. A Random Walk Down Wall Street

27. A _____ is an exchange of promises between two or more parties to do an act which is enforceable in a court of law. It is where an unqualified offer meets a qualified acceptance and the parties reach Consensus ad Idem. The parties must have the necessary capacity to _____ and the _____ must not be either trifling, indeterminate, impossible or illegal.

a. 4-4-5 Calendar
b. 7-Eleven
c. 529 plan
d. Contract

28. In finance, a _____ is a standardized contract, to buy or sell a specified commodity of standardized quality at a certain date in the future, at a market determined price (the futures price.)

The price is determined by the instantaneous equilibrium between the forces of supply and demand among competing buy and sell orders on the exchange at the time of the purchase or sale of the contract.

Chapter 16. Mutual Funds, Insurance Companies, Investment Banks, and Other Financial Firms

In many cases, the items may be such non-traditional 'commodities' as foreign currencies, commercial or government paper [e.g., bonds], or 'baskets' of corporate equity ['stock indices'] or other financial instruments.

a. Financial future
b. Heston model
c. Repurchase agreement
d. Futures contract

29. _____ is trading executed after the standard local national exchanges have closed. This is distinct from after-hours trading, as they have in context specific meanings, the former may be illegal while the latter is legal.

In the mutual fund context, _____ involves placing orders for mutual fund shares after the close of the stock market, 4:00 p.m for the New York Stock Exchange, but still getting that day's closing price, rather than the next day's opening price.

a. Divestment
b. Certificate in Investment Performance Measurement
c. Tactical asset allocation
d. Late trading

30. _____ is the strategy of making buy or sell decisions of financial assets (often stocks) by attempting to predict future market price movements. The prediction may be based on an outlook of market or economic conditions resulting from technical or fundamental analysis. This is an investment strategy based on the outlook for an aggregate market, rather than for a particular financial asset.

a. Market timing
b. Divestment
c. Portable alpha
d. Late trading

31. In economics, a _____ is a type of retirement plan in which the amount of the employer's annual contribution is specified. Individual accounts are set up for participants and benefits are based on the amounts credited to these accounts (through employer contributions and, if applicable, employee contributions) plus any investment earnings on the money in the account. Only employer contributions to the account are guaranteed, not the future benefits. In _____s, future benefits fluctuate on the basis of investment earnings.

a. Fixed asset turnover
b. Capital costs
c. Total revenue
d. Defined contribution plan

32. A _____ is a pool of assets forming an independent legal entity that are bought with the contributions to a pension plan for the exclusive purpose of financing pension plan benefits.

_____s are important shareholders of listed and private companies. They are especially important to the stock market where large institutional investors like the Ontario Teachers' Pension Plan dominate.

a. Leverage
b. Limited liability company
c. Leveraged buyout
d. Pension fund

33. In business and accounting, _____s are everything of value that is owned by a person or company. The balance sheet of a firm records the monetary value of the _____s owned by the firm. The two major _____ classes are tangible _____s and intangible _____s.

Chapter 16. Mutual Funds, Insurance Companies, Investment Banks, and Other Financial Firms

a. Accounts payable
b. EBITDA
c. Income
d. Asset

34. The institution most often referenced by the word '_____' is a public or publicly traded _____, the shares of which are traded on a public stock exchange (e.g., the New York Stock Exchange or Nasdaq in the United States) where shares of stock of _____s are bought and sold by and to the general public. Most of the largest businesses in the world are publicly traded _____s. However, the majority of _____s are said to be closely held, privately held or close _____s, meaning that no ready market exists for the trading of shares.

a. Depository Trust Company
b. Protect
c. Federal Home Loan Mortgage Corporation
d. Corporation

35.

A _____ is a type of financial intermediary and a type of bank. Commercial banking is also known as business banking. It is a bank that provides checking accounts, savings accounts, and money market accounts and that accepts time deposits.

a. 4-4-5 Calendar
b. 7-Eleven
c. Commercial bank
d. 529 plan

36. The role of the _____ is to issue accounting standards in the United Kingdom. It is recognised for that purpose under the Companies Act 1985. It took over the task of setting accounting standards from the Accounting Standards Committee (ASC) in 1990.

a. A Random Walk Down Wall Street
b. AAB
c. Accounting Standards Board
d. ABN Amro

37. The _____ of 1974 (Pub.L. 93-406, 88 Stat. 829, enacted September 2, 1974) is an American federal statute that establishes minimum standards for pension plans in private industry and provides for extensive rules on the federal income tax effects of transactions associated with employee benefit plans.

a. Articles of Partnership
b. Expedited Funds Availability Act
c. Express warranty
d. Employee Retirement Income Security Act

38. The _____ is a private, not-for-profit organization whose primary purpose is to develop generally accepted accounting principles (GAAP) within the United States in the public's interest. The Securities and Exchange Commission (SEC) designated the _____ as the organization responsible for setting accounting standards for public companies in the U.S. It was created in 1973, replacing the Accounting Principles Board and the Committee on Accounting Procedure of the American Institute of Certified Public Accountants. The _____'s mission is 'to establish and improve standards of financial accounting and reporting for the guidance and education of the public, including issuers, auditors, and users of financial information.'

The _____ is not a governmental body.

a. MRU Holdings
b. PlaNet Finance
c. Credit karma
d. FASB

Chapter 16. Mutual Funds, Insurance Companies, Investment Banks, and Other Financial Firms

39. _____ is the field of accountancy concerned with the preparation of financial statements for decision makers, such as stockholders, suppliers, banks, employees, government agencies, owners, and other stakeholders. The fundamental need for _____ is to reduce principal-agent problem by measuring and monitoring agents' performance and reporting the results to interested users.

_____ is used to prepare accounting information for people outside the organization or not involved in the day to day running of the company.

a. 7-Eleven
b. 529 plan
c. Financial Accounting
d. 4-4-5 Calendar

40. The _____ is a private, not-for-profit organization whose primary purpose is to develop generally accepted accounting principles (GAAP) within the United States in the public's interest. The Securities and Exchange Commission (SEC) designated the _____ as the organization responsible for setting accounting standards for public companies in the U.S. It was created in 1973, replacing the Accounting Principles Board and the Committee on Accounting Procedure of the American Institute of Certified Public Accountants. The _____'s mission is 'to establish and improve standards of financial accounting and reporting for the guidance and education of the public, including issuers, auditors, and users of financial information.'

The _____ is not a governmental body.

a. KPMG
b. World Congress of Accountants
c. Financial Accounting Standards Board
d. Federal Deposit Insurance Corporation

41. A _____ is a fungible, negotiable instrument representing financial value. They are broadly categorized into debt securities (such as banknotes, bonds and debentures), and equity securities; e.g., common stocks. The company or other entity issuing the _____ is called the issuer.

a. Security
b. Book entry
c. Securities lending
d. Tracking stock

42. _____ is a legally declared inability or impairment of ability of an individual or organization to pay their creditors. Creditors may file a _____ petition against a debtor ('involuntary _____') in an effort to recoup a portion of what they are owed or initiate a restructuring. In the majority of cases, however, _____ is initiated by the debtor (a 'voluntary _____' that is filed by the bankrupt individual or organization.)

a. 529 plan
b. Bankruptcy
c. Debt settlement
d. 4-4-5 Calendar

43. An _____ can be defined as a contract which provides an income stream in return for an initial payment.

An immediate _____ is an _____ for which the time between the contract date and the date of the first payment is not longer than the time interval between payments. A common use for an immediate _____ is to provide a pension to a retired person or persons.

a. Amortization
b. AT'T Inc.
c. Intrinsic value
d. Annuity

Chapter 16. Mutual Funds, Insurance Companies, Investment Banks, and Other Financial Firms

44. _____s are full-fledged pension plans for self-employed people in the United States. They are sometimes called HR10 plans and are not Individual Retirement Accounts (IRA.)

Since a _____ is a full-fledged pension, there is a Keogh for every employer-sponsored pension-plan design.

a. 7-Eleven
b. 4-4-5 Calendar
c. Keogh plan
d. 529 plan

45. _____, in bookkeeping, refers to assets, liabilities, income, and expenses recorded on individual pages of the so called book of final entry or ledger. Changes in _____ value are made by chronologically posting debit (DR) and credit (CR) entries to its page. Examples of _____s are cash, _____s receivable, mortgages, loans, land and buildings, common stock, sales, services provided, wages, and payroll overhead.

a. Option
b. Alpha
c. Accretion
d. Account

46. A _____ is a bond issued by a corporation. The term is usually applied to longer-term debt instruments, generally with a maturity date falling at least a year after their issue date. (The term 'commercial paper' is sometimes used for instruments with a shorter maturity.)

a. Brady bonds
b. Government bond
c. Serial bond
d. Corporate bond

47. In finance, a _____ (non-investment grade bond, speculative grade bond or junk bond) is a bond that is rated below investment grade at the time of purchase. These bonds have a higher risk of default or other adverse credit events, but typically pay higher yields than better quality bonds in order to make them attractive to investors.

a. Sharpe ratio
b. Volatility
c. High yield bond
d. Private equity

48. The _____ is the market for securities, where companies and governments can raise longterm funds. The _____ includes the stock market and the bond market. Financial regulators, such as the U.S. Securities and Exchange Commission, oversee the _____s in their designated countries to ensure that investors are protected against fraud.

a. Capital market
b. Delta neutral
c. Spot rate
d. Forward market

49. _____ is a life insurance policy that remains in force for the insured's whole life and requires (in most cases) premiums to be paid every year into the policy.

All life insurance was originally term insurance. However, because term life insurance only pays a claim upon death within the stated term, most term insurance policy holders became upset over the idea that they could be paying premiums for 20 or 30 years and then wind up with nothing to show for it.

a. Whole life insurance
b. 529 plan
c. 4-4-5 Calendar
d. Term life insurance

Chapter 16. Mutual Funds, Insurance Companies, Investment Banks, and Other Financial Firms

50. _____, in accrual accounting, is any account where the asset or liability is not realized until a future date, e.g. annuities, charges, taxes, income, etc. The _____ item may be carried, dependent on type of deferral, as either an asset or liability. See also: accrual

_____ is also used in the university admissions process. It is the action by which a school rejects a student for early admission but still opts to review that student in the general admissions pool.

- a. Revenue
- b. Net profit
- c. Current asset
- d. Deferred

51. _____ is a type of permanent life insurance based on a cash value. That is, the policy is established with the insurer where premium payments above the cost of insurance are credited to the cash value. The cash value is credited each month with interest, and the policy is debited each month by a cost of insurance (COI) charge, and any other policy charges and fees which are drawn from the cash value if no premium payment is made that month.

- a. A Random Walk Down Wall Street
- b. AAB
- c. ABN Amro
- d. Universal life

52. _____ is a type of private equity capital typically provided to early-stage, high-potential, growth companies in the interest of generating a return through an eventual realization event such as an IPO or trade sale of the company. _____ investments are generally made as cash in exchange for shares in the invested company. It is typical for _____ investors to identify and back companies in high technology industries such as biotechnology and ICT.

- a. Tail risk
- b. Treasury Inflation-Protected Securities
- c. Probability distribution
- d. Venture capital

53. _____ are similar to certificates of deposit that can be purchased at banks; however, they are sold by insurance companies. Like money market funds, they're very safe investments; and like all investments that are considered to be 'very safe', they won't make you very much money. Also known by other names - fixed-income fund, stable value fund, capital-preservation fund, or guaranteed fund, for example -- they generally pay interest from one- to five years.

- a. CODA plc
- b. Reputational risk
- c. Vati-Con
- d. Guaranteed investment contracts

54. _____ is a fee paid on borrowed assets. It is the price paid for the use of borrowed money, or, money earned by deposited funds. Assets that are sometimes lent with _____ include money, shares, consumer goods through hire purchase, major assets such as aircraft, and even entire factories in finance lease arrangements.

- a. AAB
- b. A Random Walk Down Wall Street
- c. Insolvency
- d. Interest

55. An _____ is the price a borrower pays for the use of money they do not own, and the return a lender receives for deferring the use of funds, by lending it to the borrower. _____s are normally expressed as a percentage rate over the period of one year.

_____s targets are also a vital tool of monetary policy and are used to control variables like investment, inflation, and unemployment.

Chapter 16. Mutual Funds, Insurance Companies, Investment Banks, and Other Financial Firms

a. ABN Amro
b. AAB
c. A Random Walk Down Wall Street
d. Interest rate

56. _____ is the risk (variability in value) borne by an interest-bearing asset, such as a loan or a bond, due to variability of interest rates. In general, as rates rise, the price of a fixed rate bond will fall, and vice versa. _____ is commonly measured by the bond's duration.

a. A Random Walk Down Wall Street
b. Interest rate risk
c. International Fisher effect
d. Official bank rate

57. _____ are risk-linked securities that transfer a specified set of risks from a sponsor to investors. They are often structured as floating rate corporate bonds whose principal is forgiven if specified trigger conditions are met. They are typically used by insurers as an alternative to traditional catastrophe reinsurance.

a. Brady bonds
b. Callable bond
c. Clean price
d. Catastrophe bonds

58. _____ is the provision of resources (such as granting a loan) by one party to another party where that second party does not reimburse the first party immediately, thereby generating a debt, and instead arranges either to repay or return those resources (or material(s) of equal value) at a later date. The first party is called a creditor, also known as a lender, while the second party is called a debtor, also known as a borrower.

Movements of financial capital are normally dependent on either _____ or equity transfers.

a. Warrant
b. Credit
c. Comparable
d. Clearing house

59. In the United States, _____ is the function of offering loans to businesses. Commercial financing is generally offered by a bank or other lender. Most commercial banks offer commercial financing, and the loans are either secured by business assets or alternatively can be unsecured, where the lender relies of the cash flows of the business to repay the facility.

a. Bonus share
b. Normative economics
c. Volatility clustering
d. Commercial finance

60. The _____ (NYSE: FRE) is an insolvent government sponsored enterprise (GSE) of the United States federal government.

The _____ was created in 1970 to expand the secondary market for mortgages in the US. Along with other GSEs, Freddie Mac buys mortgages on the secondary market, pools them, and sells them as mortgage-backed securities to investors on the open market.

a. Public company
b. The Depository Trust ' Clearing Corporation
c. Governmental Accounting Standards Board
d. Federal Home Loan Mortgage Corporation

61. The _____ (NYSE: FNM), commonly known as Fannie Mae, is a stockholder-owned corporation chartered by Congress in 1968 as a government sponsored enterprise (GSE), but founded in 1938 during the Great Depression. The corporation's purpose is to purchase and securitize mortgages in order to ensure that funds are consistently available to the institutions that lend money to home buyers.

Chapter 16. Mutual Funds, Insurance Companies, Investment Banks, and Other Financial Firms

On September 7, 2008, James Lockhart, director of the Federal Housing Finance Agency (FHFA), announced that Fannie Mae and Freddie Mac were being placed into conservatorship of the FHFA.

a. SPDR
b. The Depository Trust ' Clearing Corporation
c. Federal National Mortgage Association
d. General partnership

62. A car _____, or simply _____, is a loan where the borrower provides their car title as collateral for a loan.

These loans are typically short-term, and tend to carry higher interest rates than other sources of credit. These loans have higher interest rates than other sources of credit due to the fact that the lender typically does not check credit and that the only consideration for the loan is the value and condition of the vehicle.

a. Title loan
b. Promissory note
c. Financial plan
d. Credit repair software

63. The _____ is a U.S. government-owned corporation within the Department of Housing and Urban Development

Ginnie Mae provides guarantees on mortgage-backed securities backed by federally insured or guaranteed loans, mainly loans issued by the Federal Housing Administration, Department of Veterans Affairs, Rural Housing Service, and Office of Public and Indian Housing. Ginnie Mae securities are the only MBS that are guaranteed by the United States government.

a. Cash budget
b. GNMA
c. Case-Shiller Home Price Indices
d. Certified Emission Reductions

64. The _____ Act is an Act of the 106th United States Congress which repealed part of the Glass-Steagall Act of 1933, opening up competition among banks, securities companies and insurance companies. The Glass-Steagall Act prohibited any one institution from acting as both an investment bank and a commercial bank, or as both a bank and an insurer.

The _____ Act (GLBA) allowed commercial and investment banks to consolidate.

a. Gramm-Leach-Bliley
b. 4-4-5 Calendar
c. 7-Eleven
d. 529 plan

65. _____ refers to the likelihood that changes in the business environment adversely affect operating profits or the value of assets in a specific country. For example, financial factors such as currency controls, devaluation or regulatory changes, or stability factors such as mass riots, civil war and other potential events contribute to companies' operational risks. This term is also sometimes referred to as political risk, however _____ is a more general term, which generally only refers to risks affecting all companies operating within a particular country.

a. Single-index model
b. Solvency
c. Capital asset
d. Country risk

Chapter 16. Mutual Funds, Insurance Companies, Investment Banks, and Other Financial Firms

66. The _____ provide stable, on-demand, low-cost funding to American financial institutions for home mortgage loans, small business, rural, agricultural, and economic development lending. With their members, the _____ank System represents the largest collective source of home mortgage and community credit in the United States. The banks do not provide loans directly to individuals, only to other banks.
   a. 7-Eleven
   c. 4-4-5 Calendar
   b. Federal Home Loan Banks
   d. 529 plan

67. A _____ or bank is a financial institution whose primary activity is to act as a payment agent for customers and to borrow and lend money.

The first modern bank was founded in Italy in Genoa in 1406, its name was Banco di San Giorgio (Bank of St. George.)

Many other financial activities were added over time.
   a. Black Sea Trade and Development Bank
   c. 4-4-5 Calendar
   b. Bought deal
   d. Banker

68. _____ or amalgamation is the act of merging many things into one. In business, it often refers to the mergers or acquisitions of many smaller companies into much larger ones. The financial accounting term of _____ refers to the aggregated financial statements of a group company as consolidated account.
   a. Retained earnings
   c. Write-off
   b. Cost of goods sold
   d. Consolidation

69. _____ is a process by which a firm can obtain the use of a certain fixed assets for which it must pay a series of contractual, periodic, tax deductable payments. The lessee is the receiver of the services or the assets under the lease contract and the lessor is the owner of the assets. The relationship between the tenant and the landlord is called a tenancy, and can be for a fixed or an indefinite period of time (called the term of the lease).
   a. Royalties
   c. Quiet period
   b. Leasing
   d. Foreign Corrupt Practices Act

70. A _____ is a tax designation for a corporation investing in real estate that reduces or eliminates corporate income taxes. In return, _____s are required to distribute 95% of their income, which may be taxable in the hands of the investors. The _____ structure was designed to provide a similar structure for investment in real estate as mutual funds provide for investment in stocks.
   a. REIT
   c. Liquidation value
   b. Real estate investing
   d. Real Estate Investment Trust

71. A _____ or _____ is a tax designation for a corporation investing in real estate that reduces or eliminates corporate income taxes. In return, _____s are required to distribute 95% of their income, which may be taxable in the hands of the investors. The _____ structure was designed to provide a similar structure for investment in real estate as mutual funds provide for investment in stocks.
   a. Tenancy
   c. Liquidation value
   b. Real estate investing
   d. Real estate investment trust

Chapter 16. Mutual Funds, Insurance Companies, Investment Banks, and Other Financial Firms

72. _____ is the removal or simplification of government rules and regulations that constrain the operation of market forces. _____ does not mean elimination of laws against fraud, but eliminating or reducing government control of how business is done, thereby moving toward a more free market.

The stated rationale for '_____' is often that fewer and simpler regulations will lead to a raised level of competitiveness, therefore higher productivity, more efficiency and lower prices overall.

a. Value added
c. Supply shock
b. Demand shock
d. Deregulation

73. In economics, a _____ is a mechanism that allows people to easily buy and sell (trade) financial securities (such as stocks and bonds), commodities (such as precious metals or agricultural goods), and other fungible items of value at low transaction costs and at prices that reflect the efficient-market hypothesis.

_____s have evolved significantly over several hundred years and are undergoing constant innovation to improve liquidity.

Both general markets (where many commodities are traded) and specialized markets (where only one commodity is traded) exist.

a. Delta hedging
c. Cost of carry
b. Secondary market
d. Financial market

Chapter 17. Regulation of the Financial Institutions' Sector

1. The institution most often referenced by the word '_____' is a public or publicly traded _____, the shares of which are traded on a public stock exchange (e.g., the New York Stock Exchange or Nasdaq in the United States) where shares of stock of _____s are bought and sold by and to the general public. Most of the largest businesses in the world are publicly traded _____s. However, the majority of _____s are said to be closely held, privately held or close _____s, meaning that no ready market exists for the trading of shares.
   a. Corporation
   b. Protect
   c. Federal Home Loan Mortgage Corporation
   d. Depository Trust Company

2. Explicit _____ is a measure implemented in many countries to protect bank depositors, in full or in part, from losses caused by a bank's inability to pay its debts when due. _____ systems are one component of a financial system safety net that promotes financial stability.
   a. Reserve requirement
   b. Banking panic
   c. Time deposit
   d. Deposit Insurance

3. The _____ is a United States government corporation created by the Glass-Steagall Act of 1933. It provides deposit insurance, which guarantees the safety of checking and savings deposits in member banks, currently up to $250,000 per depositor per bank. Insured deposits are backed by the full faith and credit of the United States.
   a. FASB
   b. Ford Foundation
   c. Federal Deposit Insurance Corporation
   d. NYSE Group

4. In financial accounting, the term _____ is most commonly used to describe any part of shareholders' equity, except for basic share capital. Sometimes, the term is used instead of the term provision; such a use, however, is inconsistent with the terminology suggested by International Accounting Standards Board. For more information about provisions, see provision (accounting.)
   a. FIFO and LIFO accounting
   b. Closing entries
   c. Treasury stock
   d. Reserve

5. _____ is the provision of resources (such as granting a loan) by one party to another party where that second party does not reimburse the first party immediately, thereby generating a debt, and instead arranges either to repay or return those resources (or material(s) of equal value) at a later date. The first party is called a creditor, also known as a lender, while the second party is called a debtor, also known as a borrower.

   Movements of financial capital are normally dependent on either _____ or equity transfers.

   a. Warrant
   b. Clearing house
   c. Comparable
   d. Credit

6. _____ is the removal or simplification of government rules and regulations that constrain the operation of market forces. _____ does not mean elimination of laws against fraud, but eliminating or reducing government control of how business is done, thereby moving toward a more free market.

   The stated rationale for '_____' is often that fewer and simpler regulations will lead to a raised level of competitiveness, therefore higher productivity, more efficiency and lower prices overall.

   a. Supply shock
   b. Demand shock
   c. Value added
   d. Deregulation

Chapter 17. Regulation of the Financial Institutions' Sector

7. In economics, business, and accounting, a _____ is the value of money that has been used up to produce something, and hence is not available for use anymore. In business, the _____ may be one of acquisition, in which case the amount of money expended to acquire it is counted as _____. In this case, money is the input that is gone in order to acquire the thing.
   a. Sliding scale fees
   b. Fixed costs
   c. Marginal cost
   d. Cost

8. _____ are defined as a crime against property, involving the unlawful conversion of property belonging to another to one's own personal use and benefit. _____ often involve fraud.

   _____ are carried out via check and credit card fraud, mortgage fraud, medical fraud, corporate fraud, bank account fraud, payment (point of sale) fraud, currency fraud, and health care fraud, and they involve acts such as insider trading, tax violations, kickbacks, embezzlement, identity theft, cyber attacks, money laundering, and social engineering.

   a. 4-4-5 Calendar
   b. Financial crimes
   c. 7-Eleven
   d. 529 plan

9. In the United States, _____ are overnight borrowings by banks to maintain their bank reserves at the Federal Reserve. Banks keep reserves at Federal Reserve Banks to meet their reserve requirements and to clear financial transactions. Transactions in the _____ market enable depository institutions with reserve balances in excess of reserve requirements to lend reserves to institutions with reserve deficiencies.
   a. Regulation T
   b. Federal funds rate
   c. 4-4-5 Calendar
   d. Federal funds

10. A _____ is a cooperative financial institution that is owned and controlled by its members, and operated for the purpose of promoting thrift, providing credit at reasonable rates, and providing other financial services to its members. Many _____s exist to further community development or sustainable international development on a local level. Worldwide, _____ systems vary significantly in terms of total system assets and average institution asset size since _____s exist in a wide range of sizes, ranging from volunteer operations with a handful of members to institutions with several billion dollars in assets and hundreds of thousands of members.
    a. Credit Union Service Organization
    b. Corporate credit union
    c. Credit Union
    d. Fi-linx

11. _____ or amalgamation is the act of merging many things into one. In business, it often refers to the mergers or acquisitions of many smaller companies into much larger ones. The financial accounting term of _____ refers to the aggregated financial statements of a group company as consolidated account.
    a. Cost of goods sold
    b. Retained earnings
    c. Write-off
    d. Consolidation

12. A _____ is a company that owns other companies' outstanding stock. It usually refers to a company which does not produce goods or services itself, rather its only purpose is owning shares of other companies. They allow the reduction of risk for the owners and can allow the ownership and control of a number of different companies.
    a. Privately held company
    b. Holding company
    c. MRU Holdings
    d. Federal National Mortgage Association

Chapter 17. Regulation of the Financial Institutions' Sector

13. The phrase _____ refers to the aspect of corporate strategy, corporate finance and management dealing with the buying, selling and combining of different companies that can aid, finance, or help a growing company in a given industry grow rapidly without having to create another business entity.

An acquisition, also known as a takeover, is the buying of one company (the 'target') by another. An acquisition may be friendly or hostile.

a. 7-Eleven
b. 529 plan
c. 4-4-5 Calendar
d. Mergers and acquisitions

14.

A _____ is a type of financial intermediary and a type of bank. Commercial banking is also known as business banking. It is a bank that provides checking accounts, savings accounts, and money market accounts and that accepts time deposits.

a. 7-Eleven
b. 529 plan
c. Commercial bank
d. 4-4-5 Calendar

15. The _____ is a U.S. government-owned corporation within the Department of Housing and Urban Development

Ginnie Mae provides guarantees on mortgage-backed securities backed by federally insured or guaranteed loans, mainly loans issued by the Federal Housing Administration, Department of Veterans Affairs, Rural Housing Service, and Office of Public and Indian Housing. Ginnie Mae securities are the only MBS that are guaranteed by the United States government.

a. Certified Emission Reductions
b. Cash budget
c. GNMA
d. Case-Shiller Home Price Indices

16. A _____ or bank is a financial institution whose primary activity is to act as a payment agent for customers and to borrow and lend money.

The first modern bank was founded in Italy in Genoa in 1406, its name was Banco di San Giorgio (Bank of St. George.)

Many other financial activities were added over time.

a. Bought deal
b. Black Sea Trade and Development Bank
c. 4-4-5 Calendar
d. Banker

17. _____ refer to services provided by the finance industry.

The finance industry encompasses a broad range of organizations that deal with the management of money. Among these organizations are banks, credit card companies, insurance companies, consumer finance companies, stock brokerages, investment funds and some government sponsored enterprises.

Chapter 17. Regulation of the Financial Institutions` Sector

a. Delta hedging
c. Financial instruments
b. Cost of carry
d. Financial Services

18. The _____ Act is an Act of the 106th United States Congress which repealed part of the Glass-Steagall Act of 1933, opening up competition among banks, securities companies and insurance companies. The Glass-Steagall Act prohibited any one institution from acting as both an investment bank and a commercial bank, or as both a bank and an insurer.

The _____ Act (GLBA) allowed commercial and investment banks to consolidate.

a. 4-4-5 Calendar
c. 529 plan
b. 7-Eleven
d. Gramm-Leach-Bliley

19. A _____ is a fungible, negotiable instrument representing financial value. They are broadly categorized into debt securities (such as banknotes, bonds and debentures), and equity securities; e.g., common stocks. The company or other entity issuing the _____ is called the issuer.

a. Security
c. Tracking stock
b. Securities lending
d. Book entry

20. The _____ of 1968 is a United States federal law designed to protect consumers in credit transactions, by requiring clear disclosure of key terms of the lending arrangement and all costs. The statute is contained in Title I of the Consumer Credit Protection Act, as amended (15 U.S.C. Â§ 1601 et seq.).

a. Fair Credit Billing Act
c. Truth in Lending Act
b. Fair Credit Reporting Act
d. Regulation Q

21. _____ is a fee paid on borrowed assets. It is the price paid for the use of borrowed money , or, money earned by deposited funds . Assets that are sometimes lent with _____ include money, shares, consumer goods through hire purchase, major assets such as aircraft, and even entire factories in finance lease arrangements.

a. Insolvency
c. Interest
b. A Random Walk Down Wall Street
d. AAB

22. An _____ is the price a borrower pays for the use of money they do not own, and the return a lender receives for deferring the use of funds, by lending it to the borrower. _____s are normally expressed as a percentage rate over the period of one year.

_____s targets are also a vital tool of monetary policy and are used to control variables like investment, inflation, and unemployment.

a. AAB
c. ABN Amro
b. Interest rate
d. A Random Walk Down Wall Street

23. _____ is the risk (variability in value) borne by an interest-bearing asset, such as a loan or a bond, due to variability of interest rates. In general, as rates rise, the price of a fixed rate bond will fall, and vice versa. _____ is commonly measured by the bond's duration.

a. Official bank rate
b. International Fisher effect
c. Interest rate risk
d. A Random Walk Down Wall Street

24. The _____ of 2002 (Pub.L. 107-204, 116 Stat. 745, enacted July 30, 2002), also known as the Public Company Accounting Reform and Investor Protection Act of 2002 and commonly called Sarbanes-Oxley, Sarbox or SOX, is a United States federal law enacted on July 30, 2002 in response to a number of major corporate and accounting scandals including those affecting Enron, Tyco International, Adelphia, Peregrine Systems and WorldCom.
  a. Foreign Corrupt Practices Act
  b. Blue sky law
  c. Duty of loyalty
  d. Sarbanes-Oxley Act

25. The _____ of 1934 is a law governing the secondary trading of securities (stocks, bonds, and debentures) in the United States of America. The Act, 48 Stat. 881 (enacted June 6, 1934), codified at 15 U.S.C. § 78a et seq., was a sweeping piece of legislation. The Act and related statutes form the basis of regulation of the financial markets and their participants in the United States.
  a. 7-Eleven
  b. 529 plan
  c. 4-4-5 Calendar
  d. Securities Exchange Act

26. _____ is the risk of loss due to a debtor's non-payment of a loan or other line of credit (either the principal or interest (coupon) or both)

Most lenders employ their own models (credit scorecards) to rank potential and existing customers according to risk, and then apply appropriate strategies. With products such as unsecured personal loans or mortgages, lenders charge a higher price for higher risk customers and vice versa. With revolving products such as credit cards and overdrafts, risk is controlled through careful setting of credit limits.

  a. Liquidity risk
  b. Market risk
  c. Credit risk
  d. Transaction risk

27. _____ is the risk that the value of an investment will decrease due to moves in market factors. The five standard _____ factors are:

  - Equity risk, the risk that stock prices will change.
  - Interest rate risk, the risk that interest rates will change.
  - Currency risk, the risk that foreign exchange rates will change.
  - Commodity risk, the risk that commodity prices (e.g. grains, metals) will change.

As with other forms of risk, _____ may be measured in a number of ways. Traditionally, this is done using a Value at Risk methodology. Value at risk is well established as a risk management technique, but it contains a number of limiting assumptions that constrain its accuracy.

  a. Transaction risk
  b. Market risk
  c. Currency risk
  d. Tracking error

28. An _____ is a risk arising from execution of a company's business functions. As such, it is a very broad concept including e.g. fraud risks, legal risks, physical or environmental risks, etc. The term _____ is most commonly found in risk management programs of financial institutions that must organize their risk management program according to Basel II.

Chapter 17. Regulation of the Financial Institutions` Sector

a. ABN Amro
c. A Random Walk Down Wall Street
b. Operational risk
d. AAB

29. _____ is the discipline of identifying, monitoring and limiting risks. In some cases the acceptable risk may be near zero. Risks can come from accidents, natural causes and disasters as well as deliberate attacks from an adversary.
  a. Penny stock
  c. FIFO
  b. 4-4-5 Calendar
  d. Risk management

30. In finance, _____ refers to quote and trade related-data associated with equity, fixed-income, financial derivatives, currency, and other investment instruments. The term _____ traditionally refers to numerical price data, reported from trading venues, such as stock exchanges. The price data is attached to a ticker symbol and additional data about the trade.
  a. 7-Eleven
  c. 4-4-5 Calendar
  b. 529 plan
  d. Market data

31. A _____ is a financial institution that specializes in accepting savings deposits and making mortgage and other loans. The S'L or thrift term is mainly used in the United States; similar institutions in the United Kingdom, Ireland and some Commonwealth countries include building societies and trustee savings banks.

They are often mutually held, meaning that the depositors and borrowers are members with voting rights, and have the ability to direct the financial and managerial goals of the organization, not unlike the poliyholders of a mutual insurance company.

  a. Person-to-person lending
  c. Savings and loan association
  b. Mutual fund
  d. Net asset value

32. _____ mature in one year or less. Like zero-coupon bonds, they do not pay interest prior to maturity; instead they are sold at a discount of the par value to create a positive yield to maturity. Many regard _____ as the least risky investment available to U.S. investors.
  a. 4-4-5 Calendar
  c. Treasury securities
  b. Treasury Inflation Protected Securities
  d. Treasury bills

33. _____ are government bonds issued by the United States Department of the Treasury through the Bureau of the Public Debt. They are the debt financing instruments of the U.S. Federal government, and they are often referred to simply as Treasuries or Treasurys. There are four types of marketable _____: Treasury bills, Treasury notes, Treasury bonds, and Treasury Inflation Protected Securities (TIPS.)
  a. Treasury Inflation Protected Securities
  c. Treasury Inflation-Protected Securities
  b. Treasury securities
  d. 4-4-5 Calendar

34. In finance, a _____ is a debt security, in which the authorized issuer owes the holders a debt and, depending on the terms of the _____, is obliged to pay interest (the coupon) and/or to repay the principal at a later date, termed maturity.

Thus a _____ is a loan: the issuer is the borrower, the _____ holder is the lender, and the coupon is the interest. _____ s provide the borrower with external funds to finance long-term investments, or, in the case of government _____ s, to finance current expenditure.

a. Convertible bond
c. Catastrophe bonds
b. Puttable bond
d. Bond

35. The _____ provide stable, on-demand, low-cost funding to American financial institutions for home mortgage loans, small business, rural, agricultural, and economic development lending. With their members, the _____ank System represents the largest collective source of home mortgage and community credit in the United States. The banks do not provide loans directly to individuals, only to other banks.
   a. 7-Eleven
   b. 4-4-5 Calendar
   c. Federal Home Loan Banks
   d. 529 plan

36. The _____, an agency of the United States Department of the Treasury, is the primary regulator of federal savings associations (sometimes referred to as federal thrifts.) Federal savings associations include both federal savings banks and federal savings and loans. The OTS is also responsible for supervising savings and loan holding companies (SLHCs) and some state-chartered institutions.
   a. ABN Amro
   b. AAB
   c. A Random Walk Down Wall Street
   d. Office of Thrift Supervision

37. In finance, the _____ is the global financial market for short-term borrowing and lending. It provides short-term liquidity funding for the global financial system. The _____ is where short-term obligations such as Treasury bills, commercial paper and bankers' acceptances are bought and sold.
   a. Debt-for-equity swap
   b. Money market
   c. Consumer debt
   d. Cramdown

38. The U.S. _____ is an independent agency of the United States government which holds primary responsibility for enforcing the federal securities laws and regulating the securities industry, the nation's stock and options exchanges, and other electronic securities markets. The SEC was created by section 4 of the SEC of 1934 (now codified as 15 U.S.C. § 78d and commonly referred to as the 1934 Act.)
   a. 7-Eleven
   b. 4-4-5 Calendar
   c. 529 plan
   d. Securities and Exchange Commission

39. A _____ assesses the credit worthiness of an individual, corporation, or even a country. _____s are calculated from financial history and current assets and liabilities. Typically, a _____ tells a lender or investor the probability of the subject being able to pay back a loan.
   a. Debenture
   b. Credit report monitoring
   c. Credit rating
   d. Credit cycle

40. A _____ is a professionally managed type of collective investment scheme that pools money from many investors and invests it in stocks, bonds, short-term money market instruments, and/or other securities. The _____ will have a fund manager that trades the pooled money on a regular basis. Currently, the worldwide value of all _____s totals more than $26 trillion.

Since 1940, there have been three basic types of investment companies in the United States: open-end funds, also known in the US as _____s; unit investment trusts (UITs); and closed-end funds.

Chapter 17. Regulation of the Financial Institutions` Sector

a. Net asset value
c. Financial intermediary
b. Trust company
d. Mutual fund

41. The _____ of 1974 (Pub.L. 93-406, 88 Stat. 829, enacted September 2, 1974) is an American federal statute that establishes minimum standards for pension plans in private industry and provides for extensive rules on the federal income tax effects of transactions associated with employee benefit plans.
  a. Articles of Partnership
  c. Expedited Funds Availability Act
  b. Express warranty
  d. Employee Retirement Income Security Act

42. _____, refers to consumption opportunity gained by an entity within a specified time frame, which is generally expressed in monetary terms. However, for households and individuals, '_____ is the sum of all the wages, salaries, profits, interests payments, rents and other forms of earnings received... in a given period of time.' For firms, _____ generally refers to net-profit: what remains of revenue after expenses have been subtracted.
  a. Annual report
  c. OIBDA
  b. Accrual
  d. Income

43. A _____ is a pool of assets forming an independent legal entity that are bought with the contributions to a pension plan for the exclusive purpose of financing pension plan benefits.

_____s are important shareholders of listed and private companies. They are especially important to the stock market where large institutional investors like the Ontario Teachers' Pension Plan dominate.

  a. Pension fund
  c. Leveraged buyout
  b. Limited liability company
  d. Leverage

44. In business and accounting, _____s are everything of value that is owned by a person or company. The balance sheet of a firm records the monetary value of the _____s owned by the firm. The two major _____ classes are tangible _____s and intangible _____s.
  a. Income
  c. EBITDA
  b. Accounts payable
  d. Asset

45. A _____ is a small, short-term loan that is intended to cover a borrower's expenses until his or her next payday. The loans are also sometimes referred to as cash advances, though that term can also refer to cash provided against a prearranged line of credit such as a credit card Legislation regarding _____s varies widely between different countries and, within the USA, between different states.
  a. Payday loan
  c. 7-Eleven
  b. 4-4-5 Calendar
  d. 529 plan

46. A car _____, or simply _____, is a loan where the borrower provides their car title as collateral for a loan.

These loans are typically short-term, and tend to carry higher interest rates than other sources of credit. These loans have higher interest rates than other sources of credit due to the fact that the lender typically does not check credit and that the only consideration for the loan is the value and condition of the vehicle.

a. Promissory note
b. Credit repair software
c. Financial plan
d. Title loan

47. In finance, a _____ is a position established in one market in an attempt to offset exposure to the price risk of an equal but opposite obligation or position in another market -- usually, but not always, in the context of one's commercial activity. Hedging is a strategy designed to minimize exposure to such business risks as a sharp contraction in demand for one's inventory, while still allowing the business to profit from producing and maintaining that inventory. A typical hedger might be a farmer with 2000 acres of unharvested wheat in the ground, who would rather tend his crop without the distraction of uncertain prices.
   a. 4-4-5 Calendar
   b. Hedge
   c. 7-Eleven
   d. 529 plan

48. A _____ is a private investment fund open to a limited range of investors that is permitted by regulators to undertake a wider range of activities than other investment funds and also pays a performance fee to its investment manager. Each fund will have its own strategy which determines the type of investments and the methods of investment it undertakes. _____ s as a class invest in a broad range of investments extending over shares, debt, commodities and beyond.
   a. 529 plan
   b. Hedge fund
   c. 4-4-5 Calendar
   d. 7-Eleven

49. An _____ is a company whose main business is holding securities of other companies purely for investment purposes. The _____ invests money on behalf of its shareholders who in turn share in the profits and losses.
   a. Unit investment trust
   b. A Random Walk Down Wall Street
   c. AAB
   d. Investment Company

50. In economic models, the _____ time frame assumes no fixed factors of production. Firms can enter or leave the marketplace, and the cost (and availability) of land, labor, raw materials, and capital goods can be assumed to vary. In contrast, in the short-run time frame, certain factors are assumed to be fixed, because there is not sufficient time for them to change.
   a. 529 plan
   b. 4-4-5 Calendar
   c. Short-run
   d. Long-run

51. In economics and contract theory, _____ deals with the study of decisions in transactions where one party has more or better information than the other. This creates an imbalance of power in transactions which can sometimes cause the transactions to go awry. Examples of this problem are adverse selection and moral hazard.
   a. AAB
   b. Information asymmetry
   c. A Random Walk Down Wall Street
   d. ABN Amro

52. The _____ is a stock exchange based in New York City, New York. It is the largest stock exchange in the world by dollar value of its listed companies securities. As of October 2008, the combined capitalization of all domestic _____ listed companies was $10.1 trillion.
   a. 4-4-5 Calendar
   b. 529 plan
   c. New York Stock Exchange
   d. 7-Eleven

Chapter 17. Regulation of the Financial Institutions' Sector

53. A _____, securities exchange or (in Europe) bourse is a corporation or mutual organization which provides 'trading' facilities for stock brokers and traders, to trade stocks and other securities. _____s also provide facilities for the issue and redemption of securities as well as other financial instruments and capital events including the payment of income and dividends. The securities traded on a _____ include: shares issued by companies, unit trusts and other pooled investment products and bonds.

a. 529 plan
b. 4-4-5 Calendar
c. 7-Eleven
d. Stock Exchange

54. The _____ is the market for securities, where companies and governments can raise longterm funds. The _____ includes the stock market and the bond market. Financial regulators, such as the U.S. Securities and Exchange Commission, oversee the _____s in their designated countries to ensure that investors are protected against fraud.

a. Capital market
b. Forward market
c. Spot rate
d. Delta neutral

55. _____ is the trading of a corporation's stock or other securities (e.g. bonds or stock options) by individuals with potential access to non-public information about the company. In most countries, trading by corporate insiders such as officers, key employees, directors, and large shareholders may be legal, if this trading is done in a way that does not take advantage of non-public information. However, the term is frequently used to refer to a practice in which an insider or a related party trades based on material non-public information obtained during the performance of the insider's duties at the corporation, or otherwise in breach of a fiduciary duty or other relationship of trust and confidence or where the non-public information was misappropriated from the company.

a. Equity investment
b. Intellidex
c. Open outcry
d. Insider trading

56. In the original and simplified sense, _____ were things of value, of uniform quality, that were produced in large quantities by many different producers; the items from each different producer are considered equivalent. It is the contract and this underlying standard that define the commodity, not any quality inherent in the product.

_____ exchanges include:

- Chicago Board of Trade
- Kansas City Board of Trade
- Euronext.liffe
- Kuala Lumpur Futures Exchange
- Bhatinda Om ' Oil Exchange
- London Metal Exchange
- New York Mercantile Exchange
- Multi Commodity Exchange
- Dalian Commodity Exchange

Markets for trading _____ can be very efficient, particularly if the division into pools matches demand segments. These markets will quickly respond to changes in supply and demand to find an equilibrium price and quantity.

a. 529 plan
c. 4-4-5 Calendar
b. 7-Eleven
d. Commodities

57. The _____ is a private, not-for-profit organization whose primary purpose is to develop generally accepted accounting principles (GAAP) within the United States in the public's interest. The Securities and Exchange Commission (SEC) designated the _____ as the organization responsible for setting accounting standards for public companies in the U.S. It was created in 1973, replacing the Accounting Principles Board and the Committee on Accounting Procedure of the American Institute of Certified Public Accountants. The _____'s mission is 'to establish and improve standards of financial accounting and reporting for the guidance and education of the public, including issuers, auditors, and users of financial information.'

The _____ is not a governmental body.

a. MRU Holdings
c. FASB
b. PlaNet Finance
d. Credit karma

58. In finance, a _____ is a standardized contract, to buy or sell a specified commodity of standardized quality at a certain date in the future, at a market determined price (the futures price.)

The price is determined by the instantaneous equilibrium between the forces of supply and demand among competing buy and sell orders on the exchange at the time of the purchase or sale of the contract.

In many cases, the items may be such non-traditional 'commodities' as foreign currencies, commercial or government paper [e.g., bonds], or 'baskets' of corporate equity ['stock indices'] or other financial instruments.

a. Futures contract
c. Heston model
b. Repurchase agreement
d. Financial future

59. In the United States, the Financial Industry Regulatory Authority (FINRA) is a self-regulatory organization (SRO) under the Securities Exchange Act of 1934, successor to the _____.

FINRA is responsible for regulatory oversight of all securities firms that do business with the public; professional training, testing and licensing of registered persons; arbitration and mediation; market regulation by contract for The NASDAQ Stock Market, Inc., the American Stock Exchange LLC, and the International Securities Exchange, LLC; and industry utilities, such as Trade Reporting Facilities and other over-the-counter operations.

a. 529 plan
c. 4-4-5 Calendar
b. 7-Eleven
d. NASD

60. In the United States, the Financial Industry Regulatory Authority (FINRA) is a self-regulatory organization (SRO) under the Securities Exchange Act of 1934, successor to the _____, Inc.

Chapter 17. Regulation of the Financial Institutions` Sector

FINRA is responsible for regulatory oversight of all securities firms that do business with the public; professional training, testing and licensing of registered persons; arbitration and mediation; market regulation by contract for The NASDAQ Stock Market, Inc., the American Stock Exchange LLC, and the International Securities Exchange, LLC; and industry utilities, such as Trade Reporting Facilities and other over-the-counter operations.

a. 7-Eleven
b. 529 plan
c. 4-4-5 Calendar
d. National Association of Securities Dealers

Chapter 18. Federal, State, and Local Governments Operating in the Financial Markets

1. _____ is the amount by which a government, private company, or individual's spending exceeds income over a particular period of time, the opposite of budget surplus.

When the expenditures of a government to individuals and corporations) are greater than its tax revenues, it creates a deficit in the government budget; such a deficit is known as _____. This causes the government to borrow capital from the 'world market', increasing further debt, debt service and interest rates

a. 529 plan
c. 7-Eleven
b. 4-4-5 Calendar
d. Deficit spending

2. _____ is that which is owed; usually referencing assets owed, but the term can cover other obligations. In the case of assets, _____ is a means of using future purchasing power in the present before a summation has been earned. Some companies and corporations use _____ as a part of their overall corporate finance strategy.

a. Debt
c. Credit cycle
b. Partial Payment
d. Cross-collateralization

3. _____ refers to government attempts to influence the direction of the economy through changes in government taxes, or through some spending (fiscal allowances.)

_____ can be contrasted with the other main type of economic policy, monetary policy, which attempts to stabilize the economy by controlling interest rates and the supply of money. The two main instruments of _____ are government spending and taxation.

a. Tax exemption
c. Tax incidence
b. Qualified residence interest
d. Fiscal policy

4. In economics, a _____ is a mechanism that allows people to easily buy and sell (trade) financial securities (such as stocks and bonds), commodities (such as precious metals or agricultural goods), and other fungible items of value at low transaction costs and at prices that reflect the efficient-market hypothesis.

_____s have evolved significantly over several hundred years and are undergoing constant innovation to improve liquidity.

Both general markets (where many commodities are traded) and specialized markets (where only one commodity is traded) exist.

a. Cost of carry
c. Delta hedging
b. Financial market
d. Secondary market

5. _____ is the difference between a lower selling price and a higher purchase price, resulting in a financial loss for the seller. Pursuant to IRS TAX TIP 2009-35 'If your _____ exceeds your capital gain, the excess can be deducted on your tax return, up to an annual limit of $3,000 ($1,500 if you are married filing separately.)'.

a. 7-Eleven
c. 4-4-5 Calendar
b. 529 plan
d. Capital loss

Chapter 18. Federal, State, and Local Governments Operating in the Financial Markets 173

6. In business, _____ is income that a company receives from its normal business activities, usually from the sale of goods and services to customers. Some companies also receive _____ from interest, dividends or royalties paid to them by other companies. _____ may refer to business income in general, or it may refer to the amount, in a monetary unit, received during a period of time, as in 'Last year, Company X had _____ of $32 million.'

In many countries, including the UK, _____ is referred to as turnover.

   a. Matching principle   b. Bottom line
   c. Furniture, Fixtures and Equipment   d. Revenue

7. In economics, _____ is a rise in the general level of prices of goods and services in an economy over a period of time. The term '_____' once referred to increases in the money supply (monetary _____); however, economic debates about the relationship between money supply and price levels have led to its primary use today in describing price _____. _____ can also be described as a decline in the real value of money--a loss of purchasing power in the medium of exchange which is also the monetary unit of account.

   a. A Random Walk Down Wall Street   b. ABN Amro
   c. AAB   d. Inflation

8. _____, in bookkeeping, refers to assets, liabilities, income, and expenses recorded on individual pages of the so called book of final entry or ledger. Changes in _____ value are made by chronologically posting debit (DR) and credit (CR) entries to its page. Examples of _____s are cash, _____s receivable, mortgages, loans, land and buildings, common stock, sales, services provided, wages, and payroll overhead.

   a. Accretion   b. Option
   c. Account   d. Alpha

9. In finance, the _____ of a financial asset measures the sensitivity of the asset's price to interest rate movements, expressed as a number of years. The reason for expressing this sensitivity in years is that the time that will elapse until a cash flow is received allows more interest to accumulate. Therefore the price of an asset with long term cashflows has more interest rate sensitivity than an asset with cashflows in the near future.

   a. 4-4-5 Calendar   b. Duration
   c. Macaulay duration   d. Yield to maturity

10. _____ is a fee paid on borrowed assets. It is the price paid for the use of borrowed money, or, money earned by deposited funds. Assets that are sometimes lent with _____ include money, shares, consumer goods through hire purchase, major assets such as aircraft, and even entire factories in finance lease arrangements.

   a. Interest   b. AAB
   c. Insolvency   d. A Random Walk Down Wall Street

11. An _____ is the price a borrower pays for the use of money they do not own, and the return a lender receives for deferring the use of funds, by lending it to the borrower. _____s are normally expressed as a percentage rate over the period of one year.

_____s targets are also a vital tool of monetary policy and are used to control variables like investment, inflation, and unemployment.

a. A Random Walk Down Wall Street
b. ABN Amro
c. AAB
d. Interest rate

12. _____ is the risk (variability in value) borne by an interest-bearing asset, such as a loan or a bond, due to variability of interest rates. In general, as rates rise, the price of a fixed rate bond will fall, and vice versa. _____ is commonly measured by the bond's duration.

a. Interest rate risk
b. Official bank rate
c. International Fisher effect
d. A Random Walk Down Wall Street

13. In finance, the term _____ describes the amount in cash that returns to the owners of a security. Normally it does not include the price variations, at the difference of the total return. _____ applies to various stated rates of return on stocks (common and preferred, and convertible), fixed income instruments (bonds, notes, bills, strips, zero coupon), and some other investment type insurance products (e.g. annuities.)

a. Yield to maturity
b. 4-4-5 Calendar
c. Yield
d. Macaulay duration

14. In finance, the _____ is the relation between the interest rate (or cost of borrowing) and the time to maturity of the debt for a given borrower in a given currency. For example, the current U.S. dollar interest rates paid on U.S. Treasury securities for various maturities are closely watched by many traders, and are commonly plotted on a graph such as the one on the right which is informally called 'the _____.' More formal mathematical descriptions of this relation are often called the term structure of interest rates.

The yield of a debt instrument is the annualized percentage increase in the value of the investment.

a. 4-4-5 Calendar
b. 7-Eleven
c. Yield curve
d. 529 plan

15. A _____ is a unit that is equal to 1/100th of a percentage point. It is frequently used to express percentage point changes of less than 1%. It avoids the ambiguity between relative and absolute discussions about rates.

a. Bond market
b. 4-4-5 Calendar
c. 529 plan
d. Basis point

16. An _____ is a contract written by a seller that conveys to the buyer the right -- but not the obligation -- to buy (in the case of a call _____) or to sell (in the case of a put _____) a particular asset, such as a piece of property such as, among others, a futures contract. In return for granting the _____, the seller collects a payment (the premium) from the buyer.

For example, buying a call _____ provides the right to buy a specified quantity of a security at a set strike price at some time on or before expiration, while buying a put _____ provides the right to sell.

a. Option
b. Amortization
c. AT'T Mobility LLC
d. Annuity

17. A _____ is a bond issued by a corporation. The term is usually applied to longer-term debt instruments, generally with a maturity date falling at least a year after their issue date. (The term 'commercial paper' is sometimes used for instruments with a shorter maturity.)

Chapter 18. Federal, State, and Local Governments Operating in the Financial Markets

a. Brady bonds
c. Serial bond
b. Government bond
d. Corporate bond

18. _____ is the risk that the value of an investment will decrease due to moves in market factors. The five standard _____ factors are:

- Equity risk, the risk that stock prices will change.
- Interest rate risk, the risk that interest rates will change.
- Currency risk, the risk that foreign exchange rates will change.
- Commodity risk, the risk that commodity prices (e.g. grains, metals) will change.

As with other forms of risk, _____ may be measured in a number of ways. Traditionally, this is done using a Value at Risk methodology. Value at risk is well established as a risk management technique, but it contains a number of limiting assumptions that constrain its accuracy.

a. Market risk
c. Transaction risk
b. Currency risk
d. Tracking error

19. _____ are government bonds issued by the United States Department of the Treasury through the Bureau of the Public Debt. They are the debt financing instruments of the U.S. Federal government, and they are often referred to simply as Treasuries or Treasurys. There are four types of marketable _____: Treasury bills, Treasury notes, Treasury bonds, and Treasury Inflation Protected Securities (TIPS.)

a. Treasury securities
c. Treasury Inflation Protected Securities
b. Treasury Inflation-Protected Securities
d. 4-4-5 Calendar

20. In finance, a _____ is a debt security, in which the authorized issuer owes the holders a debt and, depending on the terms of the _____, is obliged to pay interest (the coupon) and/or to repay the principal at a later date, termed maturity.

Thus a _____ is a loan: the issuer is the borrower, the _____ holder is the lender, and the coupon is the interest. _____s provide the borrower with external funds to finance long-term investments, or, in the case of government _____s, to finance current expenditure.

a. Catastrophe bonds
c. Puttable bond
b. Convertible bond
d. Bond

21. In finance, _____ occurs when a debtor has not met its legal obligations according to the debt contract, e.g. it has not made a scheduled payment, or has violated a loan covenant (condition) of the debt contract. _____ may occur if the debtor is either unwilling or unable to pay their debt. This can occur with all debt obligations including bonds, mortgages, loans, and promissory notes.

a. Debt validation
c. Vendor finance
b. Default
d. Credit crunch

22. _____ is the risk of loss due to a debtor's non-payment of a loan or other line of credit (either the principal or interest (coupon) or both)

Most lenders employ their own models (credit scorecards) to rank potential and existing customers according to risk, and then apply appropriate strategies. With products such as unsecured personal loans or mortgages, lenders charge a higher price for higher risk customers and vice versa. With revolving products such as credit cards and overdrafts, risk is controlled through careful setting of credit limits.

a. Credit risk
b. Transaction risk
c. Liquidity risk
d. Market risk

23. A _____ is a fungible, negotiable instrument representing financial value. They are broadly categorized into debt securities (such as banknotes, bonds and debentures), and equity securities; e.g., common stocks. The company or other entity issuing the _____ is called the issuer.

a. Tracking stock
b. Book entry
c. Security
d. Securities lending

24. The _____ was a worldwide economic downturn starting in most places in 1929 and ending at different times in the 1930s or early 1940s for different countries. It was the largest and most important economic depression in the 20th century, and is used in the 21st century as an example of how far the world's economy can fall. The _____ originated in the United States; historians most often use as a starting date the stock market crash on October 29, 1929, known as Black Tuesday.

a. Great Depression
b. 529 plan
c. 4-4-5 Calendar
d. 7-Eleven

25. The _____ is one of the measures of national income and input for a given country's economy. _____ is defined as the total cost of all finished goods and services produced within the country in a stipulated period of time (usually a 365-day year.) It is sometimes regarded as the sum of profits added at every level of production (the intermediate stages) of all final goods and services produced within a country in a stipulated timeframe, and it is rarely given a monetary value.

a. Macroeconomics
b. Recession
c. Behavioral finance
d. Gross domestic product

26. _____ is the price at which an asset would trade in a competitive Walrasian auction setting. _____ is often used interchangeably with open _____, fair value or fair _____, although these terms have distinct definitions in different standards, and may differ in some circumstances.

International Valuation Standards defines _____ as 'the estimated amount for which a property should exchange on the date of valuation between a willing buyer and a willing seller in an arm'e;s-length transaction after proper marketing wherein the parties had each acted knowledgeably, prudently, and without compulsion.'

_____ is a concept distinct from market price, which is 'e;the price at which one can transact'e;, while _____ is 'e;the true underlying value'e; according to theoretical standards.

a. T-Model
b. Debt restructuring
c. Wrap account
d. Market value

27. _____, in finance and accounting, means stated value or face value. From this comes the expressions at par (at the _____), over par (over _____) and under par (under _____.)

Chapter 18. Federal, State, and Local Governments Operating in the Financial Markets 177

The term '_____' has several meanings depending on context and geography.

a. Sinking fund
b. Global Squeeze
c. FIDC
d. Par value

28. In business and accounting, _____s are everything of value that is owned by a person or company. The balance sheet of a firm records the monetary value of the _____s owned by the firm. The two major _____ classes are tangible _____s and intangible _____s.

a. EBITDA
b. Income
c. Asset
d. Accounts payable

29. _____ are liabilities that may or may not be incurred by an entity depending on the outcome of a future event such as a court case. These liabilities are recorded in a company's accounts and shown in the balance sheet when both probable and reasonably estimable. A footnote to the balance sheet describes the nature and extent of the _____.

a. Due-on-sale clause
b. Contingent liabilities
c. 4-4-5 Calendar
d. 529 plan

30. _____ mature in one year or less. Like zero-coupon bonds, they do not pay interest prior to maturity; instead they are sold at a discount of the par value to create a positive yield to maturity. Many regard _____ as the least risky investment available to U.S. investors.

a. 4-4-5 Calendar
b. Treasury Inflation Protected Securities
c. Treasury securities
d. Treasury bills

31. _____ are securities that can be easily converted into cash. Such securities will generally have highly liquid markets allowing the security to be sold at a reasonable price very quickly. This is a usual feature in real estate .

a. Book entry
b. Marketable
c. Tracking stock
d. Securities lending

32. A _____ is a measure of the average price of consumer goods and services purchased by households. The _____ can be used to index (i.e., adjust for the effects of inflation) wages, salaries, pensions, or regulated or contracted prices. The _____ is, along with the population census and the National Income and Product Accounts, one of the most closely watched national economic statistics.

a. Divisia index
b. 4-4-5 Calendar
c. Consumer price index
d. 529 plan

33. A _____ is a normalized average (typically a weighted average) of prices for a given class of goods or services in a given region, during a given interval of time. It is a statistic designed to help to compare how these prices, taken as a whole, differ between time periods or geographical locations.

a. Price discrimination
b. Discounts and allowances
c. Price Index
d. Transfer pricing

34. _____ is a mathematical science pertaining to the collection, analysis, interpretation or explanation, and presentation of data. It also provides tools for prediction and forecasting based on data. It is applicable to a wide variety of academic disciplines, from the natural and social sciences to the humanities, government and business.

a. Covariance
b. Sample size
c. Mean
d. Statistics

35. _____ are the inflation-indexed bonds issued by the U.S. Treasury. The principal is adjusted to the Consumer Price Index, the commonly used measure of inflation. The coupon rate is constant, but generates a different amount of interest when multiplied by the inflation-adjusted principal, thus protecting the holder against inflation. _____ are currently offered in 5-year, 10-year and 20-year maturities.
a. Treasury securities
b. Treasury Inflation-Protected Securities
c. 4-4-5 Calendar
d. Treasury Inflation Protected Securities

36. In banking and finance, _____ denotes all activities from the time a commitment is made for a transaction until it is settled. _____ is necessary because the speed of trades is much faster than the cycle time for completing the underlying transaction.

In its widest sense _____ involves the management of post-trading, pre-settlement credit exposures, to ensure that trades are settled in accordance with market rules, even if a buyer or seller should become insolvent prior to settlement.

a. Share
b. Clearing
c. Procter ' Gamble
d. Clearing house

37. The institution most often referenced by the word '_____' is a public or publicly traded _____, the shares of which are traded on a public stock exchange (e.g., the New York Stock Exchange or Nasdaq in the United States) where shares of stock of _____s are bought and sold by and to the general public. Most of the largest businesses in the world are publicly traded _____s. However, the majority of _____s are said to be closely held, privately held or close _____s, meaning that no ready market exists for the trading of shares.
a. Corporation
b. Federal Home Loan Mortgage Corporation
c. Protect
d. Depository Trust Company

38. _____ refers to any type of investment that yields a regular (or fixed) return.

For example, if you lend money to a borrower and the borrower has to pay interest once a month, you have been issued a fixed-income security. When a company does this, it is often called a bond or corporate bank debt (although preferred stock is also sometimes considered to be _____).

a. 4-4-5 Calendar
b. Bond market
c. Fixed Income
d. 529 plan

39. _____, refers to consumption opportunity gained by an entity within a specified time frame, which is generally expressed in monetary terms. However, for households and individuals, '_____ is the sum of all the wages, salaries, profits, interests payments, rents and other forms of earnings received... in a given period of time.' For firms, _____ generally refers to net-profit: what remains of revenue after expenses have been subtracted.
a. Accrual
b. OIBDA
c. Annual report
d. Income

Chapter 18. Federal, State, and Local Governments Operating in the Financial Markets

40. In economic models, the _____ time frame assumes no fixed factors of production. Firms can enter or leave the marketplace, and the cost (and availability) of land, labor, raw materials, and capital goods can be assumed to vary. In contrast, in the short-run time frame, certain factors are assumed to be fixed, because there is not sufficient time for them to change.
a. 529 plan
b. Long-run
c. Short-run
d. 4-4-5 Calendar

41. In economics, a _____ is a general slowdown in economic activity in a country over a sustained period of time, or a business cycle contraction. During _____s, many macroeconomic indicators vary in a similar way. Production as measured by Gross Domestic Product (GDP), employment, investment spending, capacity utilization, household incomes and business profits all fall during _____s.
a. Mercantilism
b. Recession
c. Behavioral finance
d. Fixed exchange rate

42. In economics, the concept of the _____ refers to the decision-making time frame of a firm in which at least one factor of production is fixed. Costs which are fixed in the _____ have no impact on a firms decisions. For example a firm can raise output by increasing the amount of labour through overtime.
a. 529 plan
b. 4-4-5 Calendar
c. Short-run
d. Long-run

43. The _____ or redemption yield is the yield promised to the bondholder on the assumption that the bond or other fixed-interest security such as gilts will be held to maturity, that all coupon and principal payments will be made and coupon payments are reinvested at the bond's promised yield at the same rate as invested. It is a measure of the return of the bond. This technique in theory allows investors to calculate the fair value of different financial instruments.
a. Yield to maturity
b. Macaulay duration
c. 4-4-5 Calendar
d. Yield

44. _____ is a life of security. It may also refer to the final payment date of a loan or other financial instrument, at which point all remaining interest and principal is due to be paid.

1, 3, 6 months _____ band can be calculated by using 30-day per month periods.

a. Replacement cost
b. False billing
c. Primary market
d. Maturity

45.

A _____ is a type of financial intermediary and a type of bank. Commercial banking is also known as business banking. It is a bank that provides checking accounts, savings accounts, and money market accounts and that accepts time deposits.

a. 7-Eleven
b. Commercial bank
c. 4-4-5 Calendar
d. 529 plan

Chapter 18. Federal, State, and Local Governments Operating in the Financial Markets

46. _____ is the provision of resources (such as granting a loan) by one party to another party where that second party does not reimburse the first party immediately, thereby generating a debt, and instead arranges either to repay or return those resources (or material(s) of equal value) at a later date. The first party is called a creditor, also known as a lender, while the second party is called a debtor, also known as a borrower.

Movements of financial capital are normally dependent on either _____ or equity transfers.

a. Comparable
c. Warrant
b. Clearing house
d. Credit

47. A _____ assesses the credit worthiness of an individual, corporation, or even a country. _____s are calculated from financial history and current assets and liabilities. Typically, a _____ tells a lender or investor the probability of the subject being able to pay back a loan.

a. Credit report monitoring
c. Debenture
b. Credit rating
d. Credit cycle

48. _____, consists of the buying and selling of products or services over electronic systems such as the Internet and other computer networks. The amount of trade conducted electronically has grown extraordinarily with widespread Internet usage. The use of commerce is conducted in this way, spurring and drawing on innovations in electronic funds transfer, supply chain management, Internet marketing, online transaction processing, electronic data interchange (EDI), inventory management systems, and automated data collection systems.

a. AAB
c. Electronic commerce
b. A Random Walk Down Wall Street
d. ABN Amro

49. In investment, the _____ assesses the credit worthiness of a corporation's debt issues. It is analogous to credit ratings for individuals and countries. The credit rating is a financial indicator to potential investors of debt securities such as bonds.

a. Floating charge
c. Reinvestment risk
b. Biweekly Mortgage
d. Bond credit rating

50. In the global money market, _____ is an unsecured promissory note with a fixed maturity of one to 270 days. _____ is a money-market security issued (sold) by large banks and corporations to get money to meet short term debt obligations (for example, payroll), and is only backed by an issuing bank or corporation's promise to pay the face amount on the maturity date specified on the note. Since it is not backed by collateral, only firms with excellent credit ratings from a recognized rating agency will be able to sell their _____ at a reasonable price.

a. Trade-off theory
c. Commercial paper
b. Book building
d. Financial distress

51. In the United States, a _____ is a bond issued by a city or other local government, or their agencies. Potential issuers of these bonds include cities, counties, redevelopment agencies, school districts, publicly owned airports and seaports, and any other governmental entity (or group of governments) below the state level. They may be general obligations of the issuer or secured by specified revenues.

a. Puttable bond
c. Senior debt
b. Premium bond
d. Municipal bond

Chapter 18. Federal, State, and Local Governments Operating in the Financial Markets

52. _____ occurs when an entity that has issued callable bonds calls those debt securities from the debt holders with the express purpose of reissuing new debt at a lower coupon rate. In essence, the issue of new, lower-interest debt allows the company to prematurely refund the older, higher-interest debt.

On the contrary, NonRefundable Bonds may be callable but they cannot be re-issued with a lower coupon rate.

a. Systematic risk
b. Market neutral
c. Refunding
d. No-arbitrage bounds

53. A _____ is a legal pledge in United States municipal finance, in which an entity pledges its full faith and credit to repay its debt, typically a _____ bond.

a. Financial Institutions Reform Recovery and Enforcement Act
b. Letter of credit
c. Covenant
d. General obligation

54. _____ are bonds issued by governments, authorities, or public benefit corporations that are guaranteed by the revenue flow of the issuing agency.

The Supreme Court decision of Pollock versus Farmer's Loan and Trust Company of 1895 initiated a wave or series of innovations for the financial services community in both tax-treatment and regulation from government. This specific case, according to a leading investment bank's research, resulted in the 'intergovernmental tax immunity doctrine,' ultimately leading to 'tax-free status.' Municipal bonds are generally exempt from federal tax on their interest payments (not capital gains.)

a. Gilts
b. Callable bond
c. Private activity bond
d. Revenue bonds

55. _____ is a structured finance process that involves pooling and repackaging of cash-flow-producing financial assets into securities, which are then sold to investors. The term '_____' is derived from the fact that the form of financial instruments used to obtain funds from the investors are securities. As a portfolio risk backed by amortizing cash flows - and unlike general corporate debt - the credit quality of securitized debt is non-stationary due to changes in volatility that are time- and structure-dependent.

a. Securitization
b. Reputational risk
c. The Glass-Steagall Act of 1933
d. Special journals

56. A _____ is an exemption from all or certain taxes of a state or nation in which part of the taxes that would normally be collected from an individual or an organization are instead foregone.

Normally a _____ is provided to an individual or organization which falls within a class which the government wishes to promote economically, such as charitable organizations. _____s are usually meant to either reduce the tax burden on a particular segment of society in the interests of fairness or to promote some type of economic activity through reducing the tax burden on those organizations or individuals who are involved in that activity.

Chapter 18. Federal, State, and Local Governments Operating in the Financial Markets

a. Tax incidence
c. Tax compliance solution
b. Federal Open Market Committee
d. Tax exemption

57. The U.S. _____ is an independent agency of the United States government which holds primary responsibility for enforcing the federal securities laws and regulating the securities industry, the nation's stock and options exchanges, and other electronic securities markets. The SEC was created by section 4 of the SEC of 1934 (now codified as 15 U.S.C. Â§ 78d and commonly referred to as the 1934 Act.)

a. 4-4-5 Calendar
c. 7-Eleven
b. 529 plan
d. Securities and Exchange Commission

58. _____ is the process of decreasing an amount over a period of time. The word comes from Middle English amortisen to kill, alienate in mortmain, from Anglo-French amorteser, alteration of amortir, from Vulgar Latin admortire to kill, from Latin ad- + mort-, mors death. Particular instances of the term include:

- _____ (business), the allocation of a lump sum amount to different time periods, particularly for loans and other forms of finance, including related interest or other finance charges.
    - _____ schedule, a table detailing each periodic payment on a loan (typically a mortgage), as generated by an _____ calculator.
    - Negative _____, an _____ schedule where the loan amount actually increases through not paying the full interest
- Amortized analysis, analyzing the execution cost of algorithms over a sequence of operations.
- _____ of capital expenditures of certain assets under accounting rules, particularly intangible assets, in a manner analogous to depreciation.
- _____ (tax law)

_____ is also used in the context of zoning regulations and describes the time in which a property owner has to relocate when the property's use constitutes a preexisting nonconforming use under zoning regulations.

- Depreciation

a. Option
c. Intrinsic value
b. AT'T Inc.
d. Amortization

59. In economics, business, and accounting, a _____ is the value of money that has been used up to produce something, and hence is not available for use anymore. In business, the _____ may be one of acquisition, in which case the amount of money expended to acquire it is counted as _____. In this case, money is the input that is gone in order to acquire the thing.

a. Cost
c. Marginal cost
b. Sliding scale fees
d. Fixed costs

60. A _____ is a futures contract on a short term interest rate (STIR.) Contracts vary, but are often defined on an interest rate index such as 3-month sterling or US dollar LIBOR.

They are traded across a wide range of currencies, including the G12 country currencies and many others.

Chapter 18. Federal, State, and Local Governments Operating in the Financial Markets

a. Dual currency deposit
b. Notional amount
c. Real estate derivatives
d. Financial future

61. A _____ is an exchange of promises between two or more parties to do an act which is enforceable in a court of law. It is where an unqualified offer meets a qualified acceptance and the parties reach Consensus ad Idem. The parties must have the necessary capacity to _____ and the _____ must not be either trifling, indeterminate, impossible or illegal.
   a. 4-4-5 Calendar
   b. 529 plan
   c. 7-Eleven
   d. Contract

62. In finance, a _____ is a standardized contract, to buy or sell a specified commodity of standardized quality at a certain date in the future, at a market determined price (the futures price.)

The price is determined by the instantaneous equilibrium between the forces of supply and demand among competing buy and sell orders on the exchange at the time of the purchase or sale of the contract.

In many cases, the items may be such non-traditional 'commodities' as foreign currencies, commercial or government paper [e.g., bonds], or 'baskets' of corporate equity ['stock indices'] or other financial instruments.

   a. Heston model
   b. Repurchase agreement
   c. Financial future
   d. Futures contract

Chapter 19. Business Borrowing: Corporate Bonds, Asset-Backed Securities, Bank Loans

1. A _____ is a bond issued by a corporation. The term is usually applied to longer-term debt instruments, generally with a maturity date falling at least a year after their issue date. (The term 'commercial paper' is sometimes used for instruments with a shorter maturity.)
   a. Corporate bond
   b. Brady bonds
   c. Government bond
   d. Serial bond

2. _____ is the provision of resources (such as granting a loan) by one party to another party where that second party does not reimburse the first party immediately, thereby generating a debt, and instead arranges either to repay or return those resources (or material(s) of equal value) at a later date. The first party is called a creditor, also known as a lender, while the second party is called a debtor, also known as a borrower.

Movements of financial capital are normally dependent on either _____ or equity transfers.

   a. Warrant
   b. Clearing house
   c. Credit
   d. Comparable

3. In finance, the _____ of a financial asset measures the sensitivity of the asset's price to interest rate movements, expressed as a number of years. The reason for expressing this sensitivity in years is that the time that will elapse until a cash flow is received allows more interest to accumulate. Therefore the price of an asset with long term cashflows has more interest rate sensitivity than an asset with cashflows in the near future.
   a. Yield to maturity
   b. Macaulay duration
   c. 4-4-5 Calendar
   d. Duration

4. In the theory of capital structure, _____ is the phrase used to describe funds that firms obtain from outside of the firm. It is contrasted to internal financing which consists mainly of profits retained by the firm for investment. There are many kinds of _____.
   a. Ownership equity
   b. External financing
   c. Adjustment
   d. Asset-backed commercial paper

5. In economics, _____ is a rise in the general level of prices of goods and services in an economy over a period of time. The term '_____' once referred to increases in the money supply (monetary _____); however, economic debates about the relationship between money supply and price levels have led to its primary use today in describing price _____. _____ can also be described as a decline in the real value of money--a loss of purchasing power in the medium of exchange which is also the monetary unit of account.
   a. A Random Walk Down Wall Street
   b. AAB
   c. ABN Amro
   d. Inflation

6. _____ is a fee paid on borrowed assets. It is the price paid for the use of borrowed money , or, money earned by deposited funds . Assets that are sometimes lent with _____ include money, shares, consumer goods through hire purchase, major assets such as aircraft, and even entire factories in finance lease arrangements.
   a. Insolvency
   b. A Random Walk Down Wall Street
   c. AAB
   d. Interest

7. An _____ is the price a borrower pays for the use of money they do not own, and the return a lender receives for deferring the use of funds, by lending it to the borrower. _____s are normally expressed as a percentage rate over the period of one year.

Chapter 19. Business Borrowing: Corporate Bonds, Asset-Backed Securities, Bank Loans

_____s targets are also a vital tool of monetary policy and are used to control variables like investment, inflation, and unemployment.

a. ABN Amro
b. AAB
c. Interest rate
d. A Random Walk Down Wall Street

8. _____ is the risk (variability in value) borne by an interest-bearing asset, such as a loan or a bond, due to variability of interest rates. In general, as rates rise, the price of a fixed rate bond will fall, and vice versa. _____ is commonly measured by the bond's duration.
a. Official bank rate
b. Interest rate risk
c. A Random Walk Down Wall Street
d. International Fisher effect

9. In the theory of capital structure _____ is the name for a firm using its profits as a source of capital for new investment, rather than a) distributing them to firm's owners or other investors and b) obtaining capital elsewhere. It is to be contrasted with external financing which consists of new money from outside of the firm brought in for investment. _____ is generally thought to be less expensive for the firm than external financing because the firm does not have to incur transaction costs to obtain it, nor does it have to pay the taxes associated with paying dividends.
a. Operating ratio
b. Employee stock option
c. Underwriting contract
d. Internal financing

10. In finance, the term _____ describes the amount in cash that returns to the owners of a security. Normally it does not include the price variations, at the difference of the total return. _____ applies to various stated rates of return on stocks (common and preferred, and convertible), fixed income instruments (bonds, notes, bills, strips, zero coupon), and some other investment type insurance products (e.g. annuities.)
a. 4-4-5 Calendar
b. Yield to maturity
c. Macaulay duration
d. Yield

11. In finance, the _____ is the relation between the interest rate (or cost of borrowing) and the time to maturity of the debt for a given borrower in a given currency. For example, the current U.S. dollar interest rates paid on U.S. Treasury securities for various maturities are closely watched by many traders, and are commonly plotted on a graph such as the one on the right which is informally called 'the _____.' More formal mathematical descriptions of this relation are often called the term structure of interest rates.

The yield of a debt instrument is the annualized percentage increase in the value of the investment.

a. 4-4-5 Calendar
b. 7-Eleven
c. Yield curve
d. 529 plan

12. An _____ is a security whose value and income payments are derived from and collateralized (or 'backed') by a specified pool of underlying assets. The pool of assets is typically a group of small and illiquid assets that are unable to be sold individually. Pooling the assets allows them to be sold to general investors, a process called securitization, and allows the risk of investing in the underlying assets to be diversified because each security will represent a fraction of the total value of the diverse pool of underlying assets.

Chapter 19. Business Borrowing: Corporate Bonds, Asset-Backed Securities, Bank Loans

a. ABN Amro
c. AAB

b. A Random Walk Down Wall Street
d. Asset-backed security

13. A _____ is a unit that is equal to 1/100th of a percentage point. It is frequently used to express percentage point changes of less than 1%. It avoids the ambiguity between relative and absolute discussions about rates.
a. Bond market
c. 4-4-5 Calendar

b. Basis point
d. 529 plan

14. In finance, a _____ is a debt security, in which the authorized issuer owes the holders a debt and, depending on the terms of the _____, is obliged to pay interest (the coupon) and/or to repay the principal at a later date, termed maturity.

Thus a _____ is a loan: the issuer is the borrower, the _____ holder is the lender, and the coupon is the interest. _____s provide the borrower with external funds to finance long-term investments, or, in the case of government _____s, to finance current expenditure.

a. Bond
c. Catastrophe bonds

b. Convertible bond
d. Puttable bond

15. _____ or financing is to provide capital (funds), which means money for a project, a person, a business or any other private or public institutions.

Those funds can be allocated for either short term or long term purposes. The health fund is a new way of _____ private healthcare centers.

a. Synthetic CDO
c. Product life cycle

b. Funding
d. Proxy fight

16. A _____ is a fungible, negotiable instrument representing financial value. They are broadly categorized into debt securities (such as banknotes, bonds and debentures), and equity securities; e.g., common stocks. The company or other entity issuing the _____ is called the issuer.
a. Book entry
c. Security

b. Tracking stock
d. Securities lending

17. The institution most often referenced by the word '_____' is a public or publicly traded _____, the shares of which are traded on a public stock exchange (e.g., the New York Stock Exchange or Nasdaq in the United States) where shares of stock of _____s are bought and sold by and to the general public. Most of the largest businesses in the world are publicly traded _____s. However, the majority of _____s are said to be closely held, privately held or close _____s, meaning that no ready market exists for the trading of shares.
a. Federal Home Loan Mortgage Corporation
c. Depository Trust Company

b. Protect
d. Corporation

18. A _____ is a fund established by a government agency or business for the purpose of reducing debt.

Chapter 19. Business Borrowing: Corporate Bonds, Asset-Backed Securities, Bank Loans 187

The _____ was first used in Great Britain in the 18th century to reduce national debt. While used by Robert Walpole in 1716 and effectively in the 1720s and early 1730s, it originated in the commercial tax syndicates of the Italian peninsula of the 14th century to retire redeemable public debt of those cities.

a. Modern portfolio theory
c. Sinking fund
b. Security interest
d. Debtor

19. A _____, in its most general sense, is a solemn promise to engage in or refrain from a specified action.

More specifically, a _____, in contrast to a contract, is a one-way agreement whereby the _____er is the only party bound by the promise. A _____ may have conditions and prerequisites that qualify the undertaking, including the actions of second or third parties, but there is no inherent agreement by such other parties to fulfill those requirements.

a. Federal Trade Commission Act
c. Covenant
b. Partnership
d. Clayton Antitrust Act

20. _____ is a life of security. It may also refer to the final payment date of a loan or other financial instrument, at which point all remaining interest and principal is due to be paid.

1, 3, 6 months _____ band can be calculated by using 30-day per month periods.

a. Primary market
c. Replacement cost
b. Maturity
d. False billing

21. In financial accounting, _____s are precautions for which the amount or probability of occurrence are not known. Typical examples are _____s for warranty costs and _____ for taxes the term reserve is used instead of term _____; such a use, however, is inconsistent with the terminology suggested by International Accounting Standards Board.

a. Money measurement concept
c. Petty cash
b. Provision
d. Momentum Accounting and Triple-Entry Bookkeeping

22. In economics, business, and accounting, a _____ is the value of money that has been used up to produce something, and hence is not available for use anymore. In business, the _____ may be one of acquisition, in which case the amount of money expended to acquire it is counted as _____. In this case, money is the input that is gone in order to acquire the thing.

a. Sliding scale fees
c. Marginal cost
b. Fixed costs
d. Cost

23. The coupon or _____ of a bond is the amount of interest paid per year expressed as a percentage of the face value of the bond.

For example if you hold $10,000 nominal of a bond described as a 4.5% loan stock, you will receive $450 in interest each year (probably in two installments of $225 each.)

Not all bonds have coupons.

   a. Revenue bonds
   b. Coupon rate
   c. Puttable bond
   d. Zero-coupon bond

24. _____ is that which is owed; usually referencing assets owed, but the term can cover other obligations. In the case of assets, _____ is a means of using future purchasing power in the present before a summation has been earned. Some companies and corporations use _____ as a part of their overall corporate finance strategy.
   a. Partial Payment
   b. Debt
   c. Cross-collateralization
   d. Credit cycle

25. _____ are government bonds issued by the United States Department of the Treasury through the Bureau of the Public Debt. They are the debt financing instruments of the U.S. Federal government, and they are often referred to simply as Treasuries or Treasurys. There are four types of marketable _____: Treasury bills, Treasury notes, Treasury bonds, and Treasury Inflation Protected Securities (TIPS.)
   a. Treasury Inflation Protected Securities
   b. Treasury securities
   c. Treasury Inflation-Protected Securities
   d. 4-4-5 Calendar

26. A _____ is defined as a certificate of agreement of loans which is given under the company's stamp and carries an undertaking that the _____ holder will get a fixed return (fixed on the basis of interest rates) and the principal amount whenever the _____ matures.

In finance, a _____ is a long-term debt instrument used by governments and large companies to obtain funds. It is defined as 'a debt secured only by the debtor's earning power, not by a lien on any specific asset.' It is similar to a bond except the securitization conditions are different.

   a. Collection agency
   b. Partial Payment
   c. Debenture
   d. Collateral Management

27. An _____ is a financial security used in aircraft finance, most commonly to take advantage of tax benefits in North America.

In a typical _____ transaction, a 'trust certificate' is sold to investors in order to finance the purchase of an aircraft by a trust managed on the investors' behalf. The trust then leases the aircraft to an airline, and the trustee routes payments through the trust to the investors.

   a. AAB
   b. A Random Walk Down Wall Street
   c. ABN Amro
   d. Equipment trust certificate

28. _____, refers to consumption opportunity gained by an entity within a specified time frame, which is generally expressed in monetary terms. However, for households and individuals, '_____ is the sum of all the wages, salaries, profits, interests payments, rents and other forms of earnings received... in a given period of time.' For firms, _____ generally refers to net-profit: what remains of revenue after expenses have been subtracted.

Chapter 19. Business Borrowing: Corporate Bonds, Asset-Backed Securities, Bank Loans

a. OIBDA
b. Accrual
c. Annual report
d. Income

29. A '_____' is a 'Charge' that is paid to obtain the right to delay a payment. Essentially, the payer purchases the right to make a given payment in the future instead of in the Present. The '_____', or 'Charge' that must be paid to delay the payment, is simply the difference between what the payment amount would be if it were paid in the present and what the payment amount would be paid if it were paid in the future.
   a. Risk modeling
   b. Risk aversion
   c. Value at risk
   d. Discount

30. A _____ is a bond bought at a price lower than its face value, with the face value repaid at the time of maturity. It does not make periodic interest payments, or so-called 'coupons,' hence the term zero-coupon bond. Investors earn return from the compounded interest all paid at maturity plus the difference between the discounted price of the bond and its par value.
   a. Zero coupon bond
   b. Callable bond
   c. Bowie bonds
   d. Municipal bond

31. _____ refers to any type of investment that yields a regular (or fixed) return.

For example, if you lend money to a borrower and the borrower has to pay interest once a month, you have been issued a fixed-income security. When a company does this, it is often called a bond or corporate bank debt (although preferred stock is also sometimes considered to be _____).

   a. Fixed income
   b. Bond market
   c. 529 plan
   d. 4-4-5 Calendar

32. A _____ is a bond bought at a price lower than its face value, with the face value repaid at the time of maturity. It does not make periodic interest payments, or have so-called 'coupons,' hence the term _____. Investors earn return from the compounded interest all paid at maturity plus the difference between the discounted price of the bond and its par value.
   a. Bond fund
   b. Corporate bond
   c. Clean price
   d. Zero-coupon bond

33. The _____ (NYSE: FNM), commonly known as Fannie Mae, is a stockholder-owned corporation chartered by Congress in 1968 as a government sponsored enterprise (GSE), but founded in 1938 during the Great Depression. The corporation's purpose is to purchase and securitize mortgages in order to ensure that funds are consistently available to the institutions that lend money to home buyers.

On September 7, 2008, James Lockhart, director of the Federal Housing Finance Agency (FHFA), announced that Fannie Mae and Freddie Mac were being placed into conservatorship of the FHFA.

   a. SPDR
   b. Federal National Mortgage Association
   c. The Depository Trust ' Clearing Corporation
   d. General partnership

34. The _____ (NYSE: FRE) is an insolvent government sponsored enterprise (GSE) of the United States federal government.

Chapter 19. Business Borrowing: Corporate Bonds, Asset-Backed Securities, Bank Loans

The _____ was created in 1970 to expand the secondary market for mortgages in the US. Along with other GSEs, Freddie Mac buys mortgages on the secondary market, pools them, and sells them as mortgage-backed securities to investors on the open market.

   a. Federal Home Loan Mortgage Corporation
   b. The Depository Trust ' Clearing Corporation
   c. Governmental Accounting Standards Board
   d. Public company

35. The _____ is a U.S. government-owned corporation within the Department of Housing and Urban Development

Ginnie Mae provides guarantees on mortgage-backed securities backed by federally insured or guaranteed loans, mainly loans issued by the Federal Housing Administration, Department of Veterans Affairs, Rural Housing Service, and Office of Public and Indian Housing. Ginnie Mae securities are the only MBS that are guaranteed by the United States government.

   a. Cash budget
   b. Certified Emission Reductions
   c. Case-Shiller Home Price Indices
   d. GNMA

36. The _____ is a U.S. government-owned corporation within the Department of Housing and Urban Development

Ginnie Mae provides guarantees on mortgage-backed securities backed by federally insured or guaranteed loans, mainly loans issued by the Federal Housing Administration, Department of Veterans Affairs, Rural Housing Service, and Office of Public and Indian Housing. Ginnie Mae securities are the only MBS that are guaranteed by the United States government.

   a. Graduated payment mortgage
   b. Jumbo mortgage
   c. 4-4-5 Calendar
   d. Government National Mortgage Association

37. _____ is a structured finance process that involves pooling and repackaging of cash-flow-producing financial assets into securities, which are then sold to investors. The term '_____' is derived from the fact that the form of financial instruments used to obtain funds from the investors are securities. As a portfolio risk backed by amortizing cash flows - and unlike general corporate debt - the credit quality of securitized debt is non-stationary due to changes in volatility that are time- and structure-dependent.

   a. Securitization
   b. Reputational risk
   c. The Glass-Steagall Act of 1933
   d. Special journals

38. In finance, a _____ (non-investment grade bond, speculative grade bond or junk bond) is a bond that is rated below investment grade at the time of purchase. These bonds have a higher risk of default or other adverse credit events, but typically pay higher yields than better quality bonds in order to make them attractive to investors.

   a. Private equity
   b. Sharpe ratio
   c. Volatility
   d. High yield bond

39. The _____ is the financial market where previously issued securities and financial instruments such as stock, bonds, options, and futures are bought and sold. The term '_____' is also used refer to the market for any used goods or assets, or an alternative use for an existing product or asset where the customer base is the second market

Chapter 19. Business Borrowing: Corporate Bonds, Asset-Backed Securities, Bank Loans

With primary issuances of securities or financial instruments, or the primary market, investors purchase these securities directly from issuers such as corporations issuing shares in an IPO or private placement, or directly from the federal government in the case of treasuries.

a. Delta neutral
b. Secondary market
c. Financial market
d. Performance attribution

40. A _____ or bank is a financial institution whose primary activity is to act as a payment agent for customers and to borrow and lend money.

The first modern bank was founded in Italy in Genoa in 1406, its name was Banco di San Giorgio (Bank of St. George.)

Many other financial activities were added over time.

a. Black Sea Trade and Development Bank
b. Banker
c. 4-4-5 Calendar
d. Bought deal

41. A _____ assesses the credit worthiness of an individual, corporation, or even a country. _____s are calculated from financial history and current assets and liabilities. Typically, a _____ tells a lender or investor the probability of the subject being able to pay back a loan.

a. Credit report monitoring
b. Debenture
c. Credit cycle
d. Credit rating

42. A _____ or market-based mechanism is any of a wide variety of ways to match up buyers and sellers.

An example of a _____ uses announced bid and ask prices. Generally speaking, when two parties wish to engage in a trade, the purchaser will announce a price he is willing to pay (the bid price) and seller will announce a price he is willing to accept (the ask price).

a. 4-4-5 Calendar
b. 529 plan
c. 7-Eleven
d. Price mechanism

43. In the global money market, _____ is an unsecured promissory note with a fixed maturity of one to 270 days. _____ is a money-market security issued (sold) by large banks and corporations to get money to meet short term debt obligations (for example, payroll), and is only backed by an issuing bank or corporation's promise to pay the face amount on the maturity date specified on the note. Since it is not backed by collateral, only firms with excellent credit ratings from a recognized rating agency will be able to sell their _____ at a reasonable price.

a. Commercial paper
b. Book building
c. Trade-off theory
d. Financial distress

44. The _____ is the difference between the amount paid by the underwriting group in a new issue of securities and the price at which securities are offered for sale to the public. It is the underwriter's gross profit margin, usually expressed in points per unit of sale (bond or stock.) Spreads may vary widely and are influenced by the underwriter's expectation of market demand for the securities offered for sale, interest rates, and so on.

Chapter 19. Business Borrowing: Corporate Bonds, Asset-Backed Securities, Bank Loans

a. A Random Walk Down Wall Street
b. ABN Amro
c. Underwriting Spread
d. AAB

45. The U.S. _____ is an independent agency of the United States government which holds primary responsibility for enforcing the federal securities laws and regulating the securities industry, the nation's stock and options exchanges, and other electronic securities markets. The SEC was created by section 4 of the SEC of 1934 (now codified as 15 U.S.C. Â§ 78d and commonly referred to as the 1934 Act.)

a. 4-4-5 Calendar
b. 7-Eleven
c. Securities and Exchange Commission
d. 529 plan

46. In the United States, a _____ is an offering of securities that are not registered with the Securities and Exchange Commission (SEC.) Such offerings exploit an exemption offered by the Securities Act of 1933 that comes with several restrictions, including a prohibition against general solicitation. This exemption allows companies to avoid quarterly reporting requirements and many of the legal liabilities associated with the Sarbanes-Oxley Act.

a. 529 plan
b. 7-Eleven
c. 4-4-5 Calendar
d. Private placement

47. The phrase _____ refers to the aspect of corporate strategy, corporate finance and management dealing with the buying, selling and combining of different companies that can aid, finance, or help a growing company in a given industry grow rapidly without having to create another business entity.

An acquisition, also known as a takeover, is the buying of one company (the 'target') by another. An acquisition may be friendly or hostile.

a. 4-4-5 Calendar
b. 7-Eleven
c. 529 plan
d. Mergers and acquisitions

48. In business and finance, a _____ (also referred to as equity _____) of stock means a _____ of ownership in a corporation (company.) In the plural, stocks is often used as a synonym for _____s especially in the United States, but it is less commonly used that way outside of North America.

In the United Kingdom, South Africa, and Australia, stock can also refer to completely different financial instruments such as government bonds or, less commonly, to all kinds of marketable securities.

a. Procter ' Gamble
b. Bucket shop
c. Margin
d. Share

49. In business, a _____ is the purchase of one company (the target) by another (the acquirer or bidder). In the UK the term refers to the acquisition of a public company whose shares are listed on a stock exchange, in contrast to the acquisition of a private company.

Before a bidder makes an offer for another company, it usually first informs that company's board of directors.

a. Takeover
b. 4-4-5 Calendar
c. Stock swap
d. 529 plan

Chapter 19. Business Borrowing: Corporate Bonds, Asset-Backed Securities, Bank Loans

50. _____ or amalgamation is the act of merging many things into one. In business, it often refers to the mergers or acquisitions of many smaller companies into much larger ones. The financial accounting term of _____ refers to the aggregated financial statements of a group company as consolidated account.
   a. Write-off
   b. Retained earnings
   c. Cost of goods sold
   d. Consolidation

51. _____ is the removal or simplification of government rules and regulations that constrain the operation of market forces. _____ does not mean elimination of laws against fraud, but eliminating or reducing government control of how business is done, thereby moving toward a more free market.

The stated rationale for '_____' is often that fewer and simpler regulations will lead to a raised level of competitiveness, therefore higher productivity, more efficiency and lower prices overall.

   a. Value added
   b. Demand shock
   c. Deregulation
   d. Supply shock

52. A _____ occurs when a financial sponsor acquires a controlling interest in a company's equity and where a significant percentage of the purchase price is financed through leverage (borrowing.) The assets of the acquired company are used as collateral for the borrowed capital, sometimes with assets of the acquiring company. The bonds or other paper issued for _____s are commonly considered not to be investment grade because of the significant risks involved.
   a. Leverage
   b. Pension fund
   c. Leveraged buyout
   d. Limited partnership

53.

A _____ is a type of financial intermediary and a type of bank. Commercial banking is also known as business banking. It is a bank that provides checking accounts, savings accounts, and money market accounts and that accepts time deposits.

   a. 529 plan
   b. 4-4-5 Calendar
   c. 7-Eleven
   d. Commercial bank

54. In economics, _____ refers to the ability of a person or a country to produce a particular good at a lower marginal cost and opportunity cost than another person or country. It is the ability to produce a product most efficiently given all the other products that could be produced. It can be contrasted with absolute advantage which refers to the ability of a person or a country to produce a particular good at a lower absolute cost than another.
   a. Comparative advantage
   b. Case-Shiller Home Price Indices
   c. Reputational risk
   d. Loans and interest, in Judaism

55. A _____ is a rate that determines pay-offs in a financial contract and that is outside the control of the parties to the contract. It is often some form of LIBOR rate, but it can take many forms, such as a consumer price index, a house price index or an unemployment rate. Parties to the contract choose a _____ that neither party has power to manipulate.
   a. TIBOR
   b. London Interbank Offered Rate
   c. Risk-free interest rate
   d. Reference rate

Chapter 19. Business Borrowing: Corporate Bonds, Asset-Backed Securities, Bank Loans

56. _____, also referred to as the discount rate, is the rate of interest which a central bank charges on the loans and advances that it extends to commercial banks and other financial intermediaries. Changes in the _____ are often used by central banks to control the money supply.

The term _____ is most commonly used by bankers to refer to the Federal Discount Rate of interest charged to Federally Chartered Savings Banks.

a. TIBOR
b. Fixed interest
c. London Interbank Offered Rate
d. Bank rate

57. A _____ is a loan made using real estate as collateral to secure repayment.

A _____ is similar to a residential mortgage, except the collateral is a commercial building or other business real estate, not residential property.

In addition, _____s are typically taken on by businesses instead of individual borrowers.

a. Fixed rate mortgage
b. Shared appreciation mortgage
c. Commercial mortgage
d. Chain of Blame

58. The _____ is the market for securities, where companies and governments can raise longterm funds. The _____ includes the stock market and the bond market. Financial regulators, such as the U.S. Securities and Exchange Commission, oversee the _____s in their designated countries to ensure that investors are protected against fraud.

a. Spot rate
b. Forward market
c. Delta neutral
d. Capital market

Chapter 20. The Market for Corporate Stock

1. _____ is a form of corporation equity ownership represented in the securities. It is dangerous in comparison to preferred shares and some other investment options, in that in the event of bankruptcy, _____ investors receive their funds after preferred stockholders, bondholders, creditors, etc. On the other hand, common shares on average perform better than preferred shares or bonds over time.

    a. Stock market bubble
    b. Stop-limit order
    c. Stock split
    d. Common stock

2. A _____ is a private or public market for the trading of company stock and derivatives of company stock at an agreed price; these are securities listed on a stock exchange as well as those only traded privately.

    The size of the world _____ is estimated at about $36.6 trillion US at the beginning of October 2008 . The world derivatives market has been estimated at about $480 trillion face or nominal value, 12 times the size of the entire world economy.

    a. Anton Gelonkin
    b. Adolph Coors
    c. Andrew Tobias
    d. Stock market

3. A _____ is the price of a single share of a no. of saleable stocks of the company. Once the stock is purchased, the owner becomes a shareholder of the company that issued the share.

    a. Trading curb
    b. Share price
    c. Stock split
    d. Whisper numbers

4. In business and finance, a _____ (also referred to as equity _____) of stock means a _____ of ownership in a corporation (company.) In the plural, stocks is often used as a synonym for _____s especially in the United States, but it is less commonly used that way outside of North America.

    In the United Kingdom, South Africa, and Australia, stock can also refer to completely different financial instruments such as government bonds or, less commonly, to all kinds of marketable securities.

    a. Margin
    b. Bucket shop
    c. Procter ' Gamble
    d. Share

5. _____, in finance and accounting, means stated value or face value. From this comes the expressions at par (at the _____), over par (over _____) and under par (under _____.)

    The term '_____' has several meanings depending on context and geography.

    a. FIDC
    b. Par value
    c. Sinking fund
    d. Global Squeeze

6. A _____ is a right to acquire certain property in preference to any other person. It usually refers to property newly coming into existence. A right to acquire existing property in preference to any other person is usually referred to as a right of first refusal.

    In practice, the most common form of _____ is the right of existing shareholders to acquire newly issued shares issued by a company in a rights issue, a usually but not always public offering.

a. Fraud deterrence
b. Court of Audit of Belgium
c. Down payment
d. Pre-emption right

7. _____ is typically a higher ranking stock than voting shares, and its terms are negotiated between the corporation and the investor.

_____ usually carry no voting rights, but may carry superior priority over common stock in the payment of dividends and upon liquidation. _____ may carry a dividend that is paid out prior to any dividends to common stock holders.

a. Preferred stock
b. Trade-off theory
c. Follow-on offering
d. Second lien loan

8. In finance, a _____ is a type of bond that can be converted into shares of stock in the issuing company, usually at some pre-announced ratio. It is a hybrid security with debt- and equity-like features. Although it typically has a low coupon rate, the holder is compensated with the ability to convert the bond to common stock, usually at a substantial discount to the stock's market value.

a. Corporate bond
b. Convertible bond
c. Bond fund
d. Gilts

9. _____ is capital stock which provides a specific dividend that is paid before any dividends are paid to common stock holders, and which takes precedence over common stock in the event of a liquidation. This form of financing is used by private equity investors and venture capital firms. Holders of _____ get both their money back (with interest) and the money that is distributable with respect to the percentage of common shares into which their preferred stock can convert.

a. Participating preferred stock
b. Shareholder value
c. Cash is king
d. Preferred stock

10. The institution most often referenced by the word '_____' is a public or publicly traded _____, the shares of which are traded on a public stock exchange (e.g., the New York Stock Exchange or Nasdaq in the United States) where shares of stock of _____s are bought and sold by and to the general public. Most of the largest businesses in the world are publicly traded _____s. However, the majority of _____s are said to be closely held, privately held or close _____s, meaning that no ready market exists for the trading of shares.

a. Federal Home Loan Mortgage Corporation
b. Protect
c. Depository Trust Company
d. Corporation

11. _____ are organizations which pool large sums of money and invest those sums in companies. They include banks, insurance companies, retirement or pension funds, hedge funds and mutual funds. Their role in the economy is to act as highly specialized investors on behalf of others.

a. AAB
b. Institutional investors
c. ABN Amro
d. A Random Walk Down Wall Street

12. A _____ is a professionally managed type of collective investment scheme that pools money from many investors and invests it in stocks, bonds, short-term money market instruments, and/or other securities. The _____ will have a fund manager that trades the pooled money on a regular basis. Currently, the worldwide value of all _____s totals more than $26 trillion.

Since 1940, there have been three basic types of investment companies in the United States: open-end funds, also known in the US as _____s; unit investment trusts (UITs); and closed-end funds.

a. Financial intermediary
c. Net asset value
b. Trust company
d. Mutual fund

13. A _____ is a pool of assets forming an independent legal entity that are bought with the contributions to a pension plan for the exclusive purpose of financing pension plan benefits.

_____s are important shareholders of listed and private companies. They are especially important to the stock market where large institutional investors like the Ontario Teachers' Pension Plan dominate.

a. Limited liability company
c. Leverage
b. Leveraged buyout
d. Pension fund

14. In business and accounting, _____s are everything of value that is owned by a person or company. The balance sheet of a firm records the monetary value of the _____s owned by the firm. The two major _____ classes are tangible _____s and intangible _____s.

a. EBITDA
c. Asset
b. Income
d. Accounts payable

15.

A _____ is a type of financial intermediary and a type of bank. Commercial banking is also known as business banking. It is a bank that provides checking accounts, savings accounts, and money market accounts and that accepts time deposits.

a. 7-Eleven
c. Commercial bank
b. 4-4-5 Calendar
d. 529 plan

16. A _____ is a payment made by a corporation to its shareholder members. When a corporation earns a profit or surplus, that money can be put to two uses: it can either be re-invested in the business (called retained earnings), or it can be paid to the shareholders as a _____. Many corporations retain a portion of their earnings and pay the remainder as a _____.

a. Dividend
c. Dividend yield
b. Special dividend
d. Dividend puzzle

17. The _____ on a company stock is the company's annual dividend payments divided by its market cap, or the dividend per share divided by the price per share. It is often expressed as a percentage.

Dividend payments on preferred shares are stipulated by the prospectus.

a. Dividend yield
c. Special dividend
b. Dividend reinvestment plan
d. Dividend imputation

Chapter 20. The Market for Corporate Stock

18. The _____ is one of several stock market indices, created by nineteenth-century Wall Street Journal editor and Dow Jones ' Company co-founder Charles Dow. Dow compiled the index to gauge the performance of the industrial sector of the American stock market. It is the second-oldest U.S. market index, after the Dow Jones Transportation Average, which Dow also created.
   a. 529 plan
   b. 4-4-5 Calendar
   c. 7-Eleven
   d. Dow Jones Industrial Average

19. The _____ is an American stock exchange. It is the largest electronic screen-based equity securities trading market in the United States. With approximately 3,200 companies, it has more trading volume per day than any other stock exchange in the world.
   a. 7-Eleven
   b. 4-4-5 Calendar
   c. 529 plan
   d. NASDAQ

20. The _____ is a stock exchange based in New York City, New York. It is the largest stock exchange in the world by dollar value of its listed companies securities. As of October 2008, the combined capitalization of all domestic _____ listed companies was $10.1 trillion.
   a. 7-Eleven
   b. 4-4-5 Calendar
   c. New York Stock Exchange
   d. 529 plan

21. A _____, securities exchange or (in Europe) bourse is a corporation or mutual organization which provides 'trading' facilities for stock brokers and traders, to trade stocks and other securities. _____s also provide facilities for the issue and redemption of securities as well as other financial instruments and capital events including the payment of income and dividends. The securities traded on a _____ include: shares issued by companies, unit trusts and other pooled investment products and bonds.
   a. 529 plan
   b. 4-4-5 Calendar
   c. 7-Eleven
   d. Stock Exchange

22. A _____ is a method of measuring a section of the stock market. Many indices are cited by news or financial services firms and are used to benchmark the performance of portfolios such as mutual funds.
   a. Stop order
   b. Program trading
   c. Trading curb
   d. Stock market index

23. _____ or amalgamation is the act of merging many things into one. In business, it often refers to the mergers or acquisitions of many smaller companies into much larger ones. The financial accounting term of _____ refers to the aggregated financial statements of a group company as consolidated account.
   a. Consolidation
   b. Retained earnings
   c. Cost of goods sold
   d. Write-off

24. An _____ is a contract written by a seller that conveys to the buyer the right -- but not the obligation -- to buy (in the case of a call _____) or to sell (in the case of a put _____) a particular asset, such as a piece of property such as, among others, a futures contract. In return for granting the _____, the seller collects a payment (the premium) from the buyer.

For example, buying a call _____ provides the right to buy a specified quantity of a security at a set strike price at some time on or before expiration, while buying a put _____ provides the right to sell.

a. Option
c. Amortization
b. AT'T Mobility LLC
d. Annuity

25. In finance, the term _____ describes the amount in cash that returns to the owners of a security. Normally it does not include the price variations, at the difference of the total return. _____ applies to various stated rates of return on stocks (common and preferred, and convertible), fixed income instruments (bonds, notes, bills, strips, zero coupon), and some other investment type insurance products (e.g. annuities.)

a. Macaulay duration
c. Yield to maturity
b. 4-4-5 Calendar
d. Yield

26. In economics, _____ is a rise in the general level of prices of goods and services in an economy over a period of time. The term '_____' once referred to increases in the money supply (monetary _____); however, economic debates about the relationship between money supply and price levels have led to its primary use today in describing price _____. _____ can also be described as a decline in the real value of money--a loss of purchasing power in the medium of exchange which is also the monetary unit of account.

a. AAB
c. A Random Walk Down Wall Street
b. ABN Amro
d. Inflation

27. _____ is a fee paid on borrowed assets. It is the price paid for the use of borrowed money, or, money earned by deposited funds. Assets that are sometimes lent with _____ include money, shares, consumer goods through hire purchase, major assets such as aircraft, and even entire factories in finance lease arrangements.

a. A Random Walk Down Wall Street
c. AAB
b. Insolvency
d. Interest

28. An _____ is the price a borrower pays for the use of money they do not own, and the return a lender receives for deferring the use of funds, by lending it to the borrower. _____s are normally expressed as a percentage rate over the period of one year.

_____s targets are also a vital tool of monetary policy and are used to control variables like investment, inflation, and unemployment.

a. Interest rate
c. ABN Amro
b. A Random Walk Down Wall Street
d. AAB

29. In finance, a _____ is a debt security, in which the authorized issuer owes the holders a debt and, depending on the terms of the _____, is obliged to pay interest (the coupon) and/or to repay the principal at a later date, termed maturity.

Thus a _____ is a loan: the issuer is the borrower, the _____ holder is the lender, and the coupon is the interest. _____s provide the borrower with external funds to finance long-term investments, or, in the case of government _____s, to finance current expenditure.

a. Convertible bond
c. Bond
b. Puttable bond
d. Catastrophe bonds

Chapter 20. The Market for Corporate Stock

30. _____ is that which is owed; usually referencing assets owed, but the term can cover other obligations. In the case of assets, _____ is a means of using future purchasing power in the present before a summation has been earned. Some companies and corporations use _____ as a part of their overall corporate finance strategy.
   a. Partial Payment
   b. Cross-collateralization
   c. Credit cycle
   d. Debt

31. A _____ is a fungible, negotiable instrument representing financial value. They are broadly categorized into debt securities (such as banknotes, bonds and debentures), and equity securities; e.g., common stocks. The company or other entity issuing the _____ is called the issuer.
   a. Book entry
   b. Security
   c. Securities lending
   d. Tracking stock

32. _____ or financing is to provide capital (funds), which means money for a project, a person, a business or any other private or public institutions.

Those funds can be allocated for either short term or long term purposes. The health fund is a new way of _____ private healthcare centers.

   a. Product life cycle
   b. Proxy fight
   c. Synthetic CDO
   d. Funding

33. _____ is the risk (variability in value) borne by an interest-bearing asset, such as a loan or a bond, due to variability of interest rates. In general, as rates rise, the price of a fixed rate bond will fall, and vice versa. _____ is commonly measured by the bond's duration.
   a. Interest rate risk
   b. A Random Walk Down Wall Street
   c. Official bank rate
   d. International Fisher effect

34. _____ are government bonds issued by the United States Department of the Treasury through the Bureau of the Public Debt. They are the debt financing instruments of the U.S. Federal government, and they are often referred to simply as Treasuries or Treasurys. There are four types of marketable _____: Treasury bills, Treasury notes, Treasury bonds, and Treasury Inflation Protected Securities (TIPS.)
   a. Treasury Inflation Protected Securities
   b. Treasury Inflation-Protected Securities
   c. 4-4-5 Calendar
   d. Treasury securities

35. The _____ is the market for securities, where companies and governments can raise longterm funds. The _____ includes the stock market and the bond market. Financial regulators, such as the U.S. Securities and Exchange Commission, oversee the _____s in their designated countries to ensure that investors are protected against fraud.
   a. Delta neutral
   b. Capital market
   c. Forward market
   d. Spot rate

36. The _____ process is the process of determining the price of an asset in the marketplace through the interactions of buyers and sellers .

_____ is different from valuation. _____ process involves buyers and sellers arriving at a transaction price for a specific item at a given time.

Chapter 20. The Market for Corporate Stock

a. Price discovery
b. Seed round
c. Pecking order theory
d. Return on capital employed

37. A _____ is a member of an exchange who is an employee of a member firm and executes orders, as agent, on the floor of the exchange for clients. The _____ receives an order via teletype machine from his firm's trading department and then proceeds to the appropriate trading post on the exchange floor. There he joins other brokers and the specialist in the security being bought or sold and executes the trade at the best competitive price available.
 a. Business valuation standards
 b. Floor broker
 c. Case-Shiller Home Price Indices
 d. Multivariate normal distribution

38. _____ is the name of a method of communication between professionals on a stock exchange or futures exchange which involves shouting and the use of hand signals to transfer information primarily about buy and sell orders. The part of the trading floor where this takes place is called a pit.

Examples of markets which use this system in the United States are the New York Mercantile Exchange, the Chicago Mercantile Exchange, the Chicago Board of Trade, and the Chicago Board Options Exchange.

 a. Open outcry
 b. Insider trading
 c. Intellidex
 d. Equity investment

39. In the United States, the Financial Industry Regulatory Authority (FINRA) is a self-regulatory organization (SRO) under the Securities Exchange Act of 1934, successor to the _____, Inc.

FINRA is responsible for regulatory oversight of all securities firms that do business with the public; professional training, testing and licensing of registered persons; arbitration and mediation; market regulation by contract for The NASDAQ Stock Market, Inc., the American Stock Exchange LLC, and the International Securities Exchange, LLC; and industry utilities, such as Trade Reporting Facilities and other over-the-counter operations.

 a. 4-4-5 Calendar
 b. 529 plan
 c. 7-Eleven
 d. National Association of Securities Dealers

40. _____ is a stock market index for the Tokyo Stock Exchange (TSE.) It has been calculated daily by the Nihon Keizai Shimbun (Nikkei) newspaper since 1950. It is a price-weighted average (the unit is Yen), and the components are reviewed once a year.
 a. 7-Eleven
 b. 4-4-5 Calendar
 c. 529 plan
 d. Nikkei 225

41. A _____ is the highest price that a buyer (i.e., bidder) is willing to pay for a good. It is usually referred to simply as the 'bid.'

In bid and ask, the _____ stands in contrast to the ask price or 'offer', and the difference between the two is called the bid/ask spread.

An unsolicited bid or offer is when a person or company receives a bid even though they are not looking to sell.

Chapter 20. The Market for Corporate Stock

a. Mid price
c. Political risk
b. Settlement date
d. Bid price

42. _____ is a measure of the ability of a debtor to pay their debts as and when they fall due. It is usually expressed as a ratio or a percentage of current liabilities.

For a corporation with a published balance sheet there are various ratios used to calculate a measure of liquidity.

a. Invested capital
c. Operating leverage
b. Operating profit margin
d. Accounting liquidity

43. In the United States, the Financial Industry Regulatory Authority (FINRA) is a self-regulatory organization (SRO) under the Securities Exchange Act of 1934, successor to the _____.

FINRA is responsible for regulatory oversight of all securities firms that do business with the public; professional training, testing and licensing of registered persons; arbitration and mediation; market regulation by contract for The NASDAQ Stock Market, Inc., the American Stock Exchange LLC, and the International Securities Exchange, LLC; and industry utilities, such as Trade Reporting Facilities and other over-the-counter operations.

a. 7-Eleven
c. 4-4-5 Calendar
b. 529 plan
d. NASD

44. In finance, a _____ is a trade that is usually at least 10,000 shares of a stock or $200,000 of bonds. It can also refer specifically to large trades that occur between institutional parties at a fixed price. For instance, an insurance company may hold a large stake in a company that they would like to liquidate completely.

a. 4-4-5 Calendar
c. 7-Eleven
b. 529 plan
d. Block trade

45. An _____ is the term used in financial circles for a type of computer system that facilitates trading of financial products outside of stock exchanges. The primary products that are traded on an _____ are stocks and currencies. They came into existence in 1998 when the SEC authorized their creation.

a. Electronic communication network
c. Insider trading
b. Intellidex
d. Open outcry

46. In finance, _____ trading is the trading of exchange listed securities in the over-the-counter (OTC) market. Bernard Madoff was engaged in _____ trading.

a. 529 plan
c. 4-4-5 Calendar
b. 7-Eleven
d. Third market

47. _____ is a branch of finance concerned with the details of how exchange occurs in markets. While the theory of _____ applies to the exchange of real or financial assets, more evidence is available on the microstructure of financial markets due to the availability of transactions data from financial markets. The major thrust of _____ research examines the ways in which the working processes of a market affects determinants of transaction costs, prices, quotes, volume, and trading behavior.

Chapter 20. The Market for Corporate Stock

a. Trade-off
b. Market microstructure
c. Fixed asset turnover
d. Break-even point

48. An _____ is defined as 'a promise which meets the requirements for the formation of a contract and limits the promisor's power to revoke an offer.' Restatement (Second) of Contracts § 25 (1981.)

Quite simply, an _____ is a type of contract that protects an offeree from an offeror's ability to revoke the contract.

Consideration for the _____ is still required as it is still a form of contract.

a. ABN Amro
b. AAB
c. Option contract
d. A Random Walk Down Wall Street

49. The _____ of 2002 (Pub.L. 107-204, 116 Stat. 745, enacted July 30, 2002), also known as the Public Company Accounting Reform and Investor Protection Act of 2002 and commonly called Sarbanes-Oxley, Sarbox or SOX, is a United States federal law enacted on July 30, 2002 in response to a number of major corporate and accounting scandals including those affecting Enron, Tyco International, Adelphia, Peregrine Systems and WorldCom.
a. Foreign Corrupt Practices Act
b. Blue sky law
c. Duty of loyalty
d. Sarbanes-Oxley Act

50. A _____ is an exchange of promises between two or more parties to do an act which is enforceable in a court of law. It is where an unqualified offer meets a qualified acceptance and the parties reach Consensus ad Idem. The parties must have the necessary capacity to _____ and the _____ must not be either trifling, indeterminate, impossible or illegal.
a. 529 plan
b. 4-4-5 Calendar
c. 7-Eleven
d. Contract

51. A _____ is a form of partnership similar to a general partnership, except that in addition to one or more general partners (GPs), there are one or more limited partners (_____s). It is a partnership in which only one partner is required to be a general partner.

The GPs are, in all major respects, in the same legal position as partners in a conventional firm, i.e. they have management control, share the right to use partnership property, share the profits of the firm in predefined proportions, and have joint and several liability for the debts of the partnership.

a. Leverage
b. Limited partnership
c. Fund of funds
d. Limited liability company

52. In finance, _____ is an asset class consisting of equity securities in operating companies that are not publicly traded on a stock exchange. Investments in _____ most often involve either an investment of capital into an operating company or the acquisition of an operating company. Capital for _____ is raised primarily from institutional investors.
a. Pecking order theory
b. Currency swap
c. Stock valuation
d. Private equity

Chapter 20. The Market for Corporate Stock

53. A _____ or bank is a financial institution whose primary activity is to act as a payment agent for customers and to borrow and lend money.

The first modern bank was founded in Italy in Genoa in 1406, its name was Banco di San Giorgio (Bank of St. George.)

Many other financial activities were added over time.

a. Banker
c. 4-4-5 Calendar
b. Bought deal
d. Black Sea Trade and Development Bank

54. A _____ is a type of business entity in which partners (owners) share with each other the profits or losses of the business undertaking in which all have invested. _____ s are often favored over corporations for taxation purposes, as the _____ structure does not generally incur a tax on profits before it is distributed to the partners (i.e. there is no dividend tax levied.) However, depending on the _____ structure and the jurisdiction in which it operates, owners of a _____ may be exposed to greater personal liability than they would as shareholders of a corporation.

a. Fiduciary
c. National Securities Markets Improvement Act of 1996
b. Clayton Antitrust Act
d. Partnership

55. A _____ is a bond issued by a corporation. The term is usually applied to longer-term debt instruments, generally with a maturity date falling at least a year after their issue date. (The term 'commercial paper' is sometimes used for instruments with a shorter maturity.)

a. Government bond
c. Brady bonds
b. Serial bond
d. Corporate bond

56. Explicit _____ is a measure implemented in many countries to protect bank depositors, in full or in part, from losses caused by a bank's inability to pay its debts when due. _____ systems are one component of a financial system safety net that promotes financial stability.

a. Deposit Insurance
c. Time deposit
b. Banking panic
d. Reserve requirement

57. The _____ is a United States government corporation created by the Glass-Steagall Act of 1933. It provides deposit insurance, which guarantees the safety of checking and savings deposits in member banks, currently up to $250,000 per depositor per bank. Insured deposits are backed by the full faith and credit of the United States.

a. Federal Deposit Insurance Corporation
c. FASB
b. NYSE Group
d. Ford Foundation

58. _____, is when a company issues common stock or shares to the public for the first time. They are often issued by smaller, younger companies seeking capital to expand, but can also be done by large privately-owned companies looking to become publicly traded.

In an _____ the issuer may obtain the assistance of an underwriting firm, which helps it determine what type of security to issue (common or preferred), best offering price and time to bring it to market.

Chapter 20. The Market for Corporate Stock

a. Asian Financial Crisis
c. Insolvency
b. Interest
d. Initial public offering

59. _____ is the risk that the value of an investment will decrease due to moves in market factors. The five standard _____ factors are:

- Equity risk, the risk that stock prices will change.
- Interest rate risk, the risk that interest rates will change.
- Currency risk, the risk that foreign exchange rates will change.
- Commodity risk, the risk that commodity prices (e.g. grains, metals) will change.

As with other forms of risk, _____ may be measured in a number of ways. Traditionally, this is done using a Value at Risk methodology. Value at risk is well established as a risk management technique, but it contains a number of limiting assumptions that constrain its accuracy.

a. Transaction risk
c. Currency risk
b. Tracking error
d. Market risk

60. In financial accounting, the term _____ is most commonly used to describe any part of shareholders' equity, except for basic share capital. Sometimes, the term is used instead of the term provision; such a use, however, is inconsistent with the terminology suggested by International Accounting Standards Board. For more information about provisions, see provision (accounting.)

a. FIFO and LIFO accounting
c. Closing entries
b. Treasury stock
d. Reserve

61. The U.S. _____ is an independent agency of the United States government which holds primary responsibility for enforcing the federal securities laws and regulating the securities industry, the nation's stock and options exchanges, and other electronic securities markets. The SEC was created by section 4 of the SEC of 1934 (now codified as 15 U.S.C. § 78d and commonly referred to as the 1934 Act.)

a. 529 plan
c. 7-Eleven
b. 4-4-5 Calendar
d. Securities and Exchange Commission

62. _____ is the provision of resources (such as granting a loan) by one party to another party where that second party does not reimburse the first party immediately, thereby generating a debt, and instead arranges either to repay or return those resources (or material(s) of equal value) at a later date. The first party is called a creditor, also known as a lender, while the second party is called a debtor, also known as a borrower.

Movements of financial capital are normally dependent on either _____ or equity transfers.

a. Warrant
c. Comparable
b. Credit
d. Clearing house

63. A _____ assesses the credit worthiness of an individual, corporation, or even a country. _____s are calculated from financial history and current assets and liabilities. Typically, a _____ tells a lender or investor the probability of the subject being able to pay back a loan.

Chapter 20. The Market for Corporate Stock

a. Credit report monitoring
b. Debenture
c. Credit rating
d. Credit cycle

64. The _____ is overseen by the _____ Association.

Tape C contains over-the-counter stocks listed on the NASDAQ National Market or NASDAQ Small Cap Market, and is overseen by the OTC/UTP Operating Committee.

a. Peer group analysis
b. Liquidating dividend
c. Consolidated tape
d. January effect

65. _____ is an arrangement with the U.S. Securities and Exchange Commission that allows a single registration document to be filed that permits the issuance of multiple securities.

_____ is a registration of a new issue which can be prepared up to two years in advance, so that the issue can be offered quickly as soon as funds are needed or market conditions are favorable.

For example, current market conditions in the housing market are not favorable for a specific firm to issue a public offering.

a. 4-4-5 Calendar
b. Shelf registration
c. Bought deal
d. Black Sea Trade and Development Bank

66. An _____ represents the ownership in the shares of a foreign company trading on US financial markets. The stock of many non-US companies trades on US exchanges through the use of _____s. _____s enable US investors to buy shares in foreign companies without undertaking cross-border transactions.
a. A Random Walk Down Wall Street
b. AAB
c. ABN Amro
d. American depository receipt

67. The _____ is an American financial and commodity derivative exchange based in Chicago. The _____ was founded in 1898 as the Chicago Butter and Egg Board. Originally, the exchange was a non-profit organization.
a. Financial Crimes Enforcement Network
b. Chicago Mercantile Exchange
c. Gamelan Council
d. Public Company Accounting Oversight Board

68. A _____ is a futures contract on a short term interest rate (STIR.) Contracts vary, but are often defined on an interest rate index such as 3-month sterling or US dollar LIBOR.

They are traded across a wide range of currencies, including the G12 country currencies and many others.

a. Dual currency deposit
b. Real estate derivatives
c. Notional amount
d. Financial future

69. In finance, a _____ is a standardized contract, to buy or sell a specified commodity of standardized quality at a certain date in the future, at a market determined price (the futures price.)

The price is determined by the instantaneous equilibrium between the forces of supply and demand among competing buy and sell orders on the exchange at the time of the purchase or sale of the contract.

In many cases, the items may be such non-traditional 'commodities' as foreign currencies, commercial or government paper [e.g., bonds], or 'baskets' of corporate equity ['stock indices'] or other financial instruments.

a. Repurchase agreement
b. Financial future
c. Heston model
d. Futures contract

70. In finance, a _____ is collateral that the holder of a position in securities, options, or futures contracts has to deposit to cover the credit risk of his counterparty (most often his broker.) This risk can arise if the holder has done any of the following:

- borrowed cash from the counterparty to buy securities or options,
- sold securities or options short, or
- entered into a futures contract.

The collateral can be in the form of cash or securities, and it is deposited in a _____ account. On U.S. futures exchanges, '_____' was formally called performance bond.

_____ buying is buying securities with cash borrowed from a broker, using other securities as collateral.

a. Credit
b. Share
c. Procter ' Gamble
d. Margin

71. _____ of a business involves analyzing its financial statements and health, its management and competitive advantages, and its competitors and markets. The term is used to distinguish such analysis from other types of investment analysis, such as quantitative analysis and technical analysis.

_____ is performed on historical and present data, but with the goal of making financial forecasts.

a. 4-4-5 Calendar
b. Growth stocks
c. Stock valuation
d. Fundamental analysis

72. A _____, is a mathematical formalization of a trajectory that consists of taking successive random steps. The results of _____ analysis have been applied to computer science, physics, ecology, economics and a number of other fields as a fundamental model for random processes in time. For example, the path traced by a molecule as it travels in a liquid or a gas, the search path of a foraging animal, the price of a fluctuating stock and the financial status of a gambler can all be modeled as _____s.

a. 4-4-5 Calendar
b. 7-Eleven
c. Random walk
d. 529 plan

73. _____ is a security analysis discipline for forecasting the future direction of prices through the study of past market data, primarily price and volume. In its purest form, _____ considers only the actual price and volume behavior of the market or instrument. Technical analysts may employ models and trading rules based on price and volume transformations, such as the relative strength index, moving averages, regressions, inter-market and intra-market price correlations, cycles or, classically, through recognition of chart patterns.
- a. Point and figure
- b. Dow theory
- c. Support and resistance
- d. Technical analysis

74. In economics and contract theory, _____ deals with the study of decisions in transactions where one party has more or better information than the other. This creates an imbalance of power in transactions which can sometimes cause the transactions to go awry. Examples of this problem are adverse selection and moral hazard.
- a. ABN Amro
- b. Information asymmetry
- c. A Random Walk Down Wall Street
- d. AAB

75. The _____ is the tendency of the stock market to rise between December 31 and the end of the first week in January. There are many theories for why this happens, the main one being that it occurs because many investors choose to sell some of their stock right before the end of the year in order to claim a capital loss for tax purposes. Once the tax calendar rolls over to a new year on January 1st these same investors quickly reinvest their money in the market, causing stock prices to rise.
- a. January effect
- b. Sector rotation
- c. Revaluation
- d. Death spiral financing

76. _____ is the trading of a corporation's stock or other securities (e.g. bonds or stock options) by individuals with potential access to non-public information about the company. In most countries, trading by corporate insiders such as officers, key employees, directors, and large shareholders may be legal, if this trading is done in a way that does not take advantage of non-public information. However, the term is frequently used to refer to a practice in which an insider or a related party trades based on material non-public information obtained during the performance of the insider's duties at the corporation, or otherwise in breach of a fiduciary duty or other relationship of trust and confidence or where the non-public information was misappropriated from the company.
- a. Equity investment
- b. Open outcry
- c. Insider trading
- d. Intellidex

Chapter 21. Consumer Lending and Borrowing

1. _____, in bookkeeping, refers to assets, liabilities, income, and expenses recorded on individual pages of the so called book of final entry or ledger. Changes in _____ value are made by chronologically posting debit (DR) and credit (CR) entries to its page. Examples of _____s are cash, _____s receivable, mortgages, loans, land and buildings, common stock, sales, services provided, wages, and payroll overhead.
   a. Option
   b. Accretion
   c. Alpha
   d. Account

2. _____ refers to making a wide range of secured and unsecured loans to consumers for consumable items such as a car, boat, manufactured home, home equity loan, home equity line of credit, signature loan, signature line of credit, recreational vehicle, or share or certificate of deposit or Stocks and Mutual Funds secured loans.

   _____ does not include mortgage loans, typically used for home purchases, which follow some different regulations than consumer loans. Also, consumer loans are different from commercial loans, which can be calculated on a daily basis, rather than 12 monthly payments, and include interest for leap day, such as in Actual/366 loan calculations.

   a. Coupon leverage
   b. Primary market
   c. Consumer lending
   d. Sogflation

3. A _____ is a pool of assets forming an independent legal entity that are bought with the contributions to a pension plan for the exclusive purpose of financing pension plan benefits.

   _____s are important shareholders of listed and private companies. They are especially important to the stock market where large institutional investors like the Ontario Teachers' Pension Plan dominate.

   a. Limited liability company
   b. Leverage
   c. Leveraged buyout
   d. Pension fund

4. In business and accounting, _____s are everything of value that is owned by a person or company. The balance sheet of a firm records the monetary value of the _____s owned by the firm. The two major _____ classes are tangible _____s and intangible _____s.
   a. EBITDA
   b. Accounts payable
   c. Income
   d. Asset

5. _____ is a legally declared inability or impairment of ability of an individual or organization to pay their creditors. Creditors may file a _____ petition against a debtor ('involuntary _____') in an effort to recoup a portion of what they are owed or initiate a restructuring. In the majority of cases, however, _____ is initiated by the debtor (a 'voluntary _____' that is filed by the bankrupt individual or organization.)
   a. 529 plan
   b. 4-4-5 Calendar
   c. Bankruptcy
   d. Debt settlement

6. _____ refers to a business or organization attempting to acquire goods or services to accomplish the goals of the enterprise. Though there are several organizations that attempt to set standards in the _____ process, processes can vary greatly between organizations. Typically the word '_____' is not used interchangeably with the word 'procurement', since procurement typically includes Expediting, Supplier Quality, and Traffic and Logistics (T'L) in addition to _____.

a. 529 plan
c. 7-Eleven
b. Purchasing
d. 4-4-5 Calendar

7. A _____ is a bond issued by a corporation. The term is usually applied to longer-term debt instruments, generally with a maturity date falling at least a year after their issue date. (The term 'commercial paper' is sometimes used for instruments with a shorter maturity.)

a. Serial bond
c. Brady bonds
b. Corporate bond
d. Government bond

8. _____ is the removal or simplification of government rules and regulations that constrain the operation of market forces. _____ does not mean elimination of laws against fraud, but eliminating or reducing government control of how business is done, thereby moving toward a more free market.

The stated rationale for '_____' is often that fewer and simpler regulations will lead to a raised level of competitiveness, therefore higher productivity, more efficiency and lower prices overall.

a. Deregulation
c. Value added
b. Demand shock
d. Supply shock

9. A _____ is a bond issued by a national government denominated in the country's own currency. Bonds issued by national governments in foreign currencies are normally referred to as sovereign bonds. The first ever _____ was issued by the British government in 1693 to raise money to fund a war against France.

a. Municipal bond
c. Government bond
b. Zero-coupon bond
d. Collateralized debt obligations

10. In finance, the _____ is the global financial market for short-term borrowing and lending. It provides short-term liquidity funding for the global financial system. The _____ is where short-term obligations such as Treasury bills, commercial paper and bankers' acceptances are bought and sold.

a. Debt-for-equity swap
c. Money market
b. Consumer debt
d. Cramdown

11. In business and finance, a _____ (also referred to as equity _____) of stock means a _____ of ownership in a corporation (company.) In the plural, stocks is often used as a synonym for _____s especially in the United States, but it is less commonly used that way outside of North America.

In the United Kingdom, South Africa, and Australia, stock can also refer to completely different financial instruments such as government bonds or, less commonly, to all kinds of marketable securities.

a. Margin
c. Bucket shop
b. Share
d. Procter ' Gamble

12. In finance, a _____ is a debt security, in which the authorized issuer owes the holders a debt and, depending on the terms of the _____, is obliged to pay interest (the coupon) and/or to repay the principal at a later date, termed maturity.

Chapter 21. Consumer Lending and Borrowing

Thus a _____ is a loan: the issuer is the borrower, the _____ holder is the lender, and the coupon is the interest. _____s provide the borrower with external funds to finance long-term investments, or, in the case of government _____s, to finance current expenditure.

a. Catastrophe bonds
c. Puttable bond
b. Convertible bond
d. Bond

13. In United States banking, _____ is a marketing term for certain services offered primarily to larger business customers. It may be used to describe all bank accounts (such as checking accounts) provided to businesses of a certain size, but it is more often used to describe specific services such as cash concentration, zero balance accounting, and automated clearing house facilities. Sometimes, private banking customers are given _____ services.

a. Capitalization rate
c. Profitability index
b. Global tactical asset allocation
d. Cash management

14. A _____ can require immediate payment by the second party to the third upon presentation of the _____. This is called a sight _____. A Cheques is a sight _____. An importer might write a _____ promising payment to an exporter for delivery of goods with payment to occur 60 days after the goods are delivered. Such a _____ is called a time _____.

a. Second lien loan
c. Gross profit margin
b. Cashflow matching
d. Draft

15. A _____ is a professionally managed type of collective investment scheme that pools money from many investors and invests it in stocks, bonds, short-term money market instruments, and/or other securities. The _____ will have a fund manager that trades the pooled money on a regular basis. Currently, the worldwide value of all _____s totals more than $26 trillion.

Since 1940, there have been three basic types of investment companies in the United States: open-end funds, also known in the US as _____s; unit investment trusts (UITs); and closed-end funds.

a. Mutual fund
c. Financial intermediary
b. Trust company
d. Net asset value

16. An _____ can be defined as a contract which provides an income stream in return for an initial payment.

An immediate _____ is an _____ for which the time between the contract date and the date of the first payment is not longer than the time interval between payments. A common use for an immediate _____ is to provide a pension to a retired person or persons.

a. AT'T Inc.
c. Amortization
b. Intrinsic value
d. Annuity

17. A _____ s a time deposit, a financial product commonly offered to consumers by banks, thrift institutions, and credit unions.

They are similar to savings accounts in that they are insured and thus virtually risk-free; they are 'money in the bank'. They are different from savings accounts in that they have a specific, fixed term (often three months, six months, or one to five years), and, usually, a fixed interest rate.

    a. Variable rate mortgage
    b. Certificate of deposit
    c. Time deposit
    d. Reserve requirement

18. Explicit _____ is a measure implemented in many countries to protect bank depositors, in full or in part, from losses caused by a bank's inability to pay its debts when due. _____ systems are one component of a financial system safety net that promotes financial stability.
    a. Reserve requirement
    b. Time deposit
    c. Deposit Insurance
    d. Banking panic

19. An _____ is a retirement plan account that provides some tax advantages for retirement savings in the United States.
    a. ABN Amro
    b. AAB
    c. A Random Walk Down Wall Street
    d. Individual Retirement Arrangement

20. _____s are full-fledged pension plans for self-employed people in the United States. They are sometimes called HR10 plans and are not Individual Retirement Accounts (IRA.)

Since a _____ is a full-fledged pension, there is a Keogh for every employer-sponsored pension-plan design.

    a. 7-Eleven
    b. 4-4-5 Calendar
    c. Keogh plan
    d. 529 plan

21. _____ is a type of permanent life insurance based on a cash value. That is, the policy is established with the insurer where premium payments above the cost of insurance are credited to the cash value. The cash value is credited each month with interest, and the policy is debited each month by a cost of insurance (COI) charge, and any other policy charges and fees which are drawn from the cash value if no premium payment is made that month.
    a. A Random Walk Down Wall Street
    b. ABN Amro
    c. Universal life
    d. AAB

22. A _____ is one in which a brokerage manages an investor's portfolio for a flat quarterly or annual fee. This fee covers all administrative, commission, and management expenses. Sometimes this also includes funds of funds. This type of account is also known as an investment platform.
    a. Wrap account
    b. Floating charge
    c. Payback period
    d. Net worth

23. A _____ is a current account at a banking institution that allows money to be deposited and withdrawn by the account holder, with the transactions and resulting balance being recorded on the bank's books. Some banks charge a fee for this service, while others may pay the customer interest on the funds deposited.

Although restrictions placed on access depend upon the terms and conditions of the account and the provider, the account holder retains rights to have their funds repaid on demand.

a. Bilateral netting
b. Contractum trinius
c. 4-4-5 Calendar
d. Deposit account

24. _____ is consumer credit which is outstanding. In macroeconomic terms, it is debt which is used to fund consumption rather than investment.

Some consider all debt incurred for anything else other than investments unwise or detrimental to the economy, while others believe that consumer credit is beneficial to the economy.

a. Consumer debt
b. Reinvestment risk
c. Retention ratio
d. Foreign exchange hedge

25. _____ is that which is owed; usually referencing assets owed, but the term can cover other obligations. In the case of assets, _____ is a means of using future purchasing power in the present before a summation has been earned. Some companies and corporations use _____ as a part of their overall corporate finance strategy.
a. Credit cycle
b. Debt
c. Partial Payment
d. Cross-collateralization

26. In finance, a _____ is the party in a loan agreement which receives money or other instrument from a lender and promises to repay the lender in a specified time.
a. Borrower
b. Cash credit
c. Line of credit
d. Debt management plan

27. _____ is the provision of resources (such as granting a loan) by one party to another party where that second party does not reimburse the first party immediately, thereby generating a debt, and instead arranges either to repay or return those resources (or material(s) of equal value) at a later date. The first party is called a creditor, also known as a lender, while the second party is called a debtor, also known as a borrower.

Movements of financial capital are normally dependent on either _____ or equity transfers.

a. Warrant
b. Clearing house
c. Comparable
d. Credit

28. _____ is the value of a homeowner's unencumbered interest in their property, i.e. the difference between the home's fair market value and the unpaid balance of the mortgage and any outstanding debt over the home. _____ increases as the mortgage is paid or as the property enjoys appreciation. This is sometimes called real property value in economics.
a. Home equity
b. Real Estate Investment Trust
c. REIT
d. Liquidation value

Chapter 21. Consumer Lending and Borrowing

29. _____ is a type of credit that does not have a fixed number of payments, in contrast to installment credit. Examples of _____s used by consumers include credit cards. Corporate _____ facilities are typically used to provide liquidity for a company's day-to-day operations.
   a. Commercial finance
   b. Reverse stock split
   c. Package loan
   d. Revolving credit

30. The term _____ or economic cycle refers to the fluctuations of economic activity (business fluctuations) around a long-term growth trend. The cycle involves shifts over time between periods of relatively rapid growth of output (recovery and prosperity), and periods of relative stagnation or decline (contraction or recession.) These fluctuations are often measured using the real gross domestic product.
   a. Fixed exchange rate
   b. Behavioral finance
   c. Business cycle
   d. Deflation

31. _____, refers to consumption opportunity gained by an entity within a specified time frame, which is generally expressed in monetary terms. However, for households and individuals, '_____ is the sum of all the wages, salaries, profits, interests payments, rents and other forms of earnings received... in a given period of time.' For firms, _____ generally refers to net-profit: what remains of revenue after expenses have been subtracted.
   a. Annual report
   b. Income
   c. OIBDA
   d. Accrual

32. In finance, the _____ of a financial asset measures the sensitivity of the asset's price to interest rate movements, expressed as a number of years. The reason for expressing this sensitivity in years is that the time that will elapse until a cash flow is received allows more interest to accumulate. Therefore the price of an asset with long term cashflows has more interest rate sensitivity than an asset with cashflows in the near future.
   a. 4-4-5 Calendar
   b. Yield to maturity
   c. Macaulay duration
   d. Duration

33. In economics, _____ is a rise in the general level of prices of goods and services in an economy over a period of time. The term '_____' once referred to increases in the money supply (monetary _____); however, economic debates about the relationship between money supply and price levels have led to its primary use today in describing price _____. _____ can also be described as a decline in the real value of money--a loss of purchasing power in the medium of exchange which is also the monetary unit of account.
   a. Inflation
   b. ABN Amro
   c. A Random Walk Down Wall Street
   d. AAB

34. _____ is a fee paid on borrowed assets. It is the price paid for the use of borrowed money , or, money earned by deposited funds . Assets that are sometimes lent with _____ include money, shares, consumer goods through hire purchase, major assets such as aircraft, and even entire factories in finance lease arrangements.
   a. Interest
   b. A Random Walk Down Wall Street
   c. Insolvency
   d. AAB

35. An _____ is the price a borrower pays for the use of money they do not own, and the return a lender receives for deferring the use of funds, by lending it to the borrower. _____s are normally expressed as a percentage rate over the period of one year.

_____s targets are also a vital tool of monetary policy and are used to control variables like investment, inflation, and unemployment.

    a. Interest rate
    b. ABN Amro
    c. A Random Walk Down Wall Street
    d. AAB

36. _____ is the risk (variability in value) borne by an interest-bearing asset, such as a loan or a bond, due to variability of interest rates. In general, as rates rise, the price of a fixed rate bond will fall, and vice versa. _____ is commonly measured by the bond's duration.

    a. Interest rate risk
    b. A Random Walk Down Wall Street
    c. Official bank rate
    d. International Fisher effect

37. In finance, the term _____ describes the amount in cash that returns to the owners of a security. Normally it does not include the price variations, at the difference of the total return. _____ applies to various stated rates of return on stocks (common and preferred, and convertible), fixed income instruments (bonds, notes, bills, strips, zero coupon), and some other investment type insurance products (e.g. annuities.)

    a. Yield to maturity
    b. Macaulay duration
    c. 4-4-5 Calendar
    d. Yield

38. In finance, the _____ is the relation between the interest rate (or cost of borrowing) and the time to maturity of the debt for a given borrower in a given currency. For example, the current U.S. dollar interest rates paid on U.S. Treasury securities for various maturities are closely watched by many traders, and are commonly plotted on a graph such as the one on the right which is informally called 'the _____.' More formal mathematical descriptions of this relation are often called the term structure of interest rates.

The yield of a debt instrument is the annualized percentage increase in the value of the investment.

    a. 4-4-5 Calendar
    b. Yield curve
    c. 7-Eleven
    d. 529 plan

39. A _____ is a unit that is equal to 1/100th of a percentage point. It is frequently used to express percentage point changes of less than 1%. It avoids the ambiguity between relative and absolute discussions about rates.

    a. Basis point
    b. 529 plan
    c. Bond market
    d. 4-4-5 Calendar

40. A _____ is a cooperative financial institution that is owned and controlled by its members, and operated for the purpose of promoting thrift, providing credit at reasonable rates, and providing other financial services to its members. Many _____s exist to further community development or sustainable international development on a local level. Worldwide, _____ systems vary significantly in terms of total system assets and average institution asset size since _____s exist in a wide range of sizes, ranging from volunteer operations with a handful of members to institutions with several billion dollars in assets and hundreds of thousands of members.

    a. Corporate credit union
    b. Credit Union Service Organization
    c. Fi-linx
    d. Credit union

41. A _____ is a financial institution that specializes in accepting savings deposits and making mortgage and other loans. The S'L or thrift term is mainly used in the United States; similar institutions in the United Kingdom, Ireland and some Commonwealth countries include building societies and trustee savings banks.

They are often mutually held, meaning that the depositors and borrowers are members with voting rights, and have the ability to direct the financial and managerial goals of the organization, not unlike the poliyholders of a mutual insurance company.

    a. Net asset value
    b. Mutual fund
    c. Person-to-person lending
    d. Savings and loan association

42. _____ or amalgamation is the act of merging many things into one. In business, it often refers to the mergers or acquisitions of many smaller companies into much larger ones. The financial accounting term of _____ refers to the aggregated financial statements of a group company as consolidated account.
    a. Cost of goods sold
    b. Write-off
    c. Retained earnings
    d. Consolidation

43. A _____ is a small, short-term loan that is intended to cover a borrower's expenses until his or her next payday. The loans are also sometimes referred to as cash advances, though that term can also refer to cash provided against a prearranged line of credit such as a credit card Legislation regarding _____s varies widely between different countries and, within the USA, between different states.
    a. 7-Eleven
    b. Payday loan
    c. 529 plan
    d. 4-4-5 Calendar

44. A car _____, or simply _____, is a loan where the borrower provides their car title as collateral for a loan.

These loans are typically short-term, and tend to carry higher interest rates than other sources of credit. These loans have higher interest rates than other sources of credit due to the fact that the lender typically does not check credit and that the only consideration for the loan is the value and condition of the vehicle.

    a. Promissory note
    b. Credit repair software
    c. Financial plan
    d. Title loan

45. The institution most often referenced by the word '_____' is a public or publicly traded _____, the shares of which are traded on a public stock exchange (e.g., the New York Stock Exchange or Nasdaq in the United States) where shares of stock of _____s are bought and sold by and to the general public. Most of the largest businesses in the world are publicly traded _____s. However, the majority of _____s are said to be closely held, privately held or close _____s, meaning that no ready market exists for the trading of shares.
    a. Federal Home Loan Mortgage Corporation
    b. Depository Trust Company
    c. Corporation
    d. Protect

46. The _____ is a United States government corporation created by the Glass-Steagall Act of 1933. It provides deposit insurance, which guarantees the safety of checking and savings deposits in member banks, currently up to $250,000 per depositor per bank. Insured deposits are backed by the full faith and credit of the United States.

Chapter 21. Consumer Lending and Borrowing

a. Ford Foundation
b. NYSE Group
c. FASB
d. Federal Deposit Insurance Corporation

47. In financial accounting, the term _____ is most commonly used to describe any part of shareholders' equity, except for basic share capital. Sometimes, the term is used instead of the term provision; such a use, however, is inconsistent with the terminology suggested by International Accounting Standards Board. For more information about provisions, see provision (accounting.)
   a. Reserve
   b. Closing entries
   c. FIFO and LIFO accounting
   d. Treasury stock

48. The _____ of 1968 is a United States federal law designed to protect consumers in credit transactions, by requiring clear disclosure of key terms of the lending arrangement and all costs. The statute is contained in Title I of the Consumer Credit Protection Act, as amended (15 U.S.C. § 1601 et seq.).
   a. Regulation Q
   b. Truth in Lending Act
   c. Fair Credit Reporting Act
   d. Fair Credit Billing Act

49. The _____ is a United States federal law enacted as an amendment to the Truth in Lending Act (codified at 15 U.S.C. § 1601 et seq.). Its purpose is to protect consumers from unfair billing practices and to provide a mechanism for addressing billing errors in 'open end' credit accounts, such as credit card or charge card accounts.
   a. Fair Credit Reporting Act
   b. Fair Credit Billing Act
   c. Regulation Q
   d. Truth in Lending Act

50. The _____ is an American federal law (codified at 15 U.S.C. § 1681 et seq.) that regulates the collection, dissemination, and use of consumer credit information.
   a. Truth in Lending Act
   b. Fair Credit Billing Act
   c. Regulation Q
   d. Fair Credit Reporting Act

51. _____ is a process by which a firm can obtain the use of a certain fixed assets for which it must pay a series of contractual, periodic, tax deductable payments. The lessee is the receiver of the services or the assets under the lease contract and the lessor is the owner of the assets. The relationship between the tenant and the landlord is called a tenancy, and can be for a fixed or an indefinite period of time (called the term of the lease).
   a. Quiet period
   b. Leasing
   c. Royalties
   d. Foreign Corrupt Practices Act

52. _____ refer to services provided by the finance industry.

The finance industry encompasses a broad range of organizations that deal with the management of money. Among these organizations are banks, credit card companies, insurance companies, consumer finance companies, stock brokerages, investment funds and some government sponsored enterprises.

   a. Delta hedging
   b. Cost of carry
   c. Financial instruments
   d. Financial Services

Chapter 21. Consumer Lending and Borrowing

53. The _____ Act is an Act of the 106th United States Congress which repealed part of the Glass-Steagall Act of 1933, opening up competition among banks, securities companies and insurance companies. The Glass-Steagall Act prohibited any one institution from acting as both an investment bank and a commercial bank, or as both a bank and an insurer.

The _____ Act (GLBA) allowed commercial and investment banks to consolidate.

a. 7-Eleven
b. 4-4-5 Calendar
c. 529 plan
d. Gramm-Leach-Bliley

54. The _____ is a United States law (codified at 15 U.S.C. § 1691 et seq.), enacted in 1974, that makes it unlawful for any creditor to discriminate against any applicant, with respect to any aspect of a credit transaction, on the basis of race, color, religion, national origin, sex, marital status, or age (provided the applicant has the capacity to contract); to the fact that all or part of the applicant's income derives from a public assistance program; or to the fact that the applicant has in good faith exercised any right under the Consumer Credit Protection Act. The law applies to any person who, in the ordinary course of business, regularly participates in a credit decision, including banks, retailers, bankcard companies, finance companies, and credit unions.

a. A Random Walk Down Wall Street
b. ABN Amro
c. Equal Credit Opportunity Act
d. AAB

55. In statistics, _____ has two related meanings:

- the arithmetic _____
- the expected value of a random variable, which is also called the population _____.

It is sometimes stated that the '_____' is average. This is incorrect if '_____' is taken in the specific sense of 'arithmetic _____' as there are different types of averages: the _____, median, and mode. Other simple statistical analyses use measures of spread, such as range, interquartile range, or standard deviation. For a real-valued random variable X, the _____ is the expectation of X. Note that not every probability distribution has a defined _____; see the Cauchy distribution for an example.

a. Sample size
b. Harmonic mean
c. Mean
d. Probability distribution

56. A _____ is a fungible, negotiable instrument representing financial value. They are broadly categorized into debt securities (such as banknotes, bonds and debentures), and equity securities; e.g., common stocks. The company or other entity issuing the _____ is called the issuer.

a. Tracking stock
b. Book entry
c. Securities lending
d. Security

Chapter 22. The Residential Mortgage Market

1. In finance, the _____ of a financial asset measures the sensitivity of the asset's price to interest rate movements, expressed as a number of years. The reason for expressing this sensitivity in years is that the time that will elapse until a cash flow is received allows more interest to accumulate. Therefore the price of an asset with long term cashflows has more interest rate sensitivity than an asset with cashflows in the near future.
   a. Macaulay duration
   b. Yield to maturity
   c. 4-4-5 Calendar
   d. Duration

2. In economics, _____ is a rise in the general level of prices of goods and services in an economy over a period of time. The term '_____' once referred to increases in the money supply (monetary _____); however, economic debates about the relationship between money supply and price levels have led to its primary use today in describing price _____. _____ can also be described as a decline in the real value of money--a loss of purchasing power in the medium of exchange which is also the monetary unit of account.
   a. ABN Amro
   b. Inflation
   c. A Random Walk Down Wall Street
   d. AAB

3. _____ is a fee paid on borrowed assets. It is the price paid for the use of borrowed money, or, money earned by deposited funds. Assets that are sometimes lent with _____ include money, shares, consumer goods through hire purchase, major assets such as aircraft, and even entire factories in finance lease arrangements.
   a. A Random Walk Down Wall Street
   b. Insolvency
   c. AAB
   d. Interest

4. An _____ is the price a borrower pays for the use of money they do not own, and the return a lender receives for deferring the use of funds, by lending it to the borrower. _____s are normally expressed as a percentage rate over the period of one year.

   _____s targets are also a vital tool of monetary policy and are used to control variables like investment, inflation, and unemployment.

   a. ABN Amro
   b. AAB
   c. A Random Walk Down Wall Street
   d. Interest rate

5. _____ is the risk (variability in value) borne by an interest-bearing asset, such as a loan or a bond, due to variability of interest rates. In general, as rates rise, the price of a fixed rate bond will fall, and vice versa. _____ is commonly measured by the bond's duration.
   a. Interest rate risk
   b. A Random Walk Down Wall Street
   c. Official bank rate
   d. International Fisher effect

6. In finance, the term _____ describes the amount in cash that returns to the owners of a security. Normally it does not include the price variations, at the difference of the total return. _____ applies to various stated rates of return on stocks (common and preferred, and convertible), fixed income instruments (bonds, notes, bills, strips, zero coupon), and some other investment type insurance products (e.g. annuities.)
   a. Yield
   b. 4-4-5 Calendar
   c. Macaulay duration
   d. Yield to maturity

7. In finance, the _____ is the relation between the interest rate (or cost of borrowing) and the time to maturity of the debt for a given borrower in a given currency. For example, the current U.S. dollar interest rates paid on U.S. Treasury securities for various maturities are closely watched by many traders, and are commonly plotted on a graph such as the one on the right which is informally called 'the _____.' More formal mathematical descriptions of this relation are often called the term structure of interest rates.

The yield of a debt instrument is the annualized percentage increase in the value of the investment.

a. 4-4-5 Calendar
b. 7-Eleven
c. 529 plan
d. Yield curve

8. A _____ is a unit that is equal to 1/100th of a percentage point. It is frequently used to express percentage point changes of less than 1%. It avoids the ambiguity between relative and absolute discussions about rates.
a. 4-4-5 Calendar
b. 529 plan
c. Bond market
d. Basis point

9. In the broadest sense of the term, a _____ is any loan where the proceeds are used to finance construction of some kind. In the United States Financial Services industry however, the term is used to describe a genre of loans designed for construction and containing features such as interest reserves, where repayment ability may be based on something that can only occour when the project is built. Thus the defining features of these loans are special monitoring and guidelines above normal loan guidelines to ensure that the project is completed so that repayment can begin to take place.
a. HELOC
b. Conforming loan
c. Blanket mortgage
d. Construction loan

10. In business and accounting, _____s are everything of value that is owned by a person or company. The balance sheet of a firm records the monetary value of the _____s owned by the firm. The two major _____ classes are tangible _____s and intangible _____s.
a. Accounts payable
b. EBITDA
c. Income
d. Asset

11. The _____ is the market for securities, where companies and governments can raise longterm funds. The _____ includes the stock market and the bond market. Financial regulators, such as the U.S. Securities and Exchange Commission, oversee the _____s in their designated countries to ensure that investors are protected against fraud.
a. Spot rate
b. Forward market
c. Delta neutral
d. Capital market

12. In financial accounting, the term _____ is most commonly used to describe any part of shareholders' equity, except for basic share capital. Sometimes, the term is used instead of the term provision; such a use, however, is inconsistent with the terminology suggested by International Accounting Standards Board. For more information about provisions, see provision (accounting.)
a. Closing entries
b. FIFO and LIFO accounting
c. Treasury stock
d. Reserve

13. A _____ or bank is a financial institution whose primary activity is to act as a payment agent for customers and to borrow and lend money.

Chapter 22. The Residential Mortgage Market

The first modern bank was founded in Italy in Genoa in 1406, its name was Banco di San Giorgio (Bank of St. George.)

Many other financial activities were added over time.

- a. 4-4-5 Calendar
- b. Black Sea Trade and Development Bank
- c. Bought deal
- d. Banker

14. The _____ provide stable, on-demand, low-cost funding to American financial institutions for home mortgage loans, small business, rural, agricultural, and economic development lending. With their members, the _____ank System represents the largest collective source of home mortgage and community credit in the United States. The banks do not provide loans directly to individuals, only to other banks.
    - a. 7-Eleven
    - b. 4-4-5 Calendar
    - c. 529 plan
    - d. Federal Home Loan Banks

15. The _____ (NYSE: FNM), commonly known as Fannie Mae, is a stockholder-owned corporation chartered by Congress in 1968 as a government sponsored enterprise (GSE), but founded in 1938 during the Great Depression. The corporation's purpose is to purchase and securitize mortgages in order to ensure that funds are consistently available to the institutions that lend money to home buyers.

On September 7, 2008, James Lockhart, director of the Federal Housing Finance Agency (FHFA), announced that Fannie Mae and Freddie Mac were being placed into conservatorship of the FHFA.

- a. General partnership
- b. The Depository Trust ' Clearing Corporation
- c. SPDR
- d. Federal National Mortgage Association

16. The _____ is a U.S. government-owned corporation within the Department of Housing and Urban Development

Ginnie Mae provides guarantees on mortgage-backed securities backed by federally insured or guaranteed loans, mainly loans issued by the Federal Housing Administration, Department of Veterans Affairs, Rural Housing Service, and Office of Public and Indian Housing. Ginnie Mae securities are the only MBS that are guaranteed by the United States government.

- a. Certified Emission Reductions
- b. Cash budget
- c. GNMA
- d. Case-Shiller Home Price Indices

17. The _____ is a U.S. government-owned corporation within the Department of Housing and Urban Development

Ginnie Mae provides guarantees on mortgage-backed securities backed by federally insured or guaranteed loans, mainly loans issued by the Federal Housing Administration, Department of Veterans Affairs, Rural Housing Service, and Office of Public and Indian Housing. Ginnie Mae securities are the only MBS that are guaranteed by the United States government.

a. 4-4-5 Calendar
b. Jumbo mortgage
c. Graduated payment mortgage
d. Government National Mortgage Association

18. _____ is a structured finance process that involves pooling and repackaging of cash-flow-producing financial assets into securities, which are then sold to investors. The term '_____' is derived from the fact that the form of financial instruments used to obtain funds from the investors are securities. As a portfolio risk backed by amortizing cash flows - and unlike general corporate debt - the credit quality of securitized debt is non-stationary due to changes in volatility that are time- and structure-dependent.
   a. Securitization
   b. Reputational risk
   c. Special journals
   d. The Glass-Steagall Act of 1933

19. The institution most often referenced by the word '_____' is a public or publicly traded _____, the shares of which are traded on a public stock exchange (e.g., the New York Stock Exchange or Nasdaq in the United States) where shares of stock of _____s are bought and sold by and to the general public. Most of the largest businesses in the world are publicly traded _____s. However, the majority of _____s are said to be closely held, privately held or close _____s, meaning that no ready market exists for the trading of shares.
   a. Corporation
   b. Federal Home Loan Mortgage Corporation
   c. Depository Trust Company
   d. Protect

20. The _____ (NYSE: FRE) is an insolvent government sponsored enterprise (GSE) of the United States federal government.

The _____ was created in 1970 to expand the secondary market for mortgages in the US. Along with other GSEs, Freddie Mac buys mortgages on the secondary market, pools them, and sells them as mortgage-backed securities to investors on the open market.

   a. Governmental Accounting Standards Board
   b. Federal Home Loan Mortgage Corporation
   c. The Depository Trust ' Clearing Corporation
   d. Public company

21. A _____ is an asset-backed security whose cash flows are backed by the principal and interest payments of a set of mortgage loans. Payments are typically made monthly over the lifetime of the underlying loans.
   a. Conforming loan
   b. Shared appreciation mortgage
   c. Home equity line of credit
   d. Mortgage-backed security

22. A _____ is a fungible, negotiable instrument representing financial value. They are broadly categorized into debt securities (such as banknotes, bonds and debentures), and equity securities; e.g., common stocks. The company or other entity issuing the _____ is called the issuer.
   a. Tracking stock
   b. Security
   c. Securities lending
   d. Book entry

23. A _____ is a financial debt vehicle that was first created in June 1983 by investment banks Salomon Brothers and First Boston for Freddie Mac. (The First Boston team was led by Dexter Senft.) Legally, a _____ is a special purpose entity that is wholly separate from the institution(s) that create it.
   a. 4-4-5 Calendar
   b. Collateralized mortgage obligation
   c. Yield curve spread
   d. Tranche

24. _____ is early repayment of a loan by a borrower.

In the case of a mortgage-backed security (MBS), _____ is perceived as a risk, because mortgage debts are often paid off early in order to incur lower total interest payments through cheaper refinancing. The new financing may be cheaper because the borrower's credit rating has improved or because interest rates are lower, but in either case, the payments that would have been made to the MBS investor would be above market rates.

a. Bankruptcy remote
b. Disposal tax effect
c. Retention ratio
d. Prepayment

25. A _____ or floating rate mortgage is a mortgage loan where the interest rate varies to reflect market conditions.

The interest rate will normally vary with changes to the base rate of the central bank and reflects changing costs on the credit markets. This method of variation directly linked to underlying costs benefits lenders by ensuring a profit by passing the interest rate risk to the borrower.

a. Basel Accord
b. Private money
c. Credit bureau
d. Variable rate mortgage

26. _____ is the process of decreasing an amount over a period of time. The word comes from Middle English amortisen to kill, alienate in mortmain, from Anglo-French amorteser, alteration of amortir, from Vulgar Latin admortire to kill, from Latin ad- + mort-, mors death. Particular instances of the term include:

- _____ (business), the allocation of a lump sum amount to different time periods, particularly for loans and other forms of finance, including related interest or other finance charges.
    - _____ schedule, a table detailing each periodic payment on a loan (typically a mortgage), as generated by an _____ calculator.
    - Negative _____, an _____ schedule where the loan amount actually increases through not paying the full interest
- Amortized analysis, analyzing the execution cost of algorithms over a sequence of operations.
- _____ of capital expenditures of certain assets under accounting rules, particularly intangible assets, in a manner analogous to depreciation.
- _____ (tax law)

_____ is also used in the context of zoning regulations and describes the time in which a property owner has to relocate when the property's use constitutes a preexisting nonconforming use under zoning regulations.

- Depreciation

a. Intrinsic value
b. Option
c. Amortization
d. AT'T Inc.

Chapter 22. The Residential Mortgage Market

27. _____ is the value of a homeowner's unencumbered interest in their property, i.e. the difference between the home's fair market value and the unpaid balance of the mortgage and any outstanding debt over the home. _____ increases as the mortgage is paid or as the property enjoys appreciation. This is sometimes called real property value in economics.
- a. Home equity
- b. REIT
- c. Liquidation value
- d. Real Estate Investment Trust

28. An _____ is a contract written by a seller that conveys to the buyer the right -- but not the obligation -- to buy (in the case of a call _____) or to sell (in the case of a put _____) a particular asset, such as a piece of property such as, among others, a futures contract. In return for granting the _____, the seller collects a payment (the premium) from the buyer.

For example, buying a call _____ provides the right to buy a specified quantity of a security at a set strike price at some time on or before expiration, while buying a put _____ provides the right to sell.

- a. Amortization
- b. AT'T Mobility LLC
- c. Option
- d. Annuity

29. A _____ is the price of a single share of a no. of saleable stocks of the company. Once the stock is purchased, the owner becomes a shareholder of the company that issued the share.
- a. Stock split
- b. Whisper numbers
- c. Share price
- d. Trading curb

30. An _____ is a mortgage loan where the interest rate on the note is periodically adjusted based on a variety of indices. Among the most common indices are the rates on 1-year constant-maturity Treasury (CMT) securities, the Cost of Funds Index (COFI), and the London Interbank Offered Rate (LIBOR.) A few lenders use their own cost of funds as an index, rather than using other indices.
- a. AAB
- b. ABN Amro
- c. A Random Walk Down Wall Street
- d. Adjustable rate mortgage

31. The _____ is an American financial and commodity derivative exchange based in Chicago. The _____ was founded in 1898 as the Chicago Butter and Egg Board. Originally, the exchange was a non-profit organization.
- a. Chicago Mercantile Exchange
- b. Financial Crimes Enforcement Network
- c. Public Company Accounting Oversight Board
- d. Gamelan Council

32. A _____ is a futures contract on a short term interest rate (STIR.) Contracts vary, but are often defined on an interest rate index such as 3-month sterling or US dollar LIBOR.

They are traded across a wide range of currencies, including the G12 country currencies and many others.

- a. Notional amount
- b. Real estate derivatives
- c. Financial future
- d. Dual currency deposit

33. An _____ is defined as 'a promise which meets the requirements for the formation of a contract and limits the promisor's power to revoke an offer.' Restatement (Second) of Contracts § 25 (1981.)

Quite simply, an _____ is a type of contract that protects an offeree from an offeror's ability to revoke the contract.

Consideration for the _____ is still required as it is still a form of contract.

a. A Random Walk Down Wall Street
c. ABN Amro
b. Option contract
d. AAB

34. A _____ is an exchange of promises between two or more parties to do an act which is enforceable in a court of law. It is where an unqualified offer meets a qualified acceptance and the parties reach Consensus ad Idem. The parties must have the necessary capacity to _____ and the _____ must not be either trifling, indeterminate, impossible or illegal.

a. 529 plan
c. 4-4-5 Calendar
b. 7-Eleven
d. Contract

35. In finance, a _____ is a standardized contract, to buy or sell a specified commodity of standardized quality at a certain date in the future, at a market determined price (the futures price.)

The price is determined by the instantaneous equilibrium between the forces of supply and demand among competing buy and sell orders on the exchange at the time of the purchase or sale of the contract.

In many cases, the items may be such non-traditional 'commodities' as foreign currencies, commercial or government paper [e.g., bonds], or 'baskets' of corporate equity ['stock indices'] or other financial instruments.

a. Heston model
c. Financial future
b. Futures contract
d. Repurchase agreement

36. In finance, a _____ is collateral that the holder of a position in securities, options, or futures contracts has to deposit to cover the credit risk of his counterparty (most often his broker.) This risk can arise if the holder has done any of the following:

- borrowed cash from the counterparty to buy securities or options,
- sold securities or options short, or
- entered into a futures contract.

The collateral can be in the form of cash or securities, and it is deposited in a _____ account. On U.S. futures exchanges, '_____' was formally called performance bond.

_____ buying is buying securities with cash borrowed from a broker, using other securities as collateral.

a. Share
c. Credit
b. Procter ' Gamble
d. Margin

37. _____ is the legal and professional proceeding in which a mortgagee usually a lender, obtains a court ordered termination of a mortgagor's equitable right of redemption. Usually a lender obtains a security interest from a borrower who mortgages or pledges an asset like a house to secure the loan. If the borrower defaults and the lender tries to repossess the property, courts of equity can grant the borrower the equitable right of redemption if the borrower repays the debt.

   a. Letter of credit   b. Federal Acquisition Regulations
   c. Foreclosure   d. Liability

38. _____ refers to the replacement of an existing debt obligation with a debt obligation bearing different terms. The most common consumer _____ is for a home mortgage.

_____ may be undertaken to reduce interest rate/interest costs (by _____ at a lower rate), to extend the repayment time, to pay off other debt(s), to reduce one's periodic payment obligations (sometimes by taking a longer-term loan), to reduce or alter risk (such as by _____ from a variable-rate to a fixed-rate loan), and/or to raise cash for investment, consumption, or the payment of a dividend.

   a. Refinancing   b. 4-4-5 Calendar
   c. 529 plan   d. 7-Eleven

Chapter 23. International Transactions and Currency Values

1. _____, in bookkeeping, refers to assets, liabilities, income, and expenses recorded on individual pages of the so called book of final entry or ledger. Changes in _____ value are made by chronologically posting debit (DR) and credit (CR) entries to its page. Examples of _____s are cash, _____s receivable, mortgages, loans, land and buildings, common stock, sales, services provided, wages, and payroll overhead.
   - a. Alpha
   - b. Option
   - c. Accretion
   - d. Account

2. A _____, also FX future or foreign exchange future, is a futures contract to exchange one currency for another at a specified date in the future at a price (exchange rate) that is fixed on the purchase date. Typically, one of the currencies is the US dollar. The price of a future is then in terms of US dollars per unit of other currency.
   - a. Currency swap
   - b. Non-deliverable forward
   - c. Foreign exchange controls
   - d. Currency future

3. In finance, a _____ is a standardized contract, to buy or sell a specified commodity of standardized quality at a certain date in the future, at a market determined price (the futures price.)

   The price is determined by the instantaneous equilibrium between the forces of supply and demand among competing buy and sell orders on the exchange at the time of the purchase or sale of the contract.

   In many cases, the items may be such non-traditional 'commodities' as foreign currencies, commercial or government paper [e.g., bonds], or 'baskets' of corporate equity ['stock indices'] or other financial instruments.

   - a. Futures contract
   - b. Repurchase agreement
   - c. Heston model
   - d. Financial future

4. In economics, the _____ is one of the two primary components of the balance of payments, the other being the capital account. It is the sum of the balance of trade (exports minus imports of goods and services), net factor income (such as interest and dividends) and net transfer payments (such as foreign aid.)

   The _____ balance is one of two major metrics of the nature of a country's foreign trade (the other being the net capital outflow).

   - a. Rights issue
   - b. Current account
   - c. Cash budget
   - d. Consols

5. In financial accounting, the term _____ is most commonly used to describe any part of shareholders' equity, except for basic share capital. Sometimes, the term is used instead of the term provision; such a use, however, is inconsistent with the terminology suggested by International Accounting Standards Board. For more information about provisions, see provision (accounting.)
   - a. Treasury stock
   - b. Reserve
   - c. Closing entries
   - d. FIFO and LIFO accounting

Chapter 23. International Transactions and Currency Values

6. _____, refers to consumption opportunity gained by an entity within a specified time frame, which is generally expressed in monetary terms. However, for households and individuals, '_____ is the sum of all the wages, salaries, profits, interests payments, rents and other forms of earnings received... in a given period of time.' For firms, _____ generally refers to net-profit: what remains of revenue after expenses have been subtracted.
    a. Annual report
    b. Accrual
    c. OIBDA
    d. Income

7. _____ in its classic form is defined as a company from one country making a physical investment into building a factory in another country. It is the establishment of an enterprise by a foreigner. Its definition can be extended to include investments made to acquire lasting interest in enterprises operating outside of the economy of the investor.
    a. Foreign direct investment
    b. Dow Jones ' Company
    c. MicroPlace
    d. Public company

8. In economics and finance, _____ represents passive holdings of securities such as foreign stocks, bonds, or other financial assets, none of which entails active management or control of the securities' issuer by the investor; where such control exists, it is known as foreign direct investment. Generally, this means the investor holds less than 10% of the total shares or less than the amount needed to hold the majority vote.

Some examples of _____ are:

- purchase of shares in a foreign company.
- purchase of bonds issued by a foreign government.
- acquisition of assets in a foreign country.

Factors affecting international _____:

- tax rates on interest or dividends (investors will normally prefer countries where the tax rates are relatively low)
- interest rates (money tends to flow to countries with high interest rates)
- exchange rates (foreign investors may be attracted if the local currency is expected to strengthen)

_____ is part of the capital account on the balance of payments statistics.

    a. Portable alpha
    b. Divestment
    c. Tactical asset allocation
    d. Portfolio investment

9. In economics, the concept of the _____ refers to the decision-making time frame of a firm in which at least one factor of production is fixed. Costs which are fixed in the _____ have no impact on a firms decisions. For example a firm can raise output by increasing the amount of labour through overtime.
    a. 529 plan
    b. Long-run
    c. 4-4-5 Calendar
    d. Short-run

10.

A _____ is a type of financial intermediary and a type of bank. Commercial banking is also known as business banking. It is a bank that provides checking accounts, savings accounts, and money market accounts and that accepts time deposits.

a. 7-Eleven
b. Commercial bank
c. 4-4-5 Calendar
d. 529 plan

11. _____ is a form of risk that arises from the change in price of one currency against another. Whenever investors or companies have assets or business operations across national borders, they face _____ if their positions are not hedged.

- Transaction risk is the risk that exchange rates will change unfavourably over time. It can be hedged against using forward currency contracts;
- Translation risk is an accounting risk, proportional to the amount of assets held in foreign currencies. Changes in the exchange rate over time will render a report inaccurate, and so assets are usually balanced by borrowings in that currency.

The exchange risk associated with a foreign denominated instrument is a key element in foreign investment. This risk flows from differential monetary policy and growth in real productivity, which results in differential inflation rates.

a. Tracking error
b. Market risk
c. Currency risk
d. Credit risk

12. The _____ is a monetary system in which a region's common medium of exchange are paper notes that are normally freely convertible into pre-set, fixed quantities of gold. The _____ is not currently used by any government, having been replaced completely by fiat currency.
a. 529 plan
b. Gold standard
c. 7-Eleven
d. 4-4-5 Calendar

13. _____ is a fee paid on borrowed assets. It is the price paid for the use of borrowed money , or, money earned by deposited funds . Assets that are sometimes lent with _____ include money, shares, consumer goods through hire purchase, major assets such as aircraft, and even entire factories in finance lease arrangements.
a. AAB
b. Insolvency
c. A Random Walk Down Wall Street
d. Interest

14. An _____ is the price a borrower pays for the use of money they do not own, and the return a lender receives for deferring the use of funds, by lending it to the borrower. _____s are normally expressed as a percentage rate over the period of one year.

_____s targets are also a vital tool of monetary policy and are used to control variables like investment, inflation, and unemployment.

a. A Random Walk Down Wall Street
b. AAB
c. ABN Amro
d. Interest rate

15. _____ is the risk (variability in value) borne by an interest-bearing asset, such as a loan or a bond, due to variability of interest rates. In general, as rates rise, the price of a fixed rate bond will fall, and vice versa. _____ is commonly measured by the bond's duration.

a. Official bank rate
b. A Random Walk Down Wall Street
c. International Fisher effect
d. Interest rate risk

16. The _____ is a bank that provides financial and technical assistance to developing countries for development programs (e.g. bridges, roads, schools, etc.) with the stated goal of reducing poverty.

The _____ differs from the _____ Group, in that the _____ comprises only two institutions:

- International Bank for Reconstruction and Development (IBRD)
- International Development Association (IDA)

Whereas the latter incorporates these two in addition to three more:

- International Finance Corporation (IFC)
- Multilateral Investment Guarantee Agency (MIGA)
- International Centre for Settlement of Investment Disputes (ICSID)

John Maynard Keynes (right) represented the UK at the conference, and Harry Dexter White represented the US.

The _____ was created following the ratification of the United Nations Monetary and Financial Conference | Bretton Woods agreement. The concept was originally conceived in July 1944 at the United Nations Monetary and Financial Conference.

a. 529 plan
b. 4-4-5 Calendar
c. 7-Eleven
d. World Bank

17. In finance, a _____ is a debt security, in which the authorized issuer owes the holders a debt and, depending on the terms of the _____, is obliged to pay interest (the coupon) and/or to repay the principal at a later date, termed maturity.

Thus a _____ is a loan: the issuer is the borrower, the _____ holder is the lender, and the coupon is the interest. _____s provide the borrower with external funds to finance long-term investments, or, in the case of government _____s, to finance current expenditure.

a. Catastrophe bonds
b. Convertible bond
c. Bond
d. Puttable bond

Chapter 23. International Transactions and Currency Values

18. The free _____ of a public company is an estimate of the proportion of shares that are not held by large owners and that are not stock with sales restrictions (restricted stock that cannot be sold until they become unrestricted stock.)

The free _____ or a public _____ is usually defined as being all shares held by investors other than:

- shares held by owners owning more than 5% of all shares (those could be institutional investors, 'strategic shareholders,' founders, executives, and other insiders' holdings)
- restricted stocks (granted to executives that can be, but don't have to be, registered insiders)
- insider holdings (it is assumed that insiders hold stock for the very long term)

The free _____ is an important criterion in quoting a share on the stock market.

To _____ a company means to list its shares on a public stock exchange through an initial public offering (or 'flotation'.)

- Open market
- Outstanding shares
- Market capitalization
- Public _____ *loat*
- Reverse takeover

a. Synthetic CDO
c. Trade finance
b. Golden parachute
d. Float

19. The _____ is the over-the-counter financial market in contracts for future delivery, so called forward contracts. Forward contracts are personalized between parties. The _____ is a general term used to describe the informal market by which these contracts are entered into.
a. Forward market
c. Spot rate
b. Limits to arbitrage
d. Delta hedging

20. The _____ or cash market is a commodities or securities market in which goods are sold for cash and delivered immediately. Contracts bought and sold on these markets are immediately effective. _____s can operate wherever the infrastructure exists to conduct the transaction.
a. Currency swap
c. Foreign exchange controls
b. Spot market
d. Non-deliverable forward

21. In finance, the _____ between two currencies specifies how much one currency is worth in terms of the other. For example an _____ of 102 Japanese yen to the United States dollar means that JPY 102 is worth the same as USD 1. The foreign exchange market is one of the largest markets in the world.
a. ABN Amro
c. A Random Walk Down Wall Street
b. Exchange rate
d. AAB

Chapter 23. International Transactions and Currency Values

22. An _____ is a contract written by a seller that conveys to the buyer the right -- but not the obligation -- to buy (in the case of a call _____) or to sell (in the case of a put _____) a particular asset, such as a piece of property such as, among others, a futures contract. In return for granting the _____, the seller collects a payment (the premium) from the buyer.

For example, buying a call _____ provides the right to buy a specified quantity of a security at a set strike price at some time on or before expiration, while buying a put _____ provides the right to sell.

   a. Annuity   b. Option
   c. AT'T Mobility LLC   d. Amortization

23. A _____ is the highest price that a buyer (i.e., bidder) is willing to pay for a good. It is usually referred to simply as the 'bid.'

In bid and ask, the _____ stands in contrast to the ask price or 'offer', and the difference between the two is called the bid/ask spread.

An unsolicited bid or offer is when a person or company receives a bid even though they are not looking to sell.

   a. Mid price   b. Settlement date
   c. Political risk   d. Bid price

24. A _____ is the price of a single share of a no. of saleable stocks of the company. Once the stock is purchased, the owner becomes a shareholder of the company that issued the share.
   a. Whisper numbers   b. Share price
   c. Stock split   d. Trading curb

25. In economics and finance, _____ is the practice of taking advantage of a price differential between two or more markets: striking a combination of matching deals that capitalize upon the imbalance, the profit being the difference between the market prices. When used by academics, an _____ is a transaction that involves no negative cash flow at any probabilistic or temporal state and a positive cash flow in at least one state; in simple terms, a risk-free profit.
   a. Arbitrage   b. Issuer
   c. Efficient-market hypothesis   d. Initial margin

26. _____ refers to a business or organization attempting to acquire goods or services to accomplish the goals of the enterprise. Though there are several organizations that attempt to set standards in the _____ process, processes can vary greatly between organizations. Typically the word '_____' is not used interchangeably with the word 'procurement', since procurement typically includes Expediting, Supplier Quality, and Traffic and Logistics (T'L) in addition to _____.
   a. Purchasing   b. 4-4-5 Calendar
   c. 529 plan   d. 7-Eleven

27. _____ is the value of goods/services compared to the amount paid with a currency. Currency can be either a commodity money, like gold or silver, or fiat currency like US dollars which are the world reserve currency. As Adam Smith noted, having money gives one the ability to 'command' others' labor, so _____ to some extent is power over other people, to the extent that they are willing to trade their labor or goods for money or currency.

Chapter 23. International Transactions and Currency Values

a. Purchasing power
c. 7-Eleven

b. 4-4-5 Calendar
d. 529 plan

28. The _____ theory uses the long-term equilibrium exchange rate of two currencies to equalize their purchasing power. Developed by Gustav Cassel in 1920, it is based on the law of one price: the theory states that, in ideally efficient markets, identical goods should have only one price.

This purchasing power SEM rate equalizes the purchasing power of different currencies in their home countries for a given basket of goods.

a. TED spread
c. Gross national product

b. 4-4-5 Calendar
d. Purchasing power parity

29. _____ (in a financial context) is the assumption of the risk of loss, in return for the uncertain possibility of a reward. Only if one may safely say that a particular position involves no risk may one say, strictly speaking, that such a position represents an 'investment.' Financial _____ involves the buying, holding, selling, and short-selling of stocks, bonds, commodities, currencies, collectibles, real estate, derivatives, or any valuable financial instrument to profit from fluctuations in its price as opposed to buying it for use or for income via methods such as dividends or interest. _____ represents one of four market roles in Western financial markets, distinct from hedging, long- or short-term investing, and arbitrage.

a. Market anomaly
c. Central Securities Depository

b. Forward market
d. Speculation

30. A _____ or market-based mechanism is any of a wide variety of ways to match up buyers and sellers.

An example of a _____ uses announced bid and ask prices. Generally speaking, when two parties wish to engage in a trade, the purchaser will announce a price he is willing to pay (the bid price) and seller will announce a price he is willing to accept (the ask price).

a. 7-Eleven
c. 4-4-5 Calendar

b. 529 plan
d. Price mechanism

31. A _____, reserve bank, or monetary authority is the entity responsible for the monetary policy of a country or of a group of member states. It is a bank that can lend money to other banks in times of need. Its primary responsibility is to maintain the stability of the national currency and money supply, but more active duties include controlling subsidized-loan interest rates, and acting as a lender of last resort to the banking sector during times of financial crisis (private banks often being integral to the national financial system.)

a. 4-4-5 Calendar
c. 7-Eleven

b. 529 plan
d. Central Bank

32. In the United States, _____ are overnight borrowings by banks to maintain their bank reserves at the Federal Reserve. Banks keep reserves at Federal Reserve Banks to meet their reserve requirements and to clear financial transactions. Transactions in the _____ market enable depository institutions with reserve balances in excess of reserve requirements to lend reserves to institutions with reserve deficiencies.

| a. Regulation T | b. Federal funds rate |
| c. Federal funds | d. 4-4-5 Calendar |

33. _____ is the process by which the government, or monetary authority of a country controls (i) the supply of money central bank (ii) availability of money, and (iii) cost of money or rate of interest, in order to attain a set of objectives oriented towards the growth and stability of the economy. Monetary theory provides insight into how to craft optimal _____.

_____ is referred to as either being an expansionary policy where an expansionary policy increases the total supply of money in the economy, and a contractionary policy decreases the total money supply.

| a. Federal Open Market Committee | b. Natural resources consumption tax |
| c. Tax exemption | d. Monetary policy |

34. A _____ is an agreement between two parties to buy or sell an asset at a specified point of time in the future. The price of the underlying instrument, in whatever form, is paid before control of the instrument changes. This is one of the many forms of buy/sell orders where the time of trade is not the time where the securities themselves are exchanged.

| a. Derivatives markets | b. Constant maturity credit default swap |
| c. Loan Credit Default Swap Index | d. Forward contract |

35. A _____ is an exchange of promises between two or more parties to do an act which is enforceable in a court of law. It is where an unqualified offer meets a qualified acceptance and the parties reach Consensus ad Idem. The parties must have the necessary capacity to _____ and the _____ must not be either trifling, indeterminate, impossible or illegal.

| a. 529 plan | b. 4-4-5 Calendar |
| c. 7-Eleven | d. Contract |

36. _____ is the investment strategy where an investor buys a financial instrument denominated in a foreign currency, and hedges his foreign exchange risk by selling a forward contract in the amount of the proceeds of the investment back into his base currency. The proceeds of the investment are only known exactly if the financial instrument is risk-free and only pays interest once, on the date of the forward sale of foreign currency. Otherwise, some foreign exchange risk remains.

| a. Triangular arbitrage | b. Currency future |
| c. Floating exchange rate | d. Covered interest arbitrage |

37. A _____ is a futures contract on a short term interest rate (STIR.) Contracts vary, but are often defined on an interest rate index such as 3-month sterling or US dollar LIBOR.

They are traded across a wide range of currencies, including the G12 country currencies and many others.

| a. Dual currency deposit | b. Real estate derivatives |
| c. Notional amount | d. Financial future |

38. _____ is an economic concept, expressed as a basic algebraic identity that relates interest rates and exchange rates. The identity is theoretical, and usually follows from assumptions imposed in economics models. There is evidence to support as well as to refute the concept.

Chapter 23. International Transactions and Currency Values 235

a. A Random Walk Down Wall Street
c. Unit price
b. AAB
d. Interest rate parity

39. An _____ is defined as 'a promise which meets the requirements for the formation of a contract and limits the promisor's power to revoke an offer.' Restatement (Second) of Contracts § 25 (1981.)

Quite simply, an _____ is a type of contract that protects an offeree from an offeror's ability to revoke the contract.

Consideration for the _____ is still required as it is still a form of contract.

a. ABN Amro
c. AAB
b. A Random Walk Down Wall Street
d. Option contract

40. _____ is subcontracting a process, such as product design or manufacturing, to a third-party company. The decision to outsource is often made in the interest of lowering cost or making better use of time and energy costs, redirecting or conserving energy directed at the competencies of a particular business, or to make more efficient use of land, labor, capital, (information) technology and resources. _____ became part of the business lexicon during the 1980s.
a. Exchange Rate Mechanism
c. AT'T Inc.
b. OTC Bulletin Board
d. Outsourcing

41. The _____ is an American financial and commodity derivative exchange based in Chicago. The _____ was founded in 1898 as the Chicago Butter and Egg Board. Originally, the exchange was a non-profit organization.
a. Gamelan Council
c. Financial Crimes Enforcement Network
b. Public Company Accounting Oversight Board
d. Chicago Mercantile Exchange

42. In finance, a _____ is a position established in one market in an attempt to offset exposure to the price risk of an equal but opposite obligation or position in another market -- usually, but not always, in the context of one's commercial activity. Hedging is a strategy designed to minimize exposure to such business risks as a sharp contraction in demand for one's inventory, while still allowing the business to profit from producing and maintaining that inventory. A typical hedger might be a farmer with 2000 acres of unharvested wheat in the ground, who would rather tend his crop without the distraction of uncertain prices.
a. 4-4-5 Calendar
c. Hedge
b. 529 plan
d. 7-Eleven

43. A _____ is a foreign exchange agreement between two parties to exchange principal and fixed rate interest payments on a loan in one currency for principal and fixed rate interest payments on an equal (regarding net present value) loan in another currency. They are motivated by comparative advantage.
a. Currency pair
c. Currency swap
b. Foreign exchange market
d. Forex swap

44. In finance, a _____ is a derivative in which two counterparties agree to exchange one stream of cash flows against another stream. These streams are called the legs of the _____.

The cash flows are calculated over a notional principal amount, which is usually not exchanged between counterparties.

a. Local volatility
b. Volatility swap
c. Swap
d. Volatility arbitrage

45. _____ is the provision of resources (such as granting a loan) by one party to another party where that second party does not reimburse the first party immediately, thereby generating a debt, and instead arranges either to repay or return those resources (or material(s) of equal value) at a later date. The first party is called a creditor, also known as a lender, while the second party is called a debtor, also known as a borrower.

Movements of financial capital are normally dependent on either _____ or equity transfers.

a. Clearing house
b. Warrant
c. Comparable
d. Credit

46. In economics, a _____ is a mechanism that allows people to easily buy and sell (trade) financial securities (such as stocks and bonds), commodities (such as precious metals or agricultural goods), and other fungible items of value at low transaction costs and at prices that reflect the efficient-market hypothesis.

_____s have evolved significantly over several hundred years and are undergoing constant innovation to improve liquidity.

Both general markets (where many commodities are traded) and specialized markets (where only one commodity is traded) exist.

a. Secondary market
b. Delta hedging
c. Cost of carry
d. Financial market

47. The _____ is where currency trading takes place. It is where banks and other official institutions facilitate the buying and selling of foreign currencies. FX transactions typically involve one party purchasing a quantity of one currency in exchange for paying a quantity of another.

a. Floating exchange rate
b. Foreign exchange option
c. Spot market
d. Foreign exchange market

Chapter 24. International Banking

1. The institution most often referenced by the word '_____' is a public or publicly traded _____, the shares of which are traded on a public stock exchange (e.g., the New York Stock Exchange or Nasdaq in the United States) where shares of stock of _____s are bought and sold by and to the general public. Most of the largest businesses in the world are publicly traded _____s. However, the majority of _____s are said to be closely held, privately held or close _____s, meaning that no ready market exists for the trading of shares.
   a. Depository Trust Company
   b. Corporation
   c. Federal Home Loan Mortgage Corporation
   d. Protect

2. A _____ is an entity formed between two or more parties to undertake economic activity together. The parties agree to create a new entity by both contributing equity, and they then share in the revenues, expenses, and control of the enterprise. The venture can be for one specific project only, or a continuing business relationship such as the Sony Ericsson _____.
   a. Pre-emption right
   b. Fair Debt Collection Practices Act
   c. Lien
   d. Joint venture

3. _____ generally refers to the buying and holding of shares of stock on a stock market by individuals and funds in anticipation of income from dividends and capital gain as the value of the stock rises. It also sometimes refers to the acquisition of equity (ownership) participation in a private (unlisted) company or a startup (a company being created or newly created.) When the investment is in infant companies, it is referred to as venture capital investing and is generally understood to be higher risk than investment in listed going-concern situations.
   a. Open outcry
   b. Intellidex
   c. Equity investment
   d. Insider trading

4. A _____ is an international bond that is denominated in a currency not native to the country where it is issued. It can be categorised according to the currency in which it is issued. London is one of the centers of the _____ market, but _____s may be traded throughout the world - for example in Singapore or Tokyo.
   a. Interest rate option
   b. Eurobond
   c. Education production function
   d. Economic entity

5. _____ is the term used to describe deposits residing in banks that are located outside the borders of the country that issues the currency the deposit is denominated in. For example a deposit denominated in US dollars residing in a Japanese bank is a _____ deposit, or more specifically a Eurodollar deposit.

Key points are the location of the bank and the denomination of the currency, not the nationality of the bank or the owner of the deposit/loan.

   a. AAB
   b. Eurocurrency
   c. ABN Amro
   d. A Random Walk Down Wall Street

6. A standard, commercial _____ is a document issued mostly by a financial institution, used primarily in trade finance, which usually provides an irrevocable payment undertaking.

The _____ can also be the source of payment for a transaction, meaning that redeeming the _____ will pay an exporter. Letters of credit are used primarily in international trade transactions of significant value, for deals between a supplier in one country and a customer in another.

a. Duty of loyalty
b. McFadden Act
c. Bond indenture
d. Letter of credit

7. _____ is the provision of resources (such as granting a loan) by one party to another party where that second party does not reimburse the first party immediately, thereby generating a debt, and instead arranges either to repay or return those resources (or material(s) of equal value) at a later date. The first party is called a creditor, also known as a lender, while the second party is called a debtor, also known as a borrower.

Movements of financial capital are normally dependent on either _____ or equity transfers.

a. Comparable
b. Clearing house
c. Credit
d. Warrant

8. A _____, reserve bank, or monetary authority is the entity responsible for the monetary policy of a country or of a group of member states. It is a bank that can lend money to other banks in times of need. Its primary responsibility is to maintain the stability of the national currency and money supply, but more active duties include controlling subsidized-loan interest rates, and acting as a lender of last resort to the banking sector during times of financial crisis (private banks often being integral to the national financial system.)

a. 4-4-5 Calendar
b. 529 plan
c. 7-Eleven
d. Central Bank

9. _____ is a structured finance process that involves pooling and repackaging of cash-flow-producing financial assets into securities, which are then sold to investors. The term '_____' is derived from the fact that the form of financial instruments used to obtain funds from the investors are securities. As a portfolio risk backed by amortizing cash flows - and unlike general corporate debt - the credit quality of securitized debt is non-stationary due to changes in volatility that are time- and structure-dependent.

a. Reputational risk
b. The Glass-Steagall Act of 1933
c. Securitization
d. Special journals

10. The _____ of 1956 (12 U.S.C. § 1841, et seq.) is a United States Act of Congress that regulates the actions of bank holding companies.

The original law (subsequently amended), specified that the Federal Reserve Board of Governors must approve the establishment of a bank holding company, and prohibited bank holding companies headquartered in one state from acquiring a bank in another state. The law was implemented in part to regulate and control banks that had formed bank holding companies in order to own both banking and non-banking businesses.

a. Bank Holding Company Act
b. Fair Credit Reporting Act
c. Truth in Lending Act
d. Fair Credit Billing Act

11. Explicit _____ is a measure implemented in many countries to protect bank depositors, in full or in part, from losses caused by a bank's inability to pay its debts when due. _____ systems are one component of a financial system safety net that promotes financial stability.

a. Deposit Insurance
b. Banking panic
c. Time deposit
d. Reserve requirement

12. The _____ is a United States government corporation created by the Glass-Steagall Act of 1933. It provides deposit insurance, which guarantees the safety of checking and savings deposits in member banks, currently up to $250,000 per depositor per bank. Insured deposits are backed by the full faith and credit of the United States.
   a. NYSE Group
   b. Ford Foundation
   c. FASB
   d. Federal Deposit Insurance Corporation

13. A _____ is a company that owns other companies' outstanding stock. It usually refers to a company which does not produce goods or services itself, rather its only purpose is owning shares of other companies. They allow the reduction of risk for the owners and can allow the ownership and control of a number of different companies.
   a. MRU Holdings
   b. Holding Company
   c. Privately held company
   d. Federal National Mortgage Association

14. In financial accounting, the term _____ is most commonly used to describe any part of shareholders' equity, except for basic share capital. Sometimes, the term is used instead of the term provision; such a use, however, is inconsistent with the terminology suggested by International Accounting Standards Board. For more information about provisions, see provision (accounting.)
   a. Reserve
   b. Closing entries
   c. FIFO and LIFO accounting
   d. Treasury stock

15. _____ is the removal or simplification of government rules and regulations that constrain the operation of market forces. _____ does not mean elimination of laws against fraud, but eliminating or reducing government control of how business is done, thereby moving toward a more free market.

The stated rationale for '_____' is often that fewer and simpler regulations will lead to a raised level of competitiveness, therefore higher productivity, more efficiency and lower prices overall.

   a. Supply shock
   b. Value added
   c. Demand shock
   d. Deregulation

16. _____ is a form of risk that arises from the change in price of one currency against another. Whenever investors or companies have assets or business operations across national borders, they face _____ if their positions are not hedged.

   - Transaction risk is the risk that exchange rates will change unfavourably over time. It can be hedged against using forward currency contracts;
   - Translation risk is an accounting risk, proportional to the amount of assets held in foreign currencies. Changes in the exchange rate over time will render a report inaccurate, and so assets are usually balanced by borrowings in that currency.

The exchange risk associated with a foreign denominated instrument is a key element in foreign investment. This risk flows from differential monetary policy and growth in real productivity, which results in differential inflation rates.

   a. Credit risk
   b. Tracking error
   c. Market risk
   d. Currency risk

17. _____ is a fee paid on borrowed assets. It is the price paid for the use of borrowed money, or, money earned by deposited funds. Assets that are sometimes lent with _____ include money, shares, consumer goods through hire purchase, major assets such as aircraft, and even entire factories in finance lease arrangements.

  a. Interest
  b. AAB
  c. Insolvency
  d. A Random Walk Down Wall Street

18. An _____ is the price a borrower pays for the use of money they do not own, and the return a lender receives for deferring the use of funds, by lending it to the borrower. _____s are normally expressed as a percentage rate over the period of one year.

_____s targets are also a vital tool of monetary policy and are used to control variables like investment, inflation, and unemployment.

  a. A Random Walk Down Wall Street
  b. AAB
  c. ABN Amro
  d. Interest rate

19. _____ is the risk (variability in value) borne by an interest-bearing asset, such as a loan or a bond, due to variability of interest rates. In general, as rates rise, the price of a fixed rate bond will fall, and vice versa. _____ is commonly measured by the bond's duration.

  a. A Random Walk Down Wall Street
  b. International Fisher effect
  c. Official bank rate
  d. Interest rate risk

20. _____ is a type of risk faced by investors, corporations, and governments. It is a risk that can be understood and managed with proper aforethought and investment.

Broadly, _____ refers to the complications businesses and governments may face as a result of what are commonly referred to as political decisions--or 'any political change that alters the expected outcome and value of a given economic action by changing the probability of achieving business objectives.'.

  a. Single-index model
  b. Mid price
  c. Capital asset
  d. Political risk

21. In a _____, a company's creditors generally agree to cancel some or all of the debt in exchange for equity in the company.

These deals often occur when large companies run into serious financial trouble, and often result in these companies being taken over by their principal creditors. This is because both the debt and the remaining assets in these companies are so large that there is no advantage for the creditors to drive the company into bankruptcy.

  a. Covestor
  b. Debt restructuring
  c. Financial Gerontology
  d. Debt-for-equity swap

22. In finance, a _____ is a derivative in which two counterparties agree to exchange one stream of cash flows against another stream. These streams are called the legs of the _____.

The cash flows are calculated over a notional principal amount, which is usually not exchanged between counterparties.

a. Swap
b. Volatility arbitrage
c. Local volatility
d. Volatility swap

23. The _____ is a bank that provides financial and technical assistance to developing countries for development programs (e.g. bridges, roads, schools, etc.) with the stated goal of reducing poverty.

The _____ differs from the _____ Group, in that the _____ comprises only two institutions:

- International Bank for Reconstruction and Development (IBRD)
- International Development Association (IDA)

Whereas the latter incorporates these two in addition to three more:

- International Finance Corporation (IFC)
- Multilateral Investment Guarantee Agency (MIGA)
- International Centre for Settlement of Investment Disputes (ICSID)

John Maynard Keynes (right) represented the UK at the conference, and Harry Dexter White represented the US.

The _____ was created following the ratification of the United Nations Monetary and Financial Conference | Bretton Woods agreement. The concept was originally conceived in July 1944 at the United Nations Monetary and Financial Conference.

a. 4-4-5 Calendar
b. 529 plan
c. 7-Eleven
d. World Bank

24. _____ is that which is owed; usually referencing assets owed, but the term can cover other obligations. In the case of assets, _____ is a means of using future purchasing power in the present before a summation has been earned. Some companies and corporations use _____ as a part of their overall corporate finance strategy.
a. Credit cycle
b. Debt
c. Partial Payment
d. Cross-collateralization

25. A _____ is a fungible, negotiable instrument representing financial value. They are broadly categorized into debt securities (such as banknotes, bonds and debentures), and equity securities; e.g., common stocks. The company or other entity issuing the _____ is called the issuer.
a. Securities lending
b. Book entry
c. Tracking stock
d. Security

26. A _____ or bank is a financial institution whose primary activity is to act as a payment agent for customers and to borrow and lend money.

Chapter 24. International Banking

The first modern bank was founded in Italy in Genoa in 1406, its name was Banco di San Giorgio (Bank of St. George.)

Many other financial activities were added over time.

- a. Bought deal
- b. Black Sea Trade and Development Bank
- c. 4-4-5 Calendar
- d. Banker

27. _____ is a type of trade policy that allows traders to act and transact without interference from government. Thus, the policy permits trading partners mutual gains from trade, with goods and services produced according to the theory of comparative advantage.

Under a _____ policy, prices are a reflection of true supply and demand, and are the sole determinant of resource allocation.

- a. Free Trade
- b. Yield spread
- c. Seasoned equity offering
- d. Monte Carlo methods

28. The phrase _____ refers to the aspect of corporate strategy, corporate finance and management dealing with the buying, selling and combining of different companies that can aid, finance, or help a growing company in a given industry grow rapidly without having to create another business entity.

An acquisition, also known as a takeover, is the buying of one company (the 'target') by another. An acquisition may be friendly or hostile.

- a. 4-4-5 Calendar
- b. 529 plan
- c. 7-Eleven
- d. Mergers and acquisitions

29. The _____ is a trilateral trade bloc in North America created by the governments of the United States, Canada, and Mexico. The agreement creating the trade bloc came into force on January 1, 1994. It superseded the Canada-United States Free Trade Agreement between the U.S. and Canada.

- a. North American Free Trade Agreement
- b. 7-Eleven
- c. 529 plan
- d. 4-4-5 Calendar

30.

A _____ is a type of financial intermediary and a type of bank. Commercial banking is also known as business banking. It is a bank that provides checking accounts, savings accounts, and money market accounts and that accepts time deposits.

- a. 4-4-5 Calendar
- b. 529 plan
- c. 7-Eleven
- d. Commercial Bank

31. The _____ is an important selective, mainly private, international organization designed by its founders to supervise and liberalize international trade. The organization officially commenced on 1 January 1995, under the Marrakesh Agreement, succeeding the 1947 General Agreement on Tariffs and Trade (GATT.)

The _____ deals with regulation of trade between participating countries; it provides a framework for negotiating and formalising trade agreements, and a dispute resolution process aimed at enforcing participants' adherence to _____ agreements which are signed by representatives of member governments and ratified by their parliaments.

   a. Gamelan Council
   c. Public Company Accounting Oversight Board
   b. World Trade Organization
   d. Financial Crimes Enforcement Network

Chapter 1

1. c	2. d	3. d	4. b	5. d	6. d	7. d	8. a	9. a	10. c
11. c	12. d	13. a	14. c	15. d	16. d	17. d	18. c	19. c	20. c
21. a	22. d	23. d	24. c	25. d	26. d	27. c	28. a	29. d	30. a
31. d	32. d	33. b	34. b	35. b	36. c	37. d	38. d	39. a	40. c
41. d	42. d	43. a	44. d	45. c	46. d	47. c	48. d		

Chapter 2

1. b	2. d	3. d	4. c	5. d	6. d	7. d	8. a	9. d	10. d
11. c	12. b	13. d	14. d	15. d	16. b	17. b	18. d	19. d	20. a
21. b	22. d	23. d	24. c	25. d	26. d	27. d	28. b	29. d	30. a
31. b	32. d	33. a	34. d	35. d	36. d	37. a	38. d	39. d	40. d
41. d	42. d	43. b	44. a	45. d	46. a	47. d	48. d	49. b	50. d
51. b	52. d	53. b	54. b	55. c	56. b	57. c	58. d	59. c	60. d
61. c	62. d	63. a	64. a	65. d	66. d	67. b	68. a	69. b	

Chapter 3

1. d	2. d	3. d	4. d	5. d	6. d	7. d	8. d	9. d	10. c
11. c	12. d	13. a	14. c	15. d	16. c	17. d	18. d	19. d	20. d
21. a	22. d	23. d	24. d	25. d	26. d	27. a	28. d	29. d	30. c
31. d	32. a	33. d	34. c	35. d	36. d	37. b	38. d	39. b	40. d
41. d	42. d	43. b	44. c	45. d	46. c	47. a	48. d	49. d	50. d
51. d	52. a	53. d	54. d	55. d	56. d	57. a	58. d	59. c	60. b
61. d	62. d	63. d	64. c	65. d	66. d	67. c	68. c	69. d	70. a
71. d	72. d	73. b	74. d	75. d	76. d	77. b	78. d	79. b	80. d
81. d									

Chapter 4

1. a	2. a	3. a	4. a	5. d	6. d	7. d	8. c	9. c	10. b
11. a	12. a	13. d	14. d	15. a	16. b	17. a	18. a	19. c	20. c
21. d	22. c	23. c	24. b	25. d	26. d	27. a	28. d	29. c	30. d
31. d	32. a	33. c	34. d	35. d	36. d	37. b	38. b	39. d	40. d
41. b	42. d	43. a	44. c	45. d	46. d	47. d	48. a	49. a	50. b
51. d									

Chapter 5

1. b	2. a	3. c	4. c	5. d	6. c	7. d	8. d	9. d	10. d
11. d	12. d	13. d	14. b	15. d	16. a	17. d	18. d	19. b	20. c
21. d	22. d	23. d	24. c	25. b	26. c	27. d	28. a	29. d	30. a
31. b	32. a	33. b	34. d	35. d	36. d	37. a	38. c	39. b	

ANSWER KEY

Chapter 6
1. d	2. a	3. a	4. b	5. a	6. b	7. c	8. c	9. d	10. d
11. d	12. a	13. c	14. b	15. c	16. b	17. d	18. d	19. d	20. b
21. d	22. c	23. d	24. b	25. d	26. d	27. d	28. b	29. d	30. d
31. b	32. b	33. c	34. a	35. d	36. c	37. c	38. d	39. d	40. d
41. a									

Chapter 7
1. d	2. c	3. c	4. a	5. d	6. a	7. d	8. d	9. a	10. a
11. c	12. d	13. c	14. d	15. c	16. c	17. b	18. d	19. d	20. c
21. b	22. d	23. b	24. b	25. a	26. b	27. d	28. a	29. d	30. d
31. d	32. d	33. a	34. a	35. a	36. a	37. c	38. d	39. c	40. d
41. d	42. a	43. c	44. d						

Chapter 8
1. b	2. d	3. d	4. b	5. c	6. a	7. b	8. c	9. d	10. a
11. d	12. b	13. d	14. b	15. d	16. c	17. c	18. b	19. b	20. a
21. b	22. d	23. a	24. b	25. d	26. d	27. c	28. a	29. c	30. d
31. b	32. d	33. b	34. d	35. a	36. b	37. b	38. c	39. d	40. b
41. b	42. d	43. d	44. a	45. c	46. a	47. d	48. d	49. a	50. b
51. d	52. d								

Chapter 9
1. c	2. d	3. c	4. c	5. a	6. b	7. b	8. c	9. a	10. d
11. a	12. c	13. d	14. d	15. a	16. b	17. a	18. a	19. d	20. b
21. c	22. a	23. c	24. a	25. c	26. d	27. d	28. d	29. c	30. c
31. b	32. d	33. c	34. a	35. d	36. d	37. b	38. d	39. b	40. b
41. d	42. b	43. d	44. b	45. d	46. a	47. c	48. b	49. b	50. b
51. d	52. d	53. d	54. a						

Chapter 10
1. b	2. c	3. c	4. b	5. d	6. d	7. d	8. a	9. a	10. d
11. d	12. a	13. b	14. b	15. d	16. a	17. a	18. a	19. a	20. b
21. d	22. d	23. d	24. d	25. a	26. d	27. d	28. a	29. b	30. d
31. a	32. d	33. d	34. c	35. d	36. d	37. a	38. a	39. a	40. d
41. c	42. d	43. b	44. d	45. d	46. a	47. d	48. a	49. d	50. a
51. d									

Chapter 11

1. d	2. c	3. c	4. b	5. b	6. d	7. d	8. d	9. d	10. d
11. c	12. d	13. d	14. d	15. a	16. d	17. c	18. d	19. d	20. b
21. c	22. a	23. c	24. d	25. c	26. a	27. d	28. d	29. d	30. d
31. a	32. d	33. c	34. b	35. d	36. a	37. d	38. a	39. b	40. d
41. b	42. d	43. c	44. a	45. d	46. b	47. a	48. d	49. d	50. d
51. b									

Chapter 12

1. d	2. b	3. b	4. d	5. d	6. d	7. c	8. d	9. b	10. d
11. a	12. d	13. d	14. d	15. d	16. d	17. a	18. a	19. a	20. d
21. c	22. d	23. d	24. d	25. d	26. b	27. d	28. b	29. d	30. d

Chapter 13

1. b	2. d	3. c	4. b	5. d	6. d	7. b	8. c	9. b	10. a
11. b	12. d	13. d	14. b	15. c	16. a	17. c	18. d	19. b	20. b
21. c	22. d	23. d	24. d	25. b	26. d	27. d	28. a	29. b	30. d
31. b	32. b	33. d	34. c	35. d	36. b	37. d	38. d	39. a	40. d
41. c									

Chapter 14

1. a	2. d	3. d	4. c	5. d	6. a	7. c	8. d	9. d	10. b
11. d	12. d	13. b	14. c	15. d	16. b	17. c	18. d	19. d	20. a
21. d	22. d	23. d	24. b	25. d	26. d	27. d	28. d	29. d	30. d
31. a	32. d	33. b	34. d	35. b	36. d	37. c	38. d	39. d	40. a
41. a	42. d	43. b	44. a	45. a	46. c	47. a	48. d	49. b	50. d
51. c	52. a	53. d							

Chapter 15

1. b	2. c	3. d	4. d	5. b	6. d	7. d	8. b	9. b	10. d
11. b	12. d	13. d	14. d	15. a	16. c	17. d	18. d	19. d	20. d
21. d	22. c	23. d	24. d	25. d	26. a	27. d	28. d	29. d	30. b
31. c	32. d	33. d	34. c	35. d	36. a	37. d	38. a	39. d	40. d
41. c	42. b	43. d	44. d	45. c	46. a	47. d			

Chapter 16

1. a	2. c	3. d	4. d	5. d	6. b	7. c	8. d	9. a	10. d
11. d	12. c	13. d	14. c	15. d	16. d	17. d	18. d	19. c	20. d
21. d	22. c	23. a	24. a	25. d	26. b	27. d	28. d	29. d	30. a
31. d	32. d	33. d	34. d	35. c	36. c	37. d	38. d	39. c	40. c
41. a	42. b	43. d	44. c	45. d	46. d	47. c	48. a	49. a	50. d
51. d	52. d	53. d	54. d	55. d	56. b	57. d	58. b	59. d	60. d
61. c	62. a	63. b	64. a	65. d	66. b	67. d	68. d	69. b	70. a
71. d	72. d	73. d							

ANSWER KEY

Chapter 17
1. a	2. d	3. c	4. d	5. d	6. d	7. d	8. b	9. d	10. c
11. d	12. b	13. d	14. c	15. c	16. d	17. d	18. d	19. a	20. c
21. c	22. b	23. c	24. d	25. d	26. c	27. b	28. b	29. d	30. d
31. c	32. d	33. b	34. d	35. c	36. d	37. b	38. d	39. c	40. d
41. d	42. d	43. a	44. d	45. a	46. d	47. b	48. b	49. d	50. d
51. b	52. c	53. d	54. a	55. d	56. d	57. c	58. a	59. d	60. d

Chapter 18
1. d	2. a	3. d	4. b	5. d	6. d	7. d	8. c	9. b	10. a
11. d	12. a	13. c	14. c	15. d	16. a	17. d	18. a	19. a	20. d
21. b	22. a	23. c	24. a	25. d	26. d	27. d	28. c	29. b	30. d
31. b	32. c	33. c	34. d	35. b	36. b	37. a	38. c	39. d	40. b
41. b	42. c	43. a	44. d	45. b	46. d	47. b	48. c	49. d	50. c
51. d	52. c	53. d	54. d	55. a	56. d	57. d	58. d	59. a	60. d
61. d	62. d								

Chapter 19
1. a	2. c	3. d	4. b	5. d	6. d	7. c	8. b	9. d	10. d
11. c	12. d	13. b	14. a	15. b	16. c	17. d	18. c	19. c	20. b
21. b	22. d	23. b	24. b	25. b	26. c	27. d	28. d	29. d	30. a
31. a	32. d	33. b	34. a	35. d	36. d	37. a	38. d	39. b	40. b
41. d	42. d	43. a	44. c	45. c	46. d	47. d	48. d	49. a	50. d
51. c	52. c	53. d	54. a	55. d	56. d	57. c	58. d		

Chapter 20
1. d	2. d	3. b	4. d	5. b	6. d	7. a	8. b	9. a	10. d
11. b	12. d	13. d	14. c	15. c	16. a	17. a	18. d	19. d	20. c
21. d	22. d	23. a	24. a	25. d	26. d	27. d	28. a	29. c	30. d
31. b	32. d	33. a	34. d	35. b	36. a	37. b	38. a	39. d	40. d
41. d	42. d	43. d	44. d	45. a	46. d	47. b	48. c	49. d	50. d
51. b	52. d	53. a	54. d	55. d	56. a	57. a	58. d	59. d	60. d
61. d	62. b	63. c	64. c	65. b	66. d	67. b	68. d	69. d	70. d
71. d	72. c	73. d	74. b	75. a	76. c				

Chapter 21
1. d	2. c	3. d	4. d	5. c	6. b	7. b	8. a	9. c	10. c
11. b	12. d	13. d	14. d	15. a	16. d	17. b	18. c	19. d	20. c
21. c	22. a	23. d	24. a	25. b	26. a	27. d	28. a	29. d	30. c
31. b	32. d	33. a	34. a	35. a	36. a	37. d	38. b	39. a	40. d
41. d	42. d	43. b	44. d	45. c	46. d	47. a	48. b	49. b	50. d
51. b	52. d	53. d	54. c	55. c	56. d				

Chapter 22

1. d	2. b	3. d	4. d	5. a	6. a	7. d	8. d	9. d	10. d
11. d	12. d	13. d	14. d	15. d	16. c	17. d	18. a	19. a	20. b
21. d	22. b	23. b	24. d	25. d	26. c	27. a	28. c	29. c	30. d
31. a	32. c	33. b	34. d	35. b	36. d	37. c	38. a		

Chapter 23

1. d	2. d	3. a	4. b	5. b	6. d	7. a	8. d	9. d	10. b
11. c	12. b	13. d	14. d	15. d	16. d	17. c	18. d	19. a	20. b
21. b	22. b	23. d	24. b	25. a	26. a	27. a	28. d	29. d	30. d
31. d	32. c	33. d	34. d	35. d	36. d	37. d	38. d	39. d	40. d
41. d	42. c	43. c	44. c	45. d	46. d	47. d			

Chapter 24

1. b	2. d	3. c	4. b	5. b	6. d	7. c	8. d	9. c	10. a
11. a	12. d	13. b	14. a	15. d	16. d	17. a	18. d	19. d	20. d
21. d	22. a	23. d	24. b	25. d	26. d	27. a	28. d	29. a	30. d
31. b									

www.ingramcontent.com/pod-product-compliance
Lightning Source LLC
Chambersburg PA
CBHW080729230426
43665CB00020B/2672